# The Three Faces of Discipline for the Elementary School Teacher

## Other Works by the Author

- *Solving Discipline Problems: Methods and Models for Today's Teachers, Third Edition*
  *ISBN: 0-205-16569-9*

- *The Three Faces of Discipline for Early Childhood: Empowering Teachers and Students*
  *ISBN: 0-205-15649-5*

- *School for Young Children: Developmentally Appropriate Practices*
  *ISBN: 0-205-13122-0*

# The Three Faces of Discipline for the Elementary School Teacher

## Empowering the Teacher and Students

Charles H. Wolfgang
*Florida State University*

**Allyn and Bacon**

**Boston   London   Toronto   Sydney   Tokyo   Singapore**

Copyright © 1996 by Allyn & Bacon
A Simon & Schuster Company
Needham Heights, Massachusetts 02194

**Library of Congress Cataloging-in-Publication Data**

Wolfgang, Charles H.
    The three faces of discipline for the elementary school teacher :
empowering the teacher and students / by Charles H. Wolfgang.
      p.  cm.
    Includes bibliographical references and index.
    ISBN 0-205-15647-9
    1. School discipline--United States.  2. Elementary school
teaching--United States.  3. Classroom management--United States.
I. Title.
LB3012.2.W655  1996
371.5--dc20                              95-47108
                                               CIP

Printed in the United States of America
10  9  8  7  6  5  4  3  2  1    00  99  98  97  96

*This book is dedicated to Riley Elementary School in Tallahasee, Florida, its principal, and its highly committed teachers.*

A few years ago, I had the opportunity to be invited by Doris Payne, principal, and Marjorie Green, assistant principal, to Riley Elementary School to give a presentation on discipline to the teachers. My presentation was based on my earlier book, *Solving Discipline Problems: Methods and Models for Today's Teachers*, which describes various models of discipline. Following my presentation, the teachers at Riley asked me a surprising question. They said, "Yeah, all those models of discipline techniques are very interesting, but what would *you* do, if you were a teacher at this school and you were working here tomorrow morning?" I was surprised by this question. I did not want to impose my "discipline model" on them, as so many other experts in discipline often do. But they persisted, and with Ms. Payne's support and encouragement, I spent the next three years working cooperatively with these teachers in an attempt to answer their question. As a result, we developed the *Three Faces of Discipline*, which provides both a philosophy and practical methods for dealing with elementary-age children. I know how important the principal is in making a school a success, and this was certainly true at Riley, where the key to our successful changes in school climate was Doris Payne's positive leadership and her complete commitment to moving beyond the mere "punishment of students" and creating a school with a total commitment to serving students' real needs. The Riley experience was the first developmental phase of the *Three Faces of Discipline* and the first field-testing of its practical applications and effects.

So I dedicate this book, *The Three Faces of Discipline for the Elementary School Teacher*, to Doris Payne—a very hard-working elementary school principal—and to all the teachers who challenged me and worked with me to design this new model. I hope you will find it helpful.

# Contents

# Preface

## WHO IS THIS BOOK FOR?

This book is for elementary school teachers and administrators who teach and work with first- to fifth-graders in a classroom setting. For those interested in kindergarten or the preschool age, you are referred to *The Three Faces of Discipline for Early Childhood* and *School for Young Children*, both written by Charles H. Wolfgang and Mary E. Wolfgang and published by Allyn and Bacon.

In the first few days of the new school year, you quickly learn that one of the children in your class—let's call this student Pat— is going to challenge your skills as a teacher and a disciplinarian. To put it more bluntly, if less professionally, you can sense that this child is going to drive you nuts this year. When fellow teachers see your class roster, they quickly state, "Oh, no, you got Pat! Better you than me! Good luck!" This child destroys others' property, fights, uses profanity to the extent that parents and classmates complain, and engages in a host of other misbehaviors that require you to deal with him repeatedly, sapping your energy. The bus driver, crossing guards, cafeteria workers, janitor, and other teachers begin a barrage of complaints about Pat, and they expect you to do something about him. Many teaching lessons are routinely disrupted by Pat, and you begin to get the terrible feeling that this child is out to get you. It is as if this difficult student deliberately sets "fires" that you are forced to put out, taking up far too much of your teaching time and ruining the pacing and continuity of the school day.

Other children are stimulated by Pat's misbehavior as they watch his actions, and they are beginning to attempt similar activities just to see if they can get away with it, in a disruptive game of "monkey see, monkey do." Sending Pat to the principal's office doesn't seem to help. Although the principal tries to put the "fear of God" into this child by figuratively talking his ears off, three minutes after returning from the office, Pat is up to his old tricks. In fact, this type of child appears to look forward to those "discipline" trips.

You feel all alone in your elementary classroom. Fellow teachers and school administrators are busy at their own tasks. You seem to be locked into your "classroom-cave" with 30 to 35 children who are beginning to challenge your authority, with one child leading the charge by throwing "hand grenades" into your daily classroom routine. You also begin to have the feeling that you are no longer in control of your classroom; depression and a feeling of "battle fatigue" are quickly setting in, and you are becoming concerned that your professional evaluations might suffer. September isn't even over yet, and you are already thinking about the end of this school year. You have no idea how to regain control of your classroom and deal effectively with Pat.

## DISCIPLINE MODELS

Many discipline approaches, or models, are available for the teacher to use with misbehaving children such as Pat. Most of these models (among them T.E.T., Value Clarification, Magic Circle, Reality Therapy, Control Theory, Behavior Analysis, Positive Discipline, and Assertive Discipline) claim to have the "right" way to discipline. They seem to be saying, *Follow my system and I will lead you to the blissful Promised Land of educational heaven, a world of perfectly disciplined classrooms populated by happy, cooperative students.* All provide some good ideas, most of them based to varying degrees on psychological theory. Each has a fairly narrow and differing view of what motivates children and their misbehavior, and each prescribes various techniques for dealing with a misbehaving student. Some models rely on very light requests of the child, while others make clear demands to stop misbehavior; some use strong controlling actions to extinguish the misbehavior, while others suggest methods of dealing with violent-assaultive acts directed at you as a teacher.

These models progress along a continuum from minimum to maximum use of power by the teacher. If we view the continuum of misbehavior in the classroom side by side with the continuum or pathway of discipline models with regard to the power these techniques give us as teachers, we can see that some models may be quite effective with some children but totally ineffective with the very difficult Pats of this world. The *Three Faces of Discipline* position is that no one model can work successfully for all children at all times, nor will the same model always succeed for the same child as he or she experiences different stimuli and exhibits different kinds of misbehavior. In fact, if we observe closely, we can see that we ourselves do not always use the same techniques with each and every child. Some children who are "out of line" need only to be looked at; if we meet them eye to eye and signal them about their behavior, they will stop. With others, we will need to move more forcefully by confronting them, and then with some discussion they can get "back in line." With still others, such as Pat, we might need to take very strong intervention actions, even using various forms of encouragement or punishment. Based on a host of variables, we tend to change our "face"—the way we present ourselves and the methods we use.

In the real world of Monday morning in the classroom with Pat, we rarely see a practicing classroom teacher who is a discipline purist—one who uses Assertive Discipline and only Assertive Discipline, or Glasser's Reality Therapy and only Glasser. More likely, we will find the teacher in the practical world, using many of the techniques from generally one model, but with his or her own "spin" on the techniques. The teacher adds other techniques previously learned and tested—techniques the teacher has determined can be successful for him or her.

We therefore adopt the approach of the teacher living and working in a practical world—an approach that holds: All of the various discipline models in vogue have some strengths and some limitations, so why not take the best techniques and use *something from each of them*? But this raises a very real follow-up question: How can this be done successfully?

First, we must define what we mean by discipline. *Discipline* is the required action by a teacher or school official toward a student (or group of students) after his or her (or their) behavior disrupts the ongoing educational activity or breaks a preestablished rule or law created by the teacher, the school administration, or general society. The educator's actions may fall into three broad categories of response:

- Relationship-Listening (a therapeutic process)

- Confronting-Contracting (an educational and counseling process)

- Rules and Consequences (a controlling process)

These three processes combine to constitute the *Three Faces of Discipline* and may be placed on a power continuum from minimum to maximum use of a pathway of power. The continuum reflects the level of autonomy and control given to the student to change his or her own behavior or the aversive actions used by the teacher or school officials to get the desired change in student behavior and reestablish order and safety in the educational setting. Figure 1 presents a list, based on a continuum regarding power, of today's discipline models. These models—based on varying degrees of psychological theory and, to a lesser extent, research-supported knowledge—serve as the knowledge base of practical techniques and skills needed to handle the wide variety of discipline situations the educator will face in today's school setting.

Chapter 1 presents a quick and minor discipline incident and shows how the teacher escalates his or her use of power across a continuum of teacher discipline techniques, moving from minimum to maximum use of power. The general categories of behavior used by the teacher are placed along a power continuum, called the Teacher Behavior Continuum. This continuum, or TBC, provides a construct that can be used to demonstrate the power inherent in the teacher techniques and actions eclecticly drawn from the models (listed in Figure 1). In essence, the TBC is a "power pathway" on which all of the techniques from various discipline models are arranged so the teacher can clearly see the specific and concrete steps suggested by each model as he or she faces another Monday morning with Pat.

## FIGURE 1   Today's Discipline Models

| ← ————————————— TEACHER'S POWER ————————————— → | | |
|---|---|---|
| **MINIMUM POWER** | | **MAXIMUM POWER** |
| **Relationship-Listening Face** | **Confronting-Contracting Face** | **Rules and Consequences Face** |
| Gordon, *T.E.T.: Teacher Effectiveness Training*[1]<br><br>Gordon, *Teaching Children Self-Discipline: At Home and at School*[2]<br><br>Harris, *I'm OK—You're OK: A Practical Guide to Transactional Analysis*[3]<br><br>Raths, Harmin, & Simon, *Values and Teaching*[4]<br><br>Bessell, *Human Development Program* ("The Magic Circle")[5]<br><br>Palomares & Ball, *Grounds for Growth: The Human Development Program's Comprehensive Theory*[6] | Dreikurs & Cassel, *Discipline Without Tears*[7]<br><br>Albert, *A Teacher's Guide to Cooperative Discipline: How to Manage Your Classroom and Promote Self-Esteem*[8]<br><br>Glasser, *Control Theory in the Classroom*[9]<br><br>Glasser, *Schools Without Failure*[10]<br><br>Glasser, *The Quality School: Managing Students without Coercion*[11] | Madsen & Madsen, *Teaching/Discipline: A Positive Approach for Educational Development*[12]<br><br>Alberto & Troutman, *Applied Behavior Analysis for Teachers*[13]<br><br>Dobson, *Dare to Discipline*[14]<br><br>Canter & Canter, *Assertive Discipline: Positive Behavior Management for Today's Classroom*[15]<br><br>Canter & Canter, *Succeeding with Difficult Students*[16]<br><br>Alberti, *Your Perfect Right: A Guide to Assertive Living*[17]<br><br>Alberti & Emmons, *Stand Up, Speak Out, Talk Back*[18]<br><br>Jones, *Positive Classroom Discipline*[19]<br><br>National Crisis Prevention Institute, "Nonviolent Crisis Intervention"[20] |

1. Gordon, T. (1974). *T.E.T.: Teacher Effectiveness Training.* New York: David McKay.
2. Gordon, T. (1989). *Teaching Children Self-Discipline: At Home and at School.* New York: Times Books.
3. Harris, T. A. (1969). *I'm OK—You're OK: A Practical Guide to Transactional Analysis.* New York: Harper & Row.
4. Raths, L. E., Harmin, M., & Simon, S. B. (1966). *Values and Teaching.* Columbus, OH: Merrill.
5. Bessell, H. (1976). *Human Development Program.* La Mesa, CA: Human Development Training Institute, Inc.
6. Palomares, U., & Ball, G. (1980). *Grounds for Growth: The Human Development Program's Comprehensive Theory.* Spring Valley, CA: Palomares and Associates.
7. Dreikurs, R., & Cassel, P. (1972). *Discipline Without Tears.* New York: Hawthorn.
8. Albert, L. (1989). *A Teacher's Guide to Cooperative Discipline: How to Manage Your Classroom and Promote Self-Esteem.* Circle Pines, MN: American Guidance Service.
9. Glasser, W. (1985). *Control Theory in the Classroom.* New York: Harper & Row.
10. Glasser, W. (1969). *Schools Without Failure.* New York: Harper & Row.
11. Glasser, W. (1992). *The Quality School: Managing Students Without Coercion* (2nd ed.). New York: Harper Perennial.
12. Madsen, C. H., & Madsen, C. K. (1981). *Teaching/Discipline: A Positive Approach for Educational Development.* Raleigh, NC: Contemporary Publishing.
13. Alberto, P. A., & Troutman, A. C. (1990). *Applied Behavior Analysis for Teachers* (3rd ed.). New York: Maxwell Macmillan International Publishing Group.
14. Dobson, J. (1970). *Dare to Discipline.* Wheaton, IL: Tyndale House.
15. Canter, L., & Canter, M. (1992). *Assertive Discipline: Positive Behavior Management for Today's Classroom.* Santa Monica, CA: Lee Canter & Associates.
16. Canter, L., & Canter, M. (1993). *Succeeding with Difficult Students.* Santa Monica, CA: Lee Canter & Associates.
17. Alberti, R. E. (1982). *Your Perfect Right: A Guide to Assertive Living.* San Luis Obispo, CA: Impact Publishers.
18. Alberti, R. E., & Emmons, M. L. (1975). *Stand Up, Speak Out, Talk Back.* New York: Pocket Books.
19. Jones, F. H. (1987). *Positive Classroom Discipline.* New York: McGraw-Hill.
20. National Crisis Prevention Institute (CPI), "Nonviolent Crisis Intervention." 3315-K North 124th St., Brookfield, WI 53005.

Through this approach, using the *Three Faces of Discipline,* the teacher will learn how to develop a pathway of techniques based on escalation and deescalation of his or her own power in working with a very difficult child who is disrupting the classroom.

*A style note*: In order to avoid the awkward writing construction of *his or her* or *he or she* to refer to the teacher or student, I often will simply use one gender at a time. Because teaching is a field shared by women and men alike, I will use both genders at various times throughout this book. The use of only one gender at a time should not be taken as an indication that the concepts being presented are more relevant for, or the problems encountered would be more often associated with, one gender rather than the other.

## ACKNOWLEDGMENTS

A special thanks to all my colleagues and the many teachers who read this manuscript and offered their insights and suggestions; to Callum Johnston for his research work; to Chuck Walsh for his practical examples and vignettes; and to Jon Peck for his excellent editing and solid and wise advice.

# Introduction

Classroom discipline is so much more than a simple question of "Does this child know how to behave?" It is intertwined with such diverse factors as the child's home life, peer pressure, the design of the classroom space, and even the childhood experiences of the teacher.

There is no single approach to classroom discipline that is *the* best approach or *the* only approach. For each teacher and each student, there is a mixed approach that calls for different methods, depending on the circumstances of each misbehavior.

How, then, can a single teacher hope to develop the skills necessary for such an undertaking? The answer lies in an understanding of the concept of discipline and of the Three Faces of Discipline—a concept that allows the teacher to change his or her approach as circumstances dictate. This approach can effectively empower the elementary school teacher to run a well-managed, well-behaved classroom in which students are free to learn without the constant interruptions and distractions that can occur when even one student is allowed to misbehave on an ongoing basis.

# 1

# Teacher Behavior, Misbehavior, and Discipline

*Mr. Leonard's fifth-grade class has 36 students in it, and every desk in the room is occupied—in fact, two students have to sit at a display table at the back of the room. The class is quietly working on an assignment from the textbook when a commotion erupts in the middle of the room. George, a small quiet student, is frantically looking around and under his desk. Several students around him are watching him, and some are starting to laugh softly. Mr. Leonard moves to George and, speaking softly so others will not be disturbed, asks, "George, what's the matter?" George replies, "Someone swiped my hat!" Kathy, who sits next to George, says, "Mike took it, I saw him!" Mike retorts, "I didn't take it. Check it out, man, I don't have his stupid hat!" Kathy insists, "You do, too!"*

*Mr. Leonard moves closer to Mike and makes eye contact.* (Step 1: Looking)

*The teacher says, "When teasing by taking someone's property occurs and disrupts the class so that everyone stops their work, we lose valuable time, and I find that quite annoying."* (Step 2: Naming) *Mr. Leonard backs out of Mike's "personal space" and gives him several moments to respond. Mike takes a baseball hat from inside his desk, places it on his head, throws his feet up onto his desk, and smiles broadly at Mr. Leonard.*

*"What is the rule regarding personal property?" the teacher asks. "What are you going to do to solve this problem, Mike, so that we may all get back to our work?"* (Step 3: Questioning) *Mr. Leonard is still speaking in a soft voice so only the students near George and Mike can hear. Mike does not respond.*

*Mr. Leonard states, "Mike, put your feet on the floor and return the hat to George."* (Step 4: Commanding) *There is still no action from Mike, so the teacher adds, "If you cannot quickly put your feet on the floor and return the cap now, I will need to call in Mr. Mack, the assistant principal, and Mr. Baker from across the hall, and we will escort you from the classroom to the principal's office."* (Promise a Consequence) *"Return George's hat now!"* (Commanding) *The four neighboring students turn to look at Mike, and slowly he pushes the hat toward George and seats himself with his feet on the floor. If Mike had not responded, Mr. Leonard would have followed through on his stated intent to remove the student.* (Acting [Physical Intervention])

For purposes of this example, we have ended the incident successfully; George's hat has been returned with limited disruption to most of the other students and to ongoing classroom activity. However, the experienced teacher realizes that more likely this lost hat incident may have degenerated into a situation requiring the teacher's acting (physical intervention) to actually remove Mike, to restrain George (who might angrily strike out), or to take some other action to get the students back to their classroom work activity. Later, I will provide methods and constructs for dealing with raw aggression and removal, but first it is important to understand the dynamics of the preceding incident in order to explain the construct of the Teacher Behavior Continuum (TBC)[1,2,3] and the concept of the teacher's escalation from minimum to maximum use of power (see Figure 1–1).

---

## ESCALATION/DEESCALATION OF POWER

The gradual movement up and down the TBC through the use of stronger or more demanding teacher behaviors (escalation of power) or a retreat back through this continuum with less intrusive behaviors (deescalation).

---

When a student acts in an inappropriate manner in the classroom, you may ask, "What should be done to stop this behavior?" The natural tendency, especially for a beginning teacher, is to rush toward the misbehaving student, state in a loud and forceful manner (*high-profile desist*)

---

| FIGURE 1–1   Teacher Behavior Continuum | |
|---|---|
| **Minimum Power** | **Maximum Power** |

Step 1   Looking
      Step 2   Naming
            Step 3   Questioning
                  Step 4   Commanding (Promise a Consequence)
                        Step 5   Acting (Physical Intervention)

what the student must not do ("Don't do that, Mike. Stop clowning around!") and then, if compliance is not obtained, begin a classroom search for the hat or physically remove Mike. This approach of telling the student what *not* to do is generally ineffective on a number of accounts.

Erikson,[4] a child development expert, characterizes the elementary school years as the period of *industry versus inferiority*. Students this age appear to be emotionally pulled between the two extremes of wanting to be treated as adults while at the same time readily regressing to childish behavior. These students are overly sensitive to how they are viewed by peers, and are especially critical of themselves or others who may be different than the dominant group in any way. Any confrontation, especially in a context where peers are onlookers, places great pressure on these children to save face, to avoid being made fools of, or to sense a challenge to their power, requiring them to demonstrate "macho" responses. When placed in this spotlight, they emotionally flood with feelings of shame, guilt, and inferiority. Their feeling of inferiority is a deeply felt emotion fully ready to effervesce, and can be quickly triggered by any demand. "Don't do it!" brings quick and strong defensive emotional feelings from students at this particular age, and is highly likely to flood the student with emotion. This flooding clouds a child's logical thinking on how to respond to the teacher's demand. Thus, the "don't do" statements are likely to cause feelings of guilt or inferiority or make a child confused and respond in an aggressive or foolish and destructive manner toward the teacher.

As you view this "don't put your feet on the desk" directive command, you must keep in mind the way in which students hear and absorb verbal communications when they are emotionally flooded. When emotionally flooded, especially when confronted by a teacher, students' thinking regresses to a form of irreversibility[5] of thinking—they do not think through the sequence of past actions and future consequences, but simply feel that they are in the spotlight and everyone is looking at them. As a result, they feel they must show that they are tough, no matter what. When flooded students are told, "Don't put your feet on the desk," what they often hear and remember is "PUT YOUR FEET ON THE DESK." Unknowingly, you might actually be suggesting that the students perform the very actions you do not want.

Words also trigger motor-meaning responses in students. If you are reading kindergartners a story that says, "The tiger growled and showed his ghastly teeth," a glance at the young audience will show most of the students "growling" and showing their teeth. Words suggest to young students a motor-meaning response that they impulsively seem unable to control. When school-aged students' thinking is flooded with emotions, their thought processes regress to the young child's way of responding and thinking. If you tell a student a sentence that ends with an action or motor meaning, even when the sentence begins with *Don't*, the result is likely to be that the student will perform the motor meaning of the last words. Therefore, you should tell the student what *to* do, not what *not* to do. In this way, you are presenting a reality solution (telling the student what actions you want) and are suggesting the motor meaning of your desired actions ("keep your feet on the floor").

---

### MOTOR MEANING (OR MOTOR RULES)

Motor actions are prompted by words. Just as objects can set off a student's impulsive motor-meaning response, so too can words. (If an adult hears someone shout, "Duck!" he will automatically put his head down.)

---

The final difficulty with the "don't do so-and-so" approach is that if this is a student motivated by the need for power, the student most likely will take you on in a power struggle, especially if he feels a need to save face. As a toddler, the student begins to test out his autonomy[6] by attempting to get around limits set by parents and other adults. If this limit setting by adults has been erratic and inconsistent, these children—now elementary school students—might have come to the conclusion that *Don't* really is a word that triggers a game of "Let's see if the adult really means what she has said, or can I beat her and do as I wish?" The "don't" statement as a part of *Commanding* on the Teacher Behavior Continuum places you with your back against the wall, requiring an immediate confrontation or *Acting (Physical Intervention)* toward the student who is challenging your power, perhaps even removing him from the classroom. The goal in using and understanding the Teacher Behavior Continuum is to grant the student maximum power to change his own behavior by beginning with a *low-profile desist* command. Only when you are *unsuccessful* in gaining compliance do you then gradually escalate the power until you get results.

---

### "DON'T" STATEMENTS

It is ineffective to tell a student what not to do; rather, the teacher is encouraged to tell the misbehaving student what to do. "No, Stop!" statements are used if the incident is serious and substantial harm may occur imminently.

---

## THE SEVERITY CLAUSE AND "STOP" STATEMENTS

For every rule there is an exception. If you see the student about to perform some action that is life threatening, is likely to produce injury, or will destroy expensive or irreplaceable property, the *severity clause* applies. In such a case, you state firmly or even shout a "No, Stop!" statement to attempt to get the student to immediately desist. If you have followed the previously discussed rule and have regularly told the student what *to* do rather than what *not* to do, your emergency "No, Stop!" statements are more likely to be immediately obeyed. But if the student has an hourly diet of "don't do this, don't do that" and is told repeatedly, "No, don't do so-and-so" a thousand times a day, he is desensitized to the prohibition contained in "No, Stop!" statements and is now less likely to immediately obey an emergency command. Save the "No" statements until they are really needed.

---

### SEVERITY CLAUSE

If the student's actions threaten to endanger himself or destroy significant property, a teacher is justified in escalating up the continuum to the most intrusive or demanding teacher behaviors of Acting (Physical Intervention).

---

## THE TEACHER BEHAVIOR CONTINUUM: THE TBC

The confrontation between Mike and Mr. Leonard over the missing hat and placement of the feet on the floor contains examples of those myriad small desist requests—which may be called *teachable moments*—that a classroom teacher faces daily in working with students. The incident is dealt with in a matter of minutes, and the teacher escalates up the TBC power continuum as he intervenes, modifying his approach as he receives—or fails to receive—certain responses. With some students, especially physically and verbally aggressive students, these teachable moments may arise five or six times in an hour and occur daily. You may be required over many weeks and months to handle such incidents with one particular student, and the many techniques found in the following chapters can be of great help to you.

What is important here is not this one particular desist request, but rather an understanding of the construct of the Teacher Behavior Continuum. The steps and general categories of behavior on the TBC suggest a power continuum of teacher action moving from the minimum use of power at *Step 1: Looking* (or *Modality Cueing*) to the maximum use of power at *Step 5: Acting (Physical Intervention)*. This escalation to more powerful techniques on the TBC also reflects a very real attitudinal change on the part of the intervening teacher. This attitude change may be characterized as the Three Faces of Discipline: *Relationship-Listening, Confronting-Contracting,* and *Rules and Consequences.*

---

### TEACHER BEHAVIOR CONTINUUM

A systematic teaching process that a teacher may use daily to intervene with the kinds of misbehavior normally seen in most students in classroom settings. The TBC contains a group of five general teacher behaviors (Looking, Naming, Questioning, Commanding, and Acting [Physical Intervention]) placed on a continuum, suggesting that actions may move from minimum teacher intrusion or power to maximum teacher control.

---

The *Relationship-Listening* Face involves the use of minimum power. This reflects a view that the student has the capability to change his own behavior, and that if the student is misbehaving, it is because of inner emotional turmoil, flooded behavior, or feelings of inner inade-

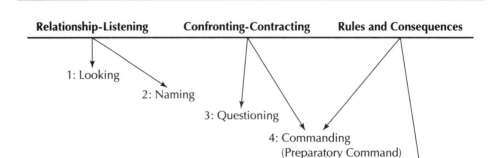

**FIGURE 1–2**  **The Three Faces of Discipline**

quacy. Your goal would be to signal or make the student aware of his actions and get him to talk out his emotional concern. This "talking it out" by the student would lead him to become more purposeful in his behavior, and the misbehavior would stop. The "face" of the Relationship-Listening teacher would rely only on such TBC minimal intervention techniques as *Looking* and *Naming* (see Figure 1–2).

The teacher's "face" when escalating to a *Confronting-Contracting* method of intervention is one of "I am the adult. I know misbehavior when I see it and will confront the student to stop this behavior. I will grant the student the power to decide how he or she will change, and encourage and contract with the student to live up to a mutual agreement for behavioral change." The Confronting-Contracting position primarily involves the use of *Questioning* techniques found on the TBC (see Figure 1–2).

The most powerful intervention technique is a teacher attitude of *Rules and Consequences*. The teacher's Rules and Consequences Face is one that communicates an attitude of "This is the rule and behavior that I want and I will set out assertively to get this action. I will teach and reward new positive behaviors acquired by the student." Drawing from the TBC, the "face" of the Rules and Consequences teacher will use the powerful techniques of *Commanding* and *Acting (Physical Intervention)*.

The Teacher Behavior Continuum and the escalation and change among these attitudes or faces of discipline may be used in two ways to help young students' behavior move to a more mature level.

- First, for the student who is simply having a rare misbehavior, you would escalate across the TBC within a few minutes. This was demonstrated in the example of Mike and the missing hat.

---

**THE THREE FACES**

- *Relationship-Listening*

The least intrusive of the three discipline faces, it views students as inherently good, and if they are misbehaving it is because they are suffering the blockage of some inner emotional need. The teacher's role is to establish a nonjudgmental relationship and encourage the student to "talk out" the problem while the teacher listens; this talking helps empower the student to solve his own problems and needs. (These methods are based on Rogerian theory.[7])

- *Confronting-Contracting*

This face attempts to maintain an adult relationship with a misbehaving student, by requesting the student to stop and change. The solution for how the student will change remains in the student's hands. (These methods are based on Glasser's Reality Therapy[8] and Adlerian theory as defined by Rudolf Dreikurs.[9])

- *Rules and Consequences*

The most powerful or controlling face, with philosophy and methodology that clearly states rules for behavior and assertively takes actions through reward to get the positive behavior sought by the teacher. These methods are based on theories of assertiveness training[10] and behavior modification.[11]

---

- Second, for the attention-getting, power-seeking, and revengeful student whose *life-stance position* is one of a day-in, day-out series of classroom disruptions, you may stay with a single face of discipline—with its accompanying techniques—for many weeks. You would gradually change your "face" to increase power if these techniques are unsuccessful, or to decrease your power to less intrusive techniques if the student's behavior begins to change and becomes more purposeful and guided.

---

**LIFE-STANCE POSITION**

When a child (or adult) becomes so overwhelmed by a world of frustration and accompanying inner emotional turmoil, he may defensively take a passive or aggressive stance, 24 hours a day, toward life experiences and toward his classmates and teacher.

---

## THE THREE FACES OF DISCIPLINE: A CONCEPT, NOT A RECIPE

The concept of the Three Faces of Discipline, with the use of the TBC power continuum and its accompanying teacher behaviors, is not for the purpose of giving the teacher a clear-cut recipe for responding to misbehavior. One example of a recipe is suggested in *Assertive Discipline,*[12] which calls for the teacher to place a student's name on the board as a warning of misbehavior, followed by a check mark for each new act of misbehavior; after three checks, the student suffers some form of punishment. This approach takes the skill out of the teacher's hand by assuming that this recipe will be effective with all students. The Teacher Behavior Continuum and the concept of the Three Faces of Discipline simply provide an orderly arrangement of teacher techniques that may be used as they relate to degrees of power. This concept permits the teacher to use her skills to decide how much power is needed for which student under what type of circumstances.

For example, with a certain misbehaving student, you may choose to ask, "Carol, what are you doing? This may not go on!" (Confronting-Contracting Face). The student, without any undue stress, realizes what she must do to comply, and the discipline incident is over. With another student who is getting out of hand, you may simply need to make eye contact (Relationship-Listening Face) for the student to gain an awareness of what he is doing wrong and how to stop doing it. Still other students require you to assertively state the rules and demand immediate compliance (Rules and Consequences Face) before they stop their improper behavior. Based on your past experiences with these students and an intimate knowledge of them, you have made a decision as to how much power and which techniques would be most effective with each individual student. The Three Faces of Discipline concept would go one step further in that with those students requiring the strong intervention of Rules and Consequences (and to a lesser extent Confronting-Contracting), over many weeks you would gradually teach or lead the students to respond by using techniques of less and less power, until the students can effectively control themselves. As a result, at the end of this process, you would need to use only the Relationship-Listening techniques, or none at all.

Subsequent chapters contain a more detailed explanation of the teacher behaviors found on the Teacher Behavior Continuum, with many new subbehavioral techniques defined and presented under each of these larger behavioral categories. Recall that in the missing hat incident, the teacher used the behavioral category of *Commanding* and then progressed to a subcommand under this category called *Promise a Consequence.* Other behaviors on the TBC will also contain subbehaviors and techniques under these broader categories. The TBC becomes a "construct" or a visual display related to degrees of power and each of the techniques taken from various discipline models (i.e., *T. E. T., Glasser, Assertive Discipline,* etc.). The TBC is presented in the following chapters, with the use of the continuum, to display the concrete techniques that are available to the teacher when dealing with a discipline incident and using one of the three "faces."

---

## TEACHER BEHAVIOR CONTINUUM (TBC)

- *Looking*

The first (minimum power) behavior on the TBC, in which the teacher uses a modality of looking, touch, or sound to signal the student to become aware of his own actions.

- *Naming*

The second behavior on the TBC, in which the teacher uses words to describe the feelings, problem, or situation the student is facing regarding some episode (difficulty with another person or objects and materials).

- *Questioning*

The third teacher behavior on the TBC, in which the student is called on to intellectually reflect on the situation and to think of new ideas to solve the situation; alternatively, questioning could be the teacher's offer to provide assistance.

- *Commanding*

The fourth behavior on the TBC, a powerful direct statement whereby the teacher tells the student what to do, not what *not* to do.

- *Promise a Consequence*

A subbehavior under the larger category of *Commanding*. Once the teacher has told the student what to do and sees that she is not getting compliance, the teacher verbally gives a promise of a consequence—a promise to follow up with a strong action (physical intervention) if the student does not quickly comply.

- *Acting (Physical Intervention)*

The strongest and most intrusive behavior on the TBC, whereby the teacher physically takes the student by the hand or restricts his body to stop an action that is occurring.

---

## TEACHER PERSONALITY TYPE

There are many teachers who do not escalate or deescalate their power along a continuum, but instead wear one "face," generally doing two to five discipline actions consistently with most students. These teachers tend to have a set philosophy or orientation.

Each teacher has a deep memory of the child within herself. This memory is an accumulation of how parents, teachers, and other significant adults disciplined her when she was young. Consequently, we parent the way we have been parented, or teach the way we have been taught. When you, as a teacher, set limits with students, you are projecting the degree of autonomy you feel comfortable giving to students to control their own behavior, or how much you need to be in control. Therefore, for some teachers, the Rules and Consequences techniques may be too strong a form of teacher control, or the Relationship-Listening face too "touchy-feely" in nature, or the Confronting-Contracting face too hokey in bringing discipline issues for group discussion. Based on their individual personalities, then, many teachers tend to naturally—and unthinkingly—use methods and techniques that cluster under one of these three schools of thought, or "faces." The question arises: Which one of these "face" philosophies best fits your personality? The Beliefs about Discipline Inventory (see Figure 1–3) is a tool that lets you answer a series of value questions to help identify which "face" philosophically comes to you naturally—based on the "child" within. Stop now and complete the inventory, so that after you are more familiar with the methods under each of these positions, you will see if your values have changed.

---

### "FACES" (TEACHER ATTITUDE)

A metaphor for the concept that a teacher may act toward a misbehaving student in a number of conscious, predetermined ways, and that the teacher's attitude and methods can change (take on a new "face") to match circumstances.

---

### FIGURE 1–3   Beliefs about Discipline Inventory

The 12 questions on this inventory will give you insights about yourself by helping you determine where your personality and the techniques you currently tend to use would cluster under the three philosophical "faces." In each numbered question you are asked to choose between two competing value statements. With some questions, you will definitely like one statement and dislike the second, and it will be easy for you to decide. With others, you will like or dislike both, leaving you with a frustrating choice—but you still must choose.

**Forced Choices**
*Instructions*: Select A or B to indicate the item you value most. You must choose between the two statements for each item. Circle item A or B.

1. a. Because students' thinking is limited, rules need to be established for them by mature adults.
   b. Each student's emotional need, rather than some preestablished rule, must be taken into consideration.

2. a. During most group time, the teacher needs to award each student his or her own desk or table space, and all students should be taught routinely to take those spaces after transitions.
   b. Groups of young students can, through class meetings, decide what rules they need to govern themselves.

3. a. During preplanning, students should be given choices as to which interest center they wish to choose that morning, and then once chosen, they must keep to that decision for most of that period.
   b. What students must learn and the tasks to be performed must be determined by the teacher, and a specific sequence of instruction to accomplish these goals must be followed.

4. The books in the classroom library are being misused, soiled, and at times destroyed. I most likely will:
   a. Hold a class meeting, show the damaged books to the class, and ask the children how we may solve this problem, including what action should be taken toward a student misusing books.
   b. Physically remove or limit the number of books available and observe closely to see who was misusing the books. I would then tell that student how such action was affecting other students and how I felt about such loss of books.

5. Two students of equal power and abilities are in a rather loud verbal conflict over classroom materials. I would:
   a. Approach the students in order to keep the situation from getting out of control, telling them of the classroom rule and demanding that they desist in their actions, promising a sanction if they fail to comply.
   b. Avoid interfering in something that the students need to resolve themselves.

6. a. The student strongly requests not to work in a group today. This would be permitted based on the teacher's feeling that this student has some emotional concerns related to the group experience.
   b. One student is being refused entrance into group activities; the teacher will raise this as an issue in a class meeting, requesting a discussion of reasons and solutions by the student and the group.

7. The noise level in the classroom is at such a high level that it is bothering me. I would:
   a. Flick the classroom lights to get the students' attention, ask them to become quiet, and later praise those who are talking quietly.
   b. Select the two or three students really making most of the noise, take them aside and question them to reflect (think) about their behavior and how it might affect others, and get an agreement with them to work quietly.

8. During the first few days of class, I would:
   a. Permit the students to test out getting along as a new group and make no predetermined teacher rules, until the students feel they are needed.
   b. Immediately teach the class rules and the fair sanction I will apply if the rules are broken.

9. My response when one student swears at another is:
   a. The student is frustrated by a classmate and has responded by swearing; I do not reprimand the student, but encourage him to talk out what is bothering him.
   b. I bring the two students together in a "knee-to-knee" confronting relationship and attempt to get them to work out this conflict while I ask questions and keep the focus on the negotiation.

*(continued)*

---

**FIGURE 1–3  Beliefs about Discipline Inventory** *(continued)*

10. If a student disrupts class while I am trying to lecture, I would:
    a. Ignore the disruption if possible and/or remove the student to the back of the room as a consequence of his misbehavior.
    b. Express my feeling of discomfort to the student about being disrupted from my task.

11. a. Each student must realize that there are some school rules that need to be obeyed, and each student who breaks them will be punished in the same fair manner.
    b. Rules are never "written in stone" and can be renegotiated by the class; sanctions will vary with each student.

12. The student refuses to put away his work or materials after using them. I most likely would:
    a. Express to the student how "not putting away" will affect future activities in this space, and how frustrating this will be to everyone. I would then leave the materials where they are for the remainder of the day.
    b. Confront the student to reflect on his behavior, think about how his non-compliance affects others, and tell him that if he cannot follow the rules he will lose the use of the materials in the future.

**Scoring Key and Interpretation**

Locate your responses for each numbered question on the table below and circle it.

| Table 1 | | Table 2 | | Table 3 | |
|---|---|---|---|---|---|
| 4b | 1b | 2b | 4a | 2a | 1a |
| 6a | 5b | 3a | 6b | 3b | 5a |
| 9a | 8a | 7b | 9b | 7a | 8b |
| 12a | 10b | 11b | 12b | 11a | 10a |

Total number of responses in Table 1 _____

Total number of responses in Table 2 _____

Total number of responses in Table 3 _____

The table with the highest total number of responses shows the "face" where your values tend to cluster. Table 1 represents Relationship-Listening, Table 2 is Confronting-Contracting, and Table 3 is Rules and Consequences. The table with the next highest score would be your secondary orientation, and the table with the least number may be the "face" that you value least. If your responses are equally distributed among all tables, you may be an eclectic teacher who picks and chooses from all philosophies. In Chapter 2, you will learn more about how this value position will relate to your "personality fit."

## SUMMARY

The wide variety of discipline models may be considered on a continuum in regard to the power they call for in order to get off-task students to change their behavior. Instead of relying on just one model, you may choose techniques from any or all of the models to build your own system or personal model of discipline. The Teacher Behavior Continuum provides a construct for viewing how much power you are using when you apply a particular technique or method with a student. You will vary in the degree of power or control you need in your classroom, and may obtain an awareness of yourself and this need for power by completing the Beliefs about Discipline Inventory.

# Related Readings

Wolfgang, C. H. (1977). *Helping Aggressive and Passive Preschoolers Through Play.* Columbus, OH: Charles E. Merrill.

Wolfgang, C. H., & Glickman, C. D. (1985). *Solving Discipline Problems: Methods and Models for Today's Teachers.* Boston: Allyn and Bacon.

Wolfgang, C. H., Mackender, B., & Wolfgang, M. E. (1981). *Growing & Learning Through Play.* Poali, PA: Judy/Instructo.

Wolfgang, C. H., and Wolfgang, M. E. (1992). *School for Young Children: Developmentally Appropriate Practices.* Boston: Allyn and Bacon.

Wolfgang, C. H., and Wolfgang, M. E. (1995). *The Three Faces of Discipline for Early Childhood: Empowering Teachers and Students.* Boston: Allyn and Bacon.

# Endnotes

1. Wolfgang, C. H. (1977). *Helping Aggressive and Passive Preschoolers Through Play.* Columbus, OH: Charles E. Merrill.
2. Wolfgang, C. H., Mackender, B., & Wolfgang, M. E. (1981). *Growing & Learning Through Play.* Poali, PA: Judy/Instructo.
3. Wolfgang, C. H., & Wolfgang, M. E. (1992). *School for Young Children: Developmentally Appropriate Practices.* Boston: Allyn and Bacon.
4. Erikson, E. H. (1950). *Childhood and Society.* New York: Norton, 1950.
5. Piaget, J. (1971). *The Construction of Reality in the Child.* New York: Ballantine Books. Piaget, J. (1971). *The Language and Thought of the Child.* New York: World Publishing.
6. Erikson, *Childhood and Society.*
7. Rogers, C. (1969). *Freedom to Learn.* Columbus, OH: Charles E. Merrill.
8. Glasser, W. (1969). *Schools Without Failure.* New York: Peter H. Wyden.
9. Dreikurs, R., & Cassel, P. (1972). *Discipline Without Tears.* New York: Hawthorn Books.
10. Canter, L., & Canter, M. (1976). *Assertive Discipline: A Take-Charge Approach for Today's Educator.* Seal Beach, CA: Lee Canter & Associates.
11. Alberto, P. A., & Troutman, A. C. (1982). *Applied Behavior Analysis for Teachers.* New York: Merrill.
12. Canter & Canter, *Assertive Discipline.*

# 2

# Describing "The Three Faces of Discipline" Systems

## THE LIMITATIONS OF PAST DISCIPLINE MODELS

A discipline situation normally requires the teacher to initiate a desist process toward a student whose behavior is off task, disruptive, or in violation of a rule. This typically involves a clash between the teacher and the student (as in the lost hat incident in Chapter 1). The teacher's desist action has historically been an intuitive action—possibly learned from his or her own childhood home and school experiences, acquired from the student-teaching experience, or learned through trial and error. These actions typically range from simply looking at the off-task student through the use of a visual prompt, to various forms of verbal actions (including mild verbal prompts, threats, and commands), and even to the use of physical intervention whereby the student is removed from the classroom.

Research has show that limit setting, through a desist action by the teacher, is the central skill in establishing positive and effective classroom discipline and classroom climate.[1] Teachers often have a clear and articulated procedure for how an instructional lesson is to be taught, but have little clear and overt cognitive understanding of why they do what they do when they issue a desist action—again, it is largely intuitive. What are you going to do if a student swears at you or tells you to shut up? To help you, the teacher, acquire the ability to make effective limit-setting responses, I offer two large categories of variables: a skill and value system related to your individual personality, and various discipline models involving how to set limits, based on psychological theories and research.

## THE TEACHER'S SKILL AND PERSONALITY TYPE

For the last quarter of the century, responsible and well-meaning district or building administrators have observed their teachers in classrooms and realized that many of these teachers could benefit by having increased training in classroom discipline. The need for discipline training has historically been a political problem, often prompted by a glaring negative incident (a high school teacher punches a tenth-grader or an injury suffered during a discipline action results in a lawsuit) that makes the front page of the local newspaper.

The district administrators, as well as people "outside the classroom," know they have a problem and want a solution. Therefore, they look around to see what is nationally available in discipline training, or what the district next door is using. This often has led them to Teacher Effectiveness Training (T. E. T.), or Glasser, or Assertive Discipline, or the many other widely known discipline models. It was considered a reasonable action to hire these discipline experts to come in to perform in-service training workshops and to purchase their books and media to be available to faculty. The pressure on the teachers, from the district or school level, to follow the techniques of this one chosen expert ranged from a suggestion, to strong encouragement, even to a command that everyone *will* use this districtwide model. One superintendent was heard to declare, "We have gone Assertive Discipline," meaning he had invested considerable money and effort into having the teachers in his district trained in a particular model and he expected every teacher to use it.

When one principal heard a presentation involving the Three Faces of Discipline model with the six or more different models it utilizes, he was overwhelmed and stated, "You expect my teachers to do all of that, when we have been 'doing Glasser' for five years and 40 percent of my teachers are still not using it?"

A parallel can be drawn using more conventional instructional materials. End-of-the-year testing in one school district showed that map skills in the fifth grade were substantially below the national average. That summer, workbooks on map skills were purchased and given to the teachers to use in the following year so that the map skill scores would be elevated. Similar responses take place in dealing with misbehavior. From outside the classroom, the question is asked, "What is the problem?" Often, the answer is poor discipline skills on the part of the teachers, and the typical response is to buy something to take care of this problem. As with the map skills workbooks, administrators are seeking an answer they can "throw at the problem," so they "buy" into one discipline model to "throw" at all the teachers in the school or district. On the surface, this approach may not seem unreasonable. But if we look closely, we will discover that soon the majority of the map skills workbooks—like the science kits and packaged science programs in vogue after the *Sputnik* national science scare—are hidden in the back of a storage closet and go largely unused.

In responding to discipline issues, a return visit to the teachers one year after their discipline model training often will reveal that the techniques have eroded. We find a small minority of teachers still using the techniques, but never in their pure form; most eclectically incorporate a few of the techniques into the basic discipline systems they have always used since the time of their student teaching. One cause may be that teachers are very conservative people and are not motivated to try new things. But if we ask a group of teachers at any school level what they want from in-service training, *discipline* will be ranked clearly at the top of this list. When Glasser or Assertive Discipline models are presented at workshops, even on Saturday mornings, teachers show up for these training sessions enthusiastic, optimistic, and eager for ideas— they are motivated.

I believe the reason most discipline training historically has failed to have a lasting effect is that (1) the training has been delivered in a verbal modality of teaching as a one-shot training with no long-term opportunity for practice and (2) the idea of one discipline orientation for all teachers was a failure of *personality fit*.

## Personality Fit

Let us first look at the concept of personality fit through the example of two mothers, Mother 1 and Mother 2, as they feed 9-month-old infants in high chairs. Mother 1 prepares and stores all warm and cold food on a counter nearby, covers herself completely with an apron, has a moist towelet nearby, and places on the infant a bib that would cover Manhattan. Mother 1 feeds the child one spoonful at a time, making sure that all food goes into the child's mouth and "down." Mother 1 is not harsh and uses fun games such as "Open up the tunnel (child's mouth)— here comes the train (a spoon full of peas)" and uses her warm and gracious personality to get the food into the infant—no spills or mess! The infant enjoys the process. By her actions, Mother 1 needs to be in control of all actions, and by her behavior, she follows a series of rules or has a structure as to how things should be done. Mother 1 has structured for "control of error" but gives limited or no "degrees of freedom" for the child to deviate from the routine.

In contrast is Mother 2. While feeding her infant, she covers the floor under the high chair with a sheet of plastic, dresses the child in a diaper and small shirt, places the food on a serving tray with suction cups secured to the high chair's table, gives the infant a spoon and shows him how to use it. But she allows him to feed himself with his hands while she carries on a "conversation" with her child as she works nearby. Mostly using his hands, the infant gets a third of the food in his mouth, a third on himself, and the other third on the floor. The child enjoys the eating experience. Mother 2 is not upset by this messiness and has observed to see that the infant has eaten an adequate amount of food. She then throws the child's shirt into the wash, kisses him warmly, gives him a bath, and hoses off the plastic sheet for the next time. Mother 2 grants the infant much autonomy, or self-control, but is not naive or permissive. She has structured for "control of error," covered the floor with plastic, dressed the child for the occasion, and organized the suction feeding bowl so the food would not get knocked from the high chair—but she also has granted the child near total "degrees of freedom" for carrying out this feeding activity. Both mothers have communicated with their children in a warm and supportive manner.

If the two mothers continue their patterns of child rearing for the next 17 years, we can clearly see that the result would be very different adult personalities. What if the children were to become teachers and incorporate nearly the exact personality characteristics, techniques, and attitudes toward children, parenting, and teaching? Continuing in this line of thinking, what if we, as school administrators, forced a model of Relationship-Listening on teacher-child 1, Mrs. Control, whereby the students were to help establish rules and sanctions? Would there be a personality fit with this teacher? The answer is no. What if teacher-child 2, Mrs. Autonomy, was required to use the obedience model of Assertive Discipline? Would there be a fit here? Most likely, the answer again would be no.

Now, what would it be like if you were to attend a dinner party at Mrs. Control's house and discover that there is no cream for your coffee? Knowing how busy the hostess is, and not wanting to trouble her, you go to her refrigerator, open it, and retrieve the cream you need. She may or may not say it to you directly but she likely thinks your action was too "forward" and impolite. ("How dare you? This is my home. What makes you think you can just go into my refrigerator?") Mrs. Autonomy, on the other hand, most likely would not even take notice that you opened her refrigerator, and might even consider it rather silly if you first asked permission to do so.

Later, in Mrs. Control's classroom, a student's pencil is broken and he needs to use the pencil sharpener. Can he just get up and use the sharpener any time he wishes? In Mrs. Control's class, the answer is no—you sharpen at the beginning or end of the period, but you do not do it during class. This classroom offers minimum "degrees of freedom." Mrs. Control also has a can of sharpened pencils nearby that students may borrow and then return, so they will have a pencil if theirs happens to break—this is "control of error." In contrast, Mrs. Autonomy permits students to sharpen pencils any time they wish, and she doesn't even seem to notice when it occurs. Both Mrs. (or Mr.) Control and Mrs. (or Mr.) Autonomy are effective teachers who are loved by their students, but they have very different personalities and run very different discipline and classroom management programs. Observers, such as school administrators, would evaluate them as excellent teachers.

The problem comes when we ask Mrs. (Mr.) Control and Mrs. (Mr.) Autonomy to be something that they are not. We mother (or father) the way we have been mothered (or fathered), and we most likely teach the way we have been taught—this is a projection of each individual's personality structure. Each of us, as teachers, has a personality core that is the "child" in us, reflecting the way we were raised, and we draw on this core when we socially interact with others. We have varying degrees of need for control and for formalizing rules to guide interactions between us and others. That core of personality will most likely be who we are for most of our lives, but with some minor changes as we mature.

As a teacher, establishing rules and setting limits with students in your classroom is a projection of your personality core of who you are as a person. Forcing you to practice techniques that are diametrically opposite to your personality core will make you false, mechanical, and ineffective—it simply won't work. We may then say that some of the discipline models, because of their degrees of power and the development of rules, are a mismatch to your own personality core. There is a lack of personality fit—they are not your "face." So, when the principal says, "We have been 'doing Glasser' for five years and 40 percent of my teachers are still not using it!" what he is really saying is that Glasser was not a personality fit for two out of every five teachers in his school— that this was not a "face" or philosophy that those teachers were psychologically comfortable in using.

The power continuum, as part of the Three Faces of Discipline, takes the position that all of these models are of value and that teachers cannot be dictated to regarding the use of one model. Instead, they must find the model or "face" that fits their personality core. Mrs. Control would be called strict by her students, while Mrs. Autonomy might be called a "softy" by the same students, but both of these teachers are effective and well liked by students and administrators.

It is Mrs. Waffle who has the serious discipline difficulties. One time she strongly disciplines a student for breaking a rule, but the next day she says nothing when the same rule is broken. Mrs. Waffle is not fair, firm, and consistent. The students will say that they can never tell "where she is coming from"—this teacher waffles. She is unpredictable and will be ineffective as a teacher and disliked by the students.

Now we may help Mrs. Waffle by assessing her personality core, by using the Beliefs about Discipline Inventory, and by helping train her in the one discipline model—one of the three "faces"—that most fits her personality (see Chapter 1 for the Inventory). This model will permit Mrs. Waffle to stop waffling, creating an orderliness to her behavior that students can understand, and thus she becomes predictable and no longer "scary" to the students. We may also use these models and three "faces" in other ways.

## THE FIVE SYSTEMS OF AN EFFECTIVE DISCIPLINE PROGRAM

The brief definition of discipline and the lost hat incident seen in Chapter 1 showed the desist or limit-setting process. This was given for purposes of introducing the concept of the Three Faces of Discipline, allowing us to see how a teacher's attitude, methods, and procedures changed in a way that became more demanding as the teacher escalated the use of power. But in order to have a complete discipline program in a classroom or school, we must go beyond limit setting by adding the aspect of classroom management. Putting together discipline and classroom management, including schoolwide management, will involve five subsystems, each of which will be described in detail in subsequent chapters.

1. Limit-Setting System (stops misbehavior)

2. Professional-Administrative Backup System (enlists the help of students, colleagues, parents, and other professionals)

3. Incentive System (maintains, increases, and speeds up desired behaviors)

4. Encouragement System (encourages positive behavior)

5. Classroom Management System (organizes objects and students to support and maintain desired behavior)

These subsystems are interdependent. In order for this process to be effective, each of the five systems must be fully implemented—no single component (such as limit setting) can stand alone.

## Limit-Setting System

Limit setting and its process of desist is the system for taking actions, in the privacy of your own classroom, toward one or more students who by their actions are preventing you from teaching and other students from learning, or who are failing to follow required procedures and rules. To put it simply, it is a request to the student that says, "Stop what you are doing, and do what I want you to do." Limit setting will start with the day-in, day-out small off-task behaviors that can also explode to conflict management (as in our Chapter 1 example of Mike and the lost hat) and blow up as outward defiance in the form of an assault against the teacher. To be effective at discipline, you must know how to set limits. Each action carries with it an inherent degree of power; your crucial skill in limit setting is knowing how much power is appropriate to use in a given situation. Employing too much power would be like using a sledgehammer to drive in a tack, whereas too little power may communicate to the students that you are afraid of them or do not mean business.[2]

## Professional-Administrative Backup System

When you have used all your limit-setting methods and techniques (described in detail later), and the student's behavior is still disrupting the classroom learning climate, you may need to declare that this student's actions and behavior are beyond your skills and abilities. You would then seek professional help from others outside your classroom, thereby making the discipline action public. Such professional help might involve the other teachers, school counselor, school psychologist, and various mental health organizations, or—in the most extreme cases—even institutionalized care for the student. The actions of the student could also involve criminal acts, which could necessitate the involvement of the administration, school board, police, juvenile authorities, and the court system.

The Professional-Administrative Backup System requires two parts (see Figure 2–1). The first entails a Professional Sphere, with clearly delineated steps and procedures designed to permit you, as the primary deliverer of educational services, to gain professional consultation, through staffing, from colleagues. The objective is to enable you to increase your skill and become more effective with a particular very difficult student.

The second part utilizes an Administrative-Legal Sphere involving a yielding of primary responsibility for the management and restraint of the student's behavior. This would occur because of the severity of the student's actions, which may be criminal or at the least threaten your safety and well-being or that of your class—or even the disruptive student himself. Understandable and clearly defined steps and procedures must be established to dictate when such crisis students should be referred to the administrative authorities or legal system.

## Incentive System

While the limit-setting system provides techniques for getting students to stop their misbehavior so ongoing teaching is not disrupted, the Incentive System is a classroom process of motivating the students to increase the speed of their work and positive behaviors, or to acquire new behaviors not already in their repertoire. Examples would include getting students to do their homework or to care for school property.

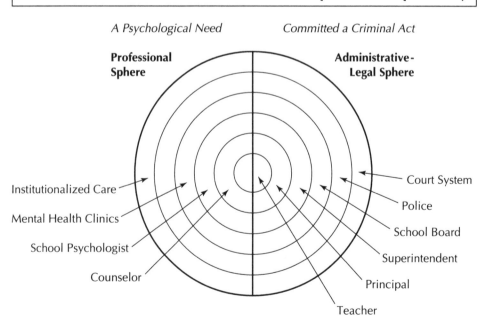

**FIGURE 2–1   Professional and Administrative Spheres of Responsibility**

### Encouragement System

We may have a very difficult student for whom the Incentive System may not work—in fact this student, by his or her behavior, may actually destroy the Incentive System. The teacher is now required to use an Encouragement System especially designed to deal with the more difficult student and to work tangentially—in something of a piggyback approach—with the Incentive System. The Encouragement System is an individualized, targeted system to deal with the very discouraged and difficult student.

### Classroom (and School) Management System

The key method of eliminating many discipline problems is the skillful management of, or the understanding and use of the technology of management of, (1) the design of classroom objects, furniture, and materials; (2) the arrangement of students in large groups, small groups, and one-to-one relationships; (3) the teaching and creation of rules; and (4) the collective and accepted procedures of the schoolwide staff and administration regarding the open field management of the total school environment (such as the hallways, cafeteria, playground, and similar areas).

The Three Faces of Discipline and the five systems demonstrate that each of the systems draws on techniques from existing discipline models, placing them into the three categories of Relationship-Listening, Confronting-Contracting, and Rules and Consequences. Techniques for managing violent and assaultive student behavior are also included.

## SUMMARY

For the experienced teacher who already has had some training in previous discipline models, such as Glasser or Assertive Discipline, the advantage of this new Three Faces of Discipline model is that you do not need to learn a totally new model, but can continue to use past practices while adding many more techniques and systems to create a complete, effective discipline program. This new, more inclusive model wraps around the experienced teacher's present techniques by adding to and expanding teaching skills. You can select and design a power pathway of techniques (the three "faces" or degrees of power) to fit your teaching style. The Beliefs about Discipline Inventory (see Chapter 1) helps you determine which techniques you find most comfortable using. One model is not forced on every teacher in the school, so each teacher can find and employ techniques that fit well with his or her values. This model is not a simplistic recipe.

Thus, obtaining good discipline in the classroom, using the Three Faces model, will involve five systems:

1. Limit-Setting System

2. Professional-Administrative Backup System

3. Incentive System

4. Encouragement System

5. Classroom Management System

The Three Faces of Discipline will enable you to teach the students rules and gain control of your classroom; gradually, the students will then be taught to be self-disciplined. The daily Incentive System allows you to relate to the students in positive ways, and the Encouragement System enables you to deal with one particularly discouraged student. Also, the Three Faces of Discipline model gives the principal or administrator a positive role as part of the Backup System. Finally, the model is not limited to the close confines of the classroom, providing techniques for managing schoolwide student behavior in such open field settings as the hallways, playground, cafeteria, and buses.

# Endnotes

1. Kounin, J. S. (1970). *Discipline and Group Management in Classrooms*. New York: Holt, Rinehart and Winston.

2. Jones, F. (1978). *Positive Discipline*. New York: McGraw-Hill.

# The Limit-Setting System

## Using the Pathway of Power as the Teacher Behavior Continuum

Ultimately, all meaningful classroom discipline must begin with setting limits. Discipline cannot survive on limit setting alone, but a teacher cannot expect students to exhibit appropriate behavior if she has not identified the boundaries that define that behavior.

Limit setting, with its process of desist, enables the teacher to take steps to minimize the disruption caused by one or more students whose actions are preventing the teacher from carrying out instruction and the other students from learning. The limit-setting system can be utilized effectively within the individual classroom or in such open field settings as the hallways, playground, or cafeteria. In its simplest terms it is a tool for the teacher to tell the misbehaving student to stop what he is doing and begin doing what the teacher wants done.

To be effective at discipline, you must know how to set limits. The crucial skill for using the Limit-Setting System is knowing how much power is appropriate to use with a given student in a given situation. Too much power can cause the misbehaving student to rebel even more, whereas too little power can signal the student that the teacher is afraid and does not mean business.

# 3

# Looking

## The Relationship-Listening Face

The following is a classroom discipline incident involving the teacher's use of limit setting and the first step on the Teacher Behavior Continuum—*looking* (sometimes called *modality cueing*). The nonitalicized words in this vignette highlight the techniques or processes being utilized, and will be defined throughout this chapter.

> *Ms. Dumas has just finished teaching a new math concept to her fourth-grade class and has directed the students to do seatwork to practice applying this concept. She moves around the room,* working the crowd *and* checking each student's work. *While working with one student, she hears muffled whispers and the slight movement of a chair coming from the far side of the room. She looks up* (check it out) *to see Nancy's eyes appear above her textbook and then disappear behind it. Again, there are whispers, and Ms. Dumas sees Nancy physically turn toward Martha, her neighbor. Nancy is busy giggling and talking to Martha, who appears to be writing. Nancy is clearly off task, requiring Ms. Dumas to take some action to get her to use the seatwork time constructively and get back to work.*

---

### CHECK IT OUT

The teacher periodically scans the classroom for off-task behavior while at the same time continues to work with students.

---

### WORKING THE CROWD

While instructing, the teacher walks around the room to make eye contact and be physically close to each student (proxemics) in order to retain control and compliance.

---

*Ms. Dumas (1) slowly stands fully erect, (2) turns her body and feet so that she is squared off with Nancy, (3) takes two controlled relaxing breaths, and attempts to (4) make eye contact with Nancy, who is not looking in her direction. Ms. Dumas remains squared off and maintains an unbroken gaze at Nancy.* The other class members see Ms. Dumas's cues, and signal Nancy to look in the teacher's direction. Nancy now makes eye contact with Ms. Dumas and sees the teacher looking straight at her. She wiggles in her chair and turns her upper body toward Ms. Dumas, but her lower body (knees and feet) still faces her neighbor. She picks up her pencil (pseudo-compliance: pencil posturing) *and places it on her paper as if to write. She looks again to see Ms. Dumas still holding the same unwavering eye contact. Nancy meets Ms. Dumas's eye contact directly and smiles at her with an open-mouth-and-teeth smile, with a slight cock of her head and raised eyebrows* ("smiley face"). *The endearing smile is one that would encourage anyone to automatically or reflexively smile back, but Ms. Dumas holds her same upright posture. She maintains the eye-to-eye visual lock with Nancy and returns Nancy's smiling overture with a flat facial expression that clearly communicates "I am not amused!"* At the same time, the teacher takes two more relaxing breaths. *It is a look worthy of England's unsmiling Queen Victoria, notorious for her icy stare.*

---

### "SMILEY FACE"

A misbehaving student's attempt to be "innocent" and appeal to the confronting teacher by showing an open-mouth-and-teeth grin (typically the student's eyebrows lift in the middle and the head is cocked to one side).

---

### EYE CONTACT

The teacher establishes eye contact with a misbehaving student and maintains it unwaveringly until the student returns to work.

---

*Nancy drops her eyes to her papers and with her pencil begins to take actions* (pseudo-compliance) *as if she is busy writing* (pencil posturing). *Ms. Dumas stands staring at Nancy for another minute, and then moves to a nearby student to inspect his work; however, in bending over the student's desk, she places herself so that she is still facing Nancy. Again, whispers are heard from Nancy's direction. With her body still bent over the student's desk, Ms. Dumas takes two more relaxing breaths and cranes her neck to scan the classroom, where she discovers that Nancy is again off task. Staying down, the teacher (1) excuses herself from the student she has been help-ing, (2) takes two more relaxing breaths, and (3) stands at a deliberate pace, slightly faster than slow motion, to an upright position. For the second time, she takes on the "I am not amused" facial expression. She (4) stares directly at Nancy across the room while (5) placing her hands behind her back* (body telegraphing).

---

### BODY TELEGRAPHING

Through nonverbal body actions (*kinestics*), the teacher communicates to the observing students her anger and fear, or that she "means business."

---

*Nancy sees Ms. Dumas and quickly returns to her* pencil posturing *pretending to do some form of writing as a form of psuedo-compliance. Ms. Dumas takes two more relaxing breaths, and waits. Seconds, or more likely minutes, click by with Nancy being aware of receiving visual "heat" from Ms. Dumas. Like a boiling pot, she becomes active in an array of actions—she tears out a sheet of paper, takes a second pencil from her desk, folds the paper, and appears to put her pencil to paper* (pseudo-compliance), *all for the purpose of convincing Ms. Dumas that she is now working and that the teacher can turn off the visual heat.*

---

### PSEUDO-COMPLIANCE

When a teacher signals a student to get back to work, the student per-forms a series of behaviors designed to convince the teacher that the stu-dent is complying when in reality he or she is not.

---

*This time, Ms. Dumas is not fooled. She takes two more of her controlled breaths and then—still holding her visual stare—begins to walk slowly across the room, directly toward Nancy. She moves with a deliberate gait straight out of the movie* High Noon. *She stops and squares off inches in front of Nancy's desk, again assuming the posture, with her hands behind her back and her face in the flat Queen Victoria "I am not amused" expression. Finally, her eyes are fixed, looking directly down at Nancy. Ms. Dumas takes her two relaxing breaths and waits.*

*Nancy responds, "Wha-a-t?" Ms. Dumas again takes two controlled breaths and maintains her fixed stare at Nancy. Seconds or even minutes pass. Nancy whines, "I wasn't doing anything. What?* (back talk: denial). *Martha wanted a pencil* (back talk: blaming), *that's all." Ms. Dumas maintains her posture and stares. Nancy drops her eyes and becomes passive. Ms. Dumas reaches out with her right hand, turns Nancy's textbook to page 45, and points to the first problem* (prompt). *She then returns to the upright Queen Victoria stare. Nancy now copies the problem onto her paper. Seeing that Ms. Dumas is still looking, Nancy whines for a second time, "I don't know how to do this"* (back talk: helplessness). *Still, Queen Victoria waits before her subject* (camping out in front). *Again, Nancy attempts another defensive ploy: "You went over this so quickly I didn't understand it"* (back talk: accusing the teacher of professional incompetence). *Queen Victoria Dumas takes two more controlled breaths, holds her position, and stares. Nancy looks attentively at the problem on her paper and puts down one number, then a second, and finally the problem is completed* (giving the teacher "part of the loaf"). *She now looks up at Queen Dumas with her second "smiley face"—open-mouth-and-teeth smile, raised eyebrows, and slight cock of the head. Except for two more controlled breaths, Mr. Dumas maintains her royal pose.*

---

### CAMPING OUT IN FRONT

A limit-setting technique through which the teacher places her palms on the misbehaving student's desk, indicating that the teacher will stay until the student's behavior changes.

---

*Ms. Dumas notices that under the table Nancy's lower body is still pointing to the neighbor who was the target of her talking. Nancy's position seems to say to the teacher, "I'll return to my talking once I get you out of my face." Nancy now appears passive and fails to continue. Ms. Dumas leans forward or eases over in a slow controlled manner and places the palms* (palms) *of her two hands flat on the far sides of Nancy's desk and seatwork, and takes two relaxing breaths.*

*The teacher remains palms-down on Nancy's desk and watches, maintaining unwavering eye contact with Nancy* (camping out in front). *Ms. Dumas is still looking when Nancy again whines, "I don't know how to do this"* (back talk: helplessness). *Queen Victoria waits before her subject* (camping out in front). *Again, Nancy retries her defensive ploy, "You went over this so quickly I didn't understand it"* (back talk: accusing the teacher of professional incompetence). *"Martha asked me for a pencil, I was only giving her a pencil."* (back talk: blaming).

*Martha, the neighbor, now joins Nancy's power team and attempts to gang up on Ms. Dumas, stating, "Yeah, get out of her face. Are you queer or something? F--- off!!"* (back talk: profanity).

*Ms. Dumas takes two more* relaxing breaths *and then, in a slow controlled manner, stands erect, does her Queen Victoria, takes two breaths, and slowly moves behind and between the girls. Ms. Dumas eases between the girls and places her elbow on Nancy's desk. She then leans over and meets Nancy in a face-to-face, eyeball-to-eyeball fixed stare, with her back to Martha* (camping out from behind). *She creates a wall between Nancy and Martha, thus splitting up this gang of two. The teacher has divided up the problem.*

---

## CAMPING OUT FROM BEHIND

A limit-setting technique through which the teacher moves behind the off-task student and places an elbow on the student's desk, putting up a wall that blocks out a second misbehaving student, all the while using limit-setting teacher behaviors.

---

*Nancy turns her lower body so her legs are now fully under her desk. She does a second, third, and fourth math problem while Ms. Dumas is "camped out." When Nancy is half-way through the second line of problems, Ms. Dumas speaks to her for the first time: "Thank you, Nancy." The teacher smiles, then picks up her elbow and turns around to face Martha. She places her other elbow and her weight on Martha's desk. Martha does not look up and is obviously working like an eager beaver on her math problems. Ms. Dumas smiles and says, "Thank you, Martha."*

*Queen Victoria Dumas begins to ease out from this confrontation; she slowly stands* (moving out), *breathes, turns, and walks to the front of Martha's desk. She takes two relaxing breaths, assumes the royal pose, and looks directly at Martha. Ms. Dumas slowly walks away from the girls* (moving out), *but first she takes five or six steps, stops, turns, takes two relaxing breaths, and looks at Nancy and then Martha. Both girls are now too busy to look up.*

*Ms. Dumas walks back to the student she originally was helping, but before bending over to help, she again takes a Queen Victoria look at Nancy and Martha. After finally being reassured, she takes two more relaxing breaths and bends over to help the nearby student, placing herself beside the new student but again in direct view of Nancy and Martha, as well as the rest of the class.*

*Once she has helped this student, Ms. Dumas slowly walks among the students' prearranged desks, traversing an interior circle around the classroom as she passes among the working students. She checks on various students' work, and passes again before Nancy and Martha.*

*While walking about, she stops, looks, checks, and in a voice soft enough that a neighbor cannot hear, makes comments about a particular student's work before moving on (working the crowd). In all, she speaks to five to seven students. When she comes to Martha, three minutes before the bell is to ring, she appears to stop, look, check, and comment in a similar fashion. But this time she whispers a different nonacademic statement: "Martha, after the bell rings I would like you to stay behind—we need to talk" (camouflage).*

---

### CAMOUFLAGE

The teacher stops and whispers to several students about their work, but when she whispers to a misbehaving student, she delivers a limit-setting statement, thus disguising the confronting behavior from the other students.

---

*Minutes later, the bell rings and the students depart, passing Ms. Dumas as she stands at the door. When Martha arrives, the teacher signals her to move to a nearby desk, then closes the door to the now empty classroom (private meeting). It is time for Ms. Dumas to deal with Martha regarding her use of profanity (don't go public!). Ms. Dumas has not forgotten Martha's words, "Yeah, get out of her face. Are you queer or something? F--- off!!"*

## LIMIT SETTING: THE TBC'S *LOOKING*

The objective for all limit setting is to calm the students and get them back on task, as Ms. Dumas did with Nancy. Research by Jones, author of *Positive Discipline*, shows that 80 percent of all discipline problems involve the off-task behavior of students talking to others when they should be working. The second most common form is goofing off or out-of-seat behaviors (15 percent), followed by such misbehaviors as note passing, playing with items smuggled into class, and tying shoelaces. When most people think of discipline problems, however, they usually think of the "big ticket" items of physical aggression, overt defiance, and destruction of property. If we use time as a central variable, we can justify and think out the value of a teacher's actions, asking, "How much does this teacher technique cost in time?" You may have wonderful discipline procedures, but if they eat up so much of your time that none is left for instruction, the techniques are of no value.

It can be reasoned that big-ticket discipline actions—assault and clear defiance of the teacher's authority—normally are very rare occurrences. These incidents take 5 minutes or less, and generally are seen by teachers no more than 5 times in a school year. By simply multiplying the 5 incidents by 5 minutes, you can see that you may spend a great deal of time worrying about big-ticket discipline incidents that might actually consume 25 minutes or less of your teaching time in an entire school year. What is more important is to watch the "nickel-and-dime" actions of talking and out-of-seat behavior, which, when combined, could eat up one-third or more of your total class time. For all the concern about big-ticket incidents, it is these nickel-and-dime misbehaviors that consume your energies and eventually wear you down. Nancy and Martha's talking may be seen as a minor incident at first, but it did cause the teacher to stop her instruction. Multiply that by 8 to 10 such incidents in a relatively short span, and they will add up, wear you out, and cut deeply into "time on task," which is correlated to academic achievement.

We may see the Nancys and Marthas of the classroom as playing a power game and doing penny-ante gambling. When these girls face Ms. Dumas for the first time, they ask, "Does she really mean what she says? Do we have to work in this classroom or can we play?" Nancy, as a *low roller* or gambler, has a Ph.D. in the "Teacher Game" to see who will hold the power in this classroom—to see how far she can go and to test this teacher to see if she means business. Nancy has learned a host of pseudo-compliance behaviors to sidetrack the teacher during power plays.

---

### LOW ROLLER

A student who attempts to play power games with the teacher in subtle ways that do not involve much risk of detection.

---

If Nancy can get the teacher to buy into these behaviors when the teacher asks her to stop playing and get to work, the teacher will lose the game and control will shift to the student's game playing. Although they look different and take various forms of being negative or positive, the techniques are all labeled as *back talk*. When confronted for compliance, Nancy and Martha began a conscious and unconscious series of back talk maneuvers to take Ms. Dumas down a blind alley toward powerlessness and defeat. This back talk took the following forms:

- *Helplessness:* "I don't know how to do this."

- *Denial:* "I wasn't doing anything. What?"

- *Blaming:* "Martha wanted a pencil, that's all!"

- *Accusing the teacher of professional incompetence:* "You went over this so quickly I didn't understand it."

- *Excusing the teacher to leave:* "Yeah, get out of her face."

- *Insult:* "Are you queer or something?"

- *Profanity*: "F--- off!"

Other forms of back talk that do not appear as such to most teachers include:

- *Crying:* The student attempts to get the teacher's sympathy.

- *Compliments:* The student makes flattering statements to the teacher.

- *Tangential statements:* The student asks a question about a topic not under discussion.

- *Pushing you aside:* When the teacher puts her hands on the desk, palms down, the student pushes them aside and off the desk.

- *Romance:* The student actually kisses the teacher or makes a sexual overture.

Every student knows the power game that is proceeding, with the ultimate prize being to see the teacher lose her cool, signaling a complete victory for the students and a total lack of control of the classroom. Remember these words: *My life is in the hands of any fool who makes me lose my temper. Calm is strenth. Upset is weakness.*[1]

## Fight or Flight Response

Think back to a time you may have tried hard to forget. You were driving your car and stopped at a red light. The light changed and you slowly pulled into the intersection, but another driver ran the light and barreled through the intersection at excessive speed. If you had not suddenly jammed on your brakes and turned your wheel quickly, you would have had a very serious accident. The adrenaline pumped through your body, your heart was in your throat, your face was warm, and your teeth were clenched. For a moment you felt as if you might throw up, and as you got out of your car 15 minutes later your legs were still wobbly. You were experiencing the results of a *fight or flight* response.

---

### FIGHT OR FLIGHT

A primal, unthinking reflex action either to dig in for a fight or to run away, all triggered by frightening or confrontational behavior.

---

Let's look at a second example—one we might have experienced but are more likely to have seen. A child, typically a two- or three-year-old, has broken from mother's hand and run into a busy street, or pushed over the white-hot charcoal grill, or released the parking brake on dad's car, or some similar action that clearly could be life-threatening for the child or others. Moments later, we see the parent, nose-to-nose with the child, screaming at the child never to do that again. The parent's emotional state and inside feelings are just as you felt when you almost had an auto accident. For all intents and purposes, the parent—quite understandably— is hysterical and out of control, and the child will be lucky to avoid being hit or shaken harshly. Teachers in schools and classrooms, of course, cannot deal with students in the same manner as the parent deals with this misbehaving child.

When you had your near-accident, your body experienced an *adrenaline dump* triggered by an external stimulus that caused a reflex body action. Like the parent, you were out of control as long as you were in this hyper-alert state, meaning that for a short period you lost your use of rational reasoning and were functioning as an automatic defensive being. Rational thinking is too slow for sudden emergencies, and your body has a built-in survival process that shuts down higher-order thinking so the defensive reflexes can act to save you. When animals are cornered, their lack of language abilities and rational thinking leaves them with only two choices—they can fight or they can flee. Humans experience a similar response when events push them out of rational thinking. This fight or flight response exacts a high price in the level of stress and burned-up energy.

---

### ADRENALINE DUMP

An emotional state, triggered by some action, causing a fight or flight state with a huge rush of adrenaline into the blood stream, resulting in extremely high and sudden levels of tension or stress.

---

Theoreticians suggest that humans have what may be thought of as three brains. This *triune brain* contains (1) a reptilian brain located at the base of the brain stem; (2) a paleocortex, an ancient cortex or "doggy-horsey brain"; and (3) a neocortex, or new cortex of higher intelligence. The Triune Brain Theory (see Figure 4–1) suggests that each of these three brains has its own functions, but under stress our thought processes downshift to lower primal brain centers for purposes of survival. Under moderate arousal, the management of behavior shifts from the neocortex to the paleocortex. Under extreme arousal, the management of behavior shifts from the paleocortex to the reptilian brain. This means that when we are angry, frightened, or upset, we become noncortical, animal-like beings, and higher thinking from the neocortex is unavailable until we calm down. The downshift occurs in two forms: an

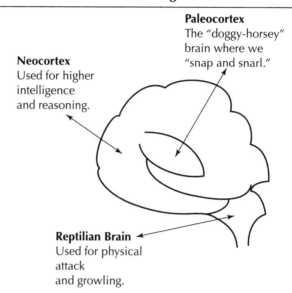

FIGURE 3–1   Truine Brain Functioning

*adrenaline dump* or a *slow "bleeding"* of adrenaline into the body system, which maintains a constant defensive state of stress.

We have seen, in the automobile near-miss and the parent reprimanding the child for a dangerous action, a full regression or downshifting to either the reptilian brain or the "doggy-horsey" brain as a result of a full adrenaline dump. In the classroom, you may face discipline incidents that are extremely confrontational toward you, as seen in Martha's implicit verbal aggression of "I'll return to my talking once I get you out of my face, so buzz off!" Other examples, admittedly less frequent, may include a student who has a weapon, who is spiteful and hurtful to others, or who exhibits a willful destruction of school property. More likely for most teachers are the day-in, day-out moderate arousals that cause the *slow bleeding* of adrenaline into their systems. The constancy of small "nickel-and-dime" discipline incidents, such as Nancy's chatting and off-task behavior, can cause an educator to continually teach and function at a moderate arousal level. For the teacher partially in a fight or flight stance with its accompanying stress, classroom life may be compared with the soldier who begins to suffer battle fatigue—a constant draining of energy.

---

### ADRENALINE "BLEED"

A state of hyper-alertness where the body is in a partial fight-or-flight state, continually producing adrenaline and causing constant tension.

---

The "slow bleed" phenomenon is caused by stress, and clear practical actions to control this stress can maintain the teacher's classroom power and effectiveness. In the student power game, the ultimate way of winning control of the classroom is for the teacher to regress to a state where she has "lost her cool," meaning the teacher is so emotional that she is reflexively acting from her reptilian brain and her higher-order thinking is unavailable. There is a high probability that this teacher, in the absence of cortex thinking, will do something very dumb. When the teacher has regressed *(gone brain stemmed)*, it is "show time" for the students. The teacher is now out of control and the students are in control, and the teacher's behavior will be quite amusing to the students as she struggles in an attempt to regain control of her classroom.

---

### "GOING BRAIN STEMMED"

In a heated conflict, the brain downshifts to the reflexive, noncognitive reptilian brain. When this occurs, it suggests the teacher is out of control and is instead controlled by emotions.

---

Let's take a look at how another professional handles a high-stress situation: a baseball umpire. It's the last of the ninth inning and the home team is down by two runs. There are two outs and the bases are loaded. The batter hits a single to right field. The runner on third base scores, and the runner on second base rounds third and heads for home as the tying run. The right fielder makes a powerful, accurate throw to home plate. It's a close play, and as the dust clears, 50,000 spectators, millions watching on television, and the players—their multimillion-dollar contracts depending on the outcome of games such as this—are all waiting for this one individual, the umpire, to call the play. The umpire looks *(see it)*, points his thumb to the heavens, shouts, "You're out!" *(sell it)*, and prepares himself as all hell breaks loose *(must live it)*. The home team's players and manager pour from the dugout and descend on the umpire—a lone man in a stressful situation who now needs to live with his decision. A power game begins with the manager shouting in the umpire's face. The manager's power game is to see if the umpire "means business" or if he can get the umpire to back down.

Clearly see what the umpire does. He removes his face mask, plants his feet firmly on the ground, and squares off to the manager, who is screaming in his face as the TV cameras zoom in for a close-up. The umpire puts his hands behind his back and crosses them, while he maintains unwavering eye contact with the hostile manager. He takes on a facial expression that says, "I am bored. I wonder what I'll have for dinner tonight," and appears to mentally leave the ball park. If he is skilled, he says nothing and stands his ground, maintaining unwavering eye contact with everyone who is back talking to him. He simply stands there and breathes deeply, waiting for the manager and players to wear themselves out with insults, blame, and questions of his professional competence (*back talk*). Doing nothing is the umpire's act of power and control. If he cannot control the adrenaline rush moving through his body, he will *go brain stemmed,* or lose his "cool," and begin to talk back to the manager and players. If this happens, he is doomed to lose control, and real violence may erupt. This would cause the most dangerous of situations among the players and fans. There is a very important lesson for the classroom teacher to learn from the baseball umpire's behavior. As a teacher, you will find yourself in confrontational situations with students involving heated and stressful interaction and back talk, but, like the umpire, you must control your behavior and maintain power. *Calm is strength. Upset is weakness.*[2]

Let's now see an example of the behavior of a teacher who has "gone brain stemmed" or "*gone chemical*" (meaning physically full of adrenaline and overcome by a fight or flight posture).

---

### "GONE CHEMICAL"

During a confrontational limit-setting process, the teacher becomes so emotional that adrenaline is heavily released into the body, making the teacher so tense that he or she cannot think correctly.

---

*In a harsh voice one step short of actually shouting, Ms. Hopkins says, "If I have told you once, Wanda and Marie, I have told you a hundred times. (The teacher stands with left hand on left hip, balancing on her left leg and tapping her right foot, as she points and shakes her index finger across the room at the girls in a threatening action). This is work time. I don't want to see you two talking, and I don't want to have to come over there! This is valuable class time and you, young ladies, are losing it. I am sick and tired of having to stop my work because of you two girls!"*

This teacher is a nagging person who is under stress and has regressed to a fight or flight position, probably with only her paleocortex (*doggy-horsey brain*) in gear. Like an animal, the teacher "snaps and snarls" and does *silly talk*; the words she says mean nothing and are even poor examples of threats. The hand pointing and similar physical actions are nonverbal territorial actions, used in the animal kingdom by creatures to intimidate and scare off rivals. The screaming baseball manager is a good example of *silly talk* as he gestures and shouts, but these are a part of the manager's powerlessness and game playing. The fans, however, are entertained because it is *show time*. Students see these behaviors in teachers and are not fearful, but are entertained by the sight of a teacher who is so weak that the students can "push her button" and get such an entertaining action from an adult who is supposed to be mature and in charge: "It's *show time,* classmates."

## EYE CONTACT AND PROXEMICS

In animal species and also among humans, contact with another individual is done by reading nonverbal body messages, and the eyes are the most expressive source of nonverbal communication. An unswerving eye lock with an individual is the most powerful confrontational stance involving real power and subservience. Eye contact with another individual is a direct challenge or exercise of power, and when the other individual breaks the visual lock, it is read as capitulation and subservience ("I don't wish to fight; I yield to your power"). One person literally stares the other down. The dominant person looks and the other person smiles back as a signal of capitulation, or "I wish to be your friend." If the dominant person smiles back, the offer of friendship is accepted. If the dominant person does not smile back or break the heat of looking, we have a direct power challenge.

> *Nancy meets Ms. Dumas's eye contact directly and smiles at her with an open-mouth-and-teeth smile, with a slight cock of her head and raised eyebrows* ("smiley face"). *The endearing smile is one that would encourage anyone to automatically or reflexively smile back, but Ms. Dumas holds her same upright posture. She maintains the eye-to-eye visual lock with Nancy, and returns Nancy's smiling overture with a flat facial expression that clearly communicates "I am not amused!" At the same time, the teacher takes two more relaxing breaths.*

The "heat" that the other person will feel from being visually confronted will depend on the spatial distance between the two people, as indicated by the *concept of proxemics*. Across the classroom, the challenge may be very strong but can be fended off by many game-playing students. However, when the teacher moves to the edge of the student's desk and leans over it, the visual heat is turned up dramatically and the student's inner kettle of emotions begins to bubble—fueled by the output of adrenaline and stress within the student. The student is now in a fight or flight confrontation with the teacher.

Most people have around them personal space, an invisible three-foot "bubble" in which they feel safe. When this space is invaded by others, the person becomes emotionally uncomfortable and feels potentially threatened. When you touch students, place your hands on what they touch, or place your face inches from theirs, you burst their bubble and the protective safety of their personal space. You force them to resist or back down (fight or flight).

We may classify space distances when visually confronting a misbehaving student as *proximity-far* when the teacher is across the room, *proximity-near* when within three feet or at the edge of the student's "comfort bubble," and *proximity-intimate* when mere inches from the student's face. As the teacher, you actually use these three distances as a technique of signaling the student to desist and return to work, and escalate the intrusion by doing a slow walk. You begin a process of *clos-*

*ing space* and start to turn up the heat in the confrontational process. The slow movement of walking and all other easing movements are for the purpose of giving the student time to recognize and understand the challenge, and to allow you to maintain and body-telegraph a calm message of "I am in charge" and "I mean business."

---

### COMFORT BUBBLE

An invisible three-foot circle around the student, in which the student is secure. The student feels threatened if someone invades this space.

---

### CLOSING SPACE

In limit setting, the teacher escalates the confrontation by moving toward the student and "accepting" the student's challenge.

---

## LIMIT SETTING ON THE WING

*Proximity is accountability. Distance is safety.*[3] The teacher who has been trained in the Three Faces of Discipline will not be found lecturing from behind her desk, seated on top of her desk, or seated in a chair. The Three Faces of Discipline style of teaching requires the teacher to be on her feet slowly walking and *working the crowd*, moving among the students who are seated at desks or tables. When walking, or *on the wing*, the teacher is aware of and uses eye contact and proximity to maintain the attentiveness or work activity of each and every student. The combination of walking and looking creates a conscious ballet of movement that will bring the teacher in *proximity-far* (as far as 10 feet) and *proximity-near* (at the edge of the 3-foot "comfort bubble" of each student). Periodically, when bending over to help one student for a few moments, the teacher is in *proximity-intimate*. Throughout the entire class period, students will always feel the teacher's presence, whether the teacher is instructing or the students are doing independent seatwork.

In order for the teacher to perform this walking ballet to work the crowd, it is critical to have well-designed staging of the students' desks, chairs, or tables. Classrooms traditionally are thought of as six rows of five or more chairs each, with the teacher's desk before a chalkboard at the front of the classroom. In such a room arrangement, however, the desks act as a defensive wall, placing distance between the teacher and the students and always maintaining the teacher at the *proximity-far*. Instead, the students' desks should be arranged with an interior loop as a pathway for the teacher to walk through (see Figure 3–2).

The use of an interior loop of free floor space, where the teacher can walk without obstruction, permits easy teacher movement and excellent supervision through the use of proximity and eye contact. We will cover

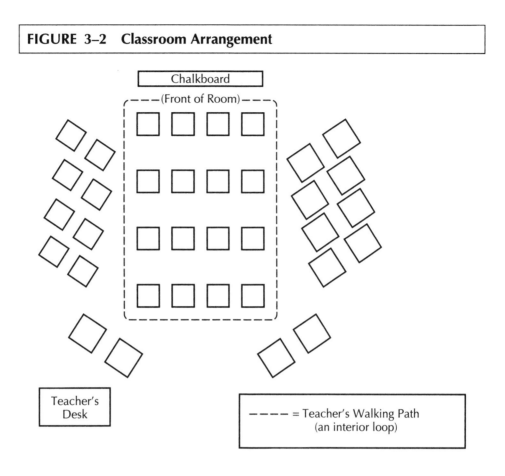

**FIGURE 3–2   Classroom Arrangement**

in great detail the effective arrangement of furniture, space, and objects in Section VI, but it is important to point out that space and its arrangement are critical for the use of proximity constructing and the TBC's *Looking*.

## *LOOKING* AND THE THREE FACES CONCEPTS

Let's now turn to practical applications of these techniques, using the same students from our earlier example but with two entirely different teacher approaches.

> *It is Monday morning and the class is working on an assignment. The quiet working atmosphere is somewhat disrupted by giggles from the far side of the room. Two students' heads bob up to look, and then return to their talking. The teacher sees Nancy and Martha's heads together across the aisle, and it is apparent that they are off task.*

Now let's observe two entirely different teachers—Ms. HIGH Profile and Ms. LOW Profile—as they attempt to get Nancy and Martha to stop their actions.

### Ms. HIGH Profile

*In an angry voice from across the classroom, Ms. HIGH Profile says, "That is enough! Stop it, and stop it right now!" She points and wags her finger at the girls.[4] "I have had enough of your behavior, and I am sick and tired of it. Get back to work immediately!" (This is the "doggy-horsey" brain speaking.)*

As a result of Ms. HIGH Profile's strong verbal broadcasting across the room, all the students in the class—who previously were working—are now looking and, like spectators at a tennis match, have their heads bouncing from the teacher to the girls, back to the teacher, and again back to the girls. Their concentration on their seatwork has been disrupted and most have experienced a mild form of fight or flight response as they initially wondered if the teacher was reprimanding them. The students then recognized that the teacher's outburst was directed at Nancy and Martha, and they now wish to see if a confrontation will develop between Ms. HIGH Profile and the girls. They wonder to themselves, "Is this *show time?*"[5]

Only a few of the classmates will now be able to focus and return their concentration to their work. The rest begin to wiggle in their chairs, check their watches, and begin mentally "gathering wool." Meanwhile, Nancy and Martha make *pseudo-compliance behaviors*[6] and pass a victory smile between themselves.

### Ms. LOW Profile

*Walking about the classroom, Ms. LOW Profile notices the off-task girls. She stops, slowly takes two relaxing breaths, stands upright with her hands clasped behind her back, and looks directly at the girls. They look up and see her looking directly at them. Ms. LOW Profile takes two more relaxing breaths and broadcasts the nonverbal facial expression of "I am not amused." Nancy opens her book as if to read, and Martha does pencil posturing.[7] Ms. LOW Profile takes another two relaxing breaths and maintains unwavering eye contact. She walks slowly across the room and stops at the edge of the girls' desks and takes two relaxing breaths. The girls now shift their legs under their desks and away from each other and begin to do real work. Ms. LOW Profile maintains her eye contact for another two minutes, then returns to her previous task. No one else in the class was even aware of this interaction.*

Kounin's[8] classic study in classroom management demonstrated that classroom teachers who used *high-profile desists* had poor classroom discipline and fewer academic gains than teachers using *low-profile correction*. It is this "nickel-and-dime" day-in, day-out limit setting, which Kounin labels *desists*, that makes or breaks a teacher's discipline and classroom management practices. The high-profile teacher in the example caused a greater disruption than the off-task girls she was disciplining. In reality, the teacher was the person who most disrupted the learning in that classroom.

Getting students to desist, or stop, requires a technique of skills and teaching abilities if these desists are to be skillful and effective. Two general problems may arise when a desist is ineffective. (1) The teacher can overpower or "slam dunk" the off-task student(s), as Ms. HIGH Profile did; (2) The teacher can use behaviors that do not have enough power, and students view the teacher as not *meaning business*. The teacher can use appropriate desist techniques but the misbehaving student may escalate the power game from minimum *pseudo-compliance* to defiant *back talk*, or may fully escalate to the point of assaulting the teacher. The practicing teacher, therefore, needs a range of techniques and teacher behaviors to deal with such varying degrees of student challenges to the teacher's authority.

The Three Faces of Discipline position with the use of the Teacher Behavior Continuum, then, is an array of techniques for teacher responses ranging from minimum to maximum use of power and intrusion by the teacher. It will be the well-trained and skilled teacher who will know how to use this power and varying degrees of techniques effectively. The result will be compliance and cooperation from the off-task student while still maintaining the teacher-student relationship and avoiding alienation.

Limit setting is the process of taking actions toward one or more students who, by their actions, are preventing the teacher from teaching or other classmates from learning, or are failing to follow required procedures and rules. To put it simply, it is a request that says to the student, "Stop what you are doing and do what I, the teacher, want you to do." Limit setting will start with the day-in, day-out small off-task behaviors, but can also expand to conflict management and blow up to outward defiance by the student in the form of an assault against the teacher. To be effective at discipline, you must know how to set limits. The crucial teacher skill in limit setting is knowing how much power, inherent in your action, is appropriate. Too much power is like using a sledgehammer to drive in a tack, whereas too little power may communicate to the students that you are afraid of them and do not *mean business*.[9]

## Private versus Public Desist

Beginning in the elementary school years and blossoming in middle childhood, students begin to assert their own autonomy in relating to adults, while at the same time they wish to find social acceptance among peers. Peer pressure and loyalty can be much stronger than teacher and adult pressure. When the teacher gives a high-profile desist, confronting Nancy or Martha with the entire class as an audience, the student feels she must stand up to the teacher to gain or maintain status in her peers' eyes. Therefore, an informed and skilled teacher will heed the cardinal rules of limit setting, as a part of the Three Faces of Discipline, and attempt to keep any desist actions *pri-*

*vate* and always *low profile* between the teacher and misbehaving student. If necessary, the teacher may escalate to more controlling *semiprivate* actions, where only the misbehaving student knows what is being said but the peers are aware that something is afoot. *Public* actions are high profile for all to see, and may include involvement of the school principal, a counselor, parents, and even law enforcement or mental health authorities.

---

### CARDINAL RULE 1

Make a desist as private as possible.

---

The second cardinal rule of limit setting, within the Three Faces desist process, is to use as little power as necessary to get the desired change in student behavior—beginning with nonintrusive Relationship-Listening techniques and, if necessary, gradually escalating to the more powerful techniques found in Confronting-Contracting and, finally, Rules and Consequences. The construct applies both of these variables, power and privacy, through the use of the Teacher Behavior Continuum.

---

### CARDINAL RULE 2

Use as little power as necessary to get positive change in the misbehaving student's behavior.

---

## Limit Setting as a Desist

The Nancy and Martha vignette shows nonverbal limit setting only while the students are doing seatwork. But other situations will also arise that demand a response, such as (1) while the teacher is lecturing; (2) while the teacher is working with a small group of students at one side of the classroom and a desist is needed for a student across the room; and (3) in an open field situation such as hallways, play yard, and cafeteria.

### Desist While Lecturing

When you are instructing or lecturing and wish the entire class to give you their total attention, you may find students (such as Martha) who are acting out in such a manner that it shows they are not paying attention or are beginning to rival you for the class's attention. You handle this first with a *redirect*, a low-profile desist. If that does not work, you then escalate to *stop in midsentence* and begin the first step of eye contact. Finally, if necessary, you may *sidestep* the confrontation.

*Ms. Dumas is near the end of a lesson on fractions when Martha's giggles and behavior begin to draw glances of 20 percent of her classmates. The class is gradually being drawn away from its focus on Ms. Dumas, with that focus shifting toward Martha. Ms. Dumas states, "Class, when you try to understand fractions such as one-half of something, or three-quarters of something, it might be helpful to think of a dollar. You know that it takes four quarters to make up a dollar, and two quarters to make a half-dollar.* <u>Martha</u>, *you will notice that . . ." Ms. Dumas pauses for a split second, makes solid eye contact as she says Martha's name, and then prompts by using her writing hand to sweep across the students with a pointing gesture. She checks for eye contact with all students, and stops this pointing and hand sweep in Martha's direction. She again makes eye contact and then moves her hand in a gesture that seems to say "follow me" back to a focal point on the chalkboard. Once the chalk hits the board, Ms. Dumas again makes eye contact with Martha and continues the lesson. "So, two quarters equals one half, in money and in everything else."*

The entire sequence is a *low-profile correction* as a redirection. The teacher said Martha's name, made eye contact, and used a prompting gesture in a matter of seconds, and did it generally unnoticed by classmates. The rest of the class continued to be mentally and perceptually focused on the point that Ms. Dumas was making, and the pacing of the lesson was maintained. At the same time, Ms. Dumas gave repeated visual and hand prompts to Martha to signal her to desist and comply. This is an example of low-profile correction during lecturing.

What if Martha did not get the message or wants to play a power game? We now view Martha as playing the transactional analysis game of "I am the boss in this classroom and I will steal your power as the teacher." There will be some teachers who would say, "Well, I would stop and tell Martha to go to the time-out chair at the back of the room, or use exclusionary time out and send her out of the room. I would not let her get away with it."

That high-profile action is dangerous if Martha is a student motivated by a desire for power or revenge.[10] The power/revengeful Martha will do a counterescalation in her behavior, possibly responding with "Make me!" challenges. If this occurs, Martha has won and the teacher and other students have lost because the lesson time will now be eaten up by a confrontational battle and the teacher will need a new bottle of antacid for her ulcer. If Martha cannot be the best "good kid," she will attempt to be the best "bad kid." Because the teacher has "gone high profile," Martha has won and is now in control of the classroom through her behavior—Martha is stealing time!

Handling the power/revengeful student who disrupts a lesson requires that the student be deprived of an audience. You can either have the student move away from the class—a dangerous and expensive risk in using time out—or have the class move away from the student.

*Ms. Dumas states, "Class, I know that I have not quite finished my point on fractions, but I am going to stop right here and give you time to get started on your homework. Turn to page 24, and I want you all to do the first two problems* (terminate instruction for purposes of discipline[11]). *I will come around in 10 minutes to see if you have done them correctly." The teacher has now controlled classmates' reinforcement of Martha by diverting them from looking at her misbehavior, and has* sidestepped *the power struggle with Martha. The teacher now moves about the class, stopping to whisper to various students* (camouflage) *until she comes to Martha. She now takes two relaxing breaths and gives the girl an* ear-warning *using* verbal desist.*)*

## Desist in Midsentence

There is one more technique, slightly more high profile in nature, that can be used with a student who is disrupting during a lecture, and that is to *stop in midsentence.* You see a student disrupting; you stop very suddenly and abruptly in midsentence. You turn, *square off* toward the student, make eye contact, and wait while taking two relaxing breaths. You wait until the student has stopped and turned around in his seat so that it is obvious you now have his attention. You take two relaxing breaths and return to your lesson.

---

### SQUARE OFF

When confronting a misbehaving student, the teacher places his or her feet parallel so they face the student.

---

When you hold your *visual burn* on this student, the class will join you by also contributing their "visual burn" toward their classmate. However, the student cannot hold this position for very long. You should continue to wait, and wait as long as the class is totally quiet and inactive, joining you in the visual burn. The moment any student giggles, the power ball is now in your court. You must drop the visual desist and move to *sidestepping,* as previously described. Get the class busy, *work the crowd* and do *camouflage,* and then end up in front of the misbehaving student to do *ear-warnings* as a form of verbal desist or limit setting. You would only want to use a *midsentence desist* after first attempting a number of *low-profile corrections* as *redirects.*

## Desist Across the Room

When working with a small group, it is best to locate the group meeting at the side of the room. In this way, you can face each student in the small group face to face, while at the same time look over their heads to get a panoramic view of the entire classroom and the students working independently. Meeting at the front or back of the room is less preferable because it forces you to scan by making repeated head movements to the left and right.

It is also important to begin independent work with students before sectioning yourself off with a small group.

1.  *The independent workers have begun their seatwork first, before you move to the group.*
2.  *You have* worked the crowd *of seatworkers and know that all seatworkers have completed the first problem.*
3.  *There is a list of at least three activities on the Assignment Board, located on one side of the chalkboard, that tells the students what to do if they finish this seatwork. (The last item is a catch-all general activity such as "read a library book.")*

*Ms. Dumas is now busy working with the small group and sees good old Martha, the disrupter, off task and disturbing others. Ms. Dumas takes a greeting-card envelope from her lesson plan book and quickly gives it to a student who is seated at the end of her small group but closest to Martha. She instructs this student to take the note, which is a* desist letter, *to Martha. Ms. Dumas then returns to the small group lesson, hardly missing a beat. Martha now has this note before her on her desk. She opens it and reads, "Stop! Get back to work!" (The teacher will collect this desist letter and envelope at the end of the period and return it to her lesson plan book, where it is always available.)*

*If this low-profile desist message is not effective with Martha and her disruptions continue, Ms. Dumas takes two relaxing breaths and terminates the lesson with the small group ("discipline before instruction"[12]). She excuses herself: "Excuse me, group, hold just one minute, please!" Ms. Dumas takes another two relaxing breaths, and then turns, stands, looks, and says Martha's first name. She takes another two relaxing breaths and then waits. If Martha's misbehavior does not stop, the teacher* sidesteps *by putting her small group to work. She then continues to move up the limit-setting steps, beginning by walking to the desk, and then progressing to prompting the off-task student and camping out from behind. If all these nonverbal limit-setting steps fail, Ms. Dumas will abandon the limit setting of* Looking *and go to verbal limit setting (explained in later chapters).*

Another cardinal rule is "Discipline comes before instruction."[13] The teacher is instructing one student at his seat and is just getting to the point of closure on her mini-lesson when a discipline situation surfaces. The teacher may think, "I will just ignore Martha for another minute until I finish this instruction with Mark, and then I will go and take care of the problem." But this will tell the students that instruction is more important than classroom discipline, and once that has been learned, they will take every opportunity for nickel-and-dime misbehaviors; they will gamble that they can get away with it, and the teacher will get little instruction done in the future. "Pay now with small change, or pay later with big dollars to remediate the problem."[14] Terminating instruction requires the teacher to apologize to the first student in a way that says she is done with him for the moment, and then "announce" that she is about to escalate her use of power by dealing with the misbehavior.

---

## CARDINAL RULE 3

Discipline comes before instruction.

---

There are those teachers who will argue that Martha has gotten away with disrupting the small group lesson. But the important principle as a part of visual limit setting is that discipline must come before instruction, or pay pennies now and save dollars later in remediation if you discipline. If Ms. Dumas would have "gone high profile," there would have been a disruption of all learning in the classroom, with a likelihood that other students would begin to act up. The procedure just described  allowed the small group to continue learning, avoided a disruption of the learning of the seatworking students, and permitted the teacher to deal with Martha. Ms. Dumas spent the time "currency" to deal with Martha in the short term, knowing that it will pay off in the long run.

To summarize the teacher techniques used in a classroom desist: While lecturing or actively involved with a small group, handle the desist first with a *redirect* (low-profile desist). If that does not work, escalate to *stopping in midsentence* and using eye contact. Finally, if need be, *sidestep* the confrontation. The overriding principle in such actions is to maintain control of your classroom and not permit the power/revengeful student to take over and determine the classroom agenda, while at the same time to stay private and use power on your own terms.

### Desist in an Open Field

There will be times when you are responsible for supervising the cafeteria, school yard or playground, hallways, lavatories, and other open field areas that are taxing and place demands on your limit-setting skills. All the general principles developed so far still hold true for these settings. You need to use the minimum amount of power possible and maintain a private process. This means that the TBC's *Looking* as a nonverbal desist will dominate your actions.

Making a desist in an open field setting can present a number of difficulties. The biggest of these is that many times you will not know the student you are confronting and have not built a relationship of good will with that student. As a result, you are primarily confronting strangers. To make such open field limit setting work, it is *critical* that the structures of the motor rules of behavior be taught to students through a schoolwide training program (described in Section VI) and that all teaching staff accept the philosophy that outside of the individual classroom, "every student is the teacher's student."[15]

Another potential problem is that since open field settings are so dynamic, with many students moving about, the teacher will not take adequate time to use *Looking* with eye contact and proximity, but too quickly will overpower the situation by moving to a verbal desist of naming, questioning, or commanding. When a student is acting out in the cafeteria or the hallway, you should follow the nonverbal limit setting of *Looking*, as previously outlined:

1. *Work the crowd.* If you are in the cafeteria talking with a colleague or student and are not walking around and looking, you are not supervising. You must be working the crowd to use proximity as an effective tool. When misbehavior does occur, you are then in the best position to intervene.

2. *Terminate instruction or whatever you are doing.*

3. *Turn (you should be standing), look, and catch the student's attention—nonverbally cue the student.* Most students who disrupt are motivated by *attention getting,*[16] and since these students are annoying and a repeated problem, your natural tendency is to move away from them. However, this is just the opposite of what is needed. If you do not know the attention-getting student's name and it is apparent that he is going to repeatedly challenge you in this supervision situation, find out his name and learn it. Personalize yourself with the student before any difficulty occurs again by chatting with him to establish good will and a solid relationship.

4. *Walk to the student.* Most likely, you will not be able to catch a student's eye, especially in an active cafeteria, from a level of proximity-far. As a result, you will be required to close space by walking to the edge of the student's "comfort bubble" (proximity-near).

5. *Prompt.* Prompting normally will be the highest step you will need to use. For example, a student departs from the cafeteria table, leaving his trash behind. You intercept him as he is about to leave the cafeteria, make eye contact, square off, take two relaxing breaths and simply point (prompt) to the table from which he came. If he still does not understand, point to the waste cans and then back to the table. Suppress the desire to lecture, threaten, or make any remarks.

6. *Camp out in front.* If need be, you must be willing to give the time to camp out.

7. *Camp out from behind.* If two or more students are involved, attempt to put a wall between them so you can deal with one student at a time.

Finally, if the student escalates his behavior and the TBC's step of *Looking* fails, move to *Step 2: Naming* as a verbal desist. When you use a verbal desist in open field settings, you must also obey the cardinal rule of "keep it private." Speak to the misbehaving student softly so classmates will not hear, or ask the student to walk with you (so you get him out of the hearing of fellow classmates before you deliver verbal limit setting). Unless it is a safety-threatening situation or one that could cause significant property damage, you should never verbally confront the student with an audience of peers in the fairly open, unstructured context of an open field setting. This nonclassroom and less formal setting will encourage the student to escalate a confrontation with you when he might never consider doing so in the classroom environment.

Effective teachers have "with-it-ness," meaning that at all times they are perceptually and cognitively aware of what is occurring in their classrooms or the open field areas such as the cafeteria. They repeatedly check out what students are doing. To be effective in doing this, the teacher must be careful where she *parks her body*. If Ms. Dumas is helping one student and is bent over with her head down and her back to 80 percent of the classroom, she will not hear Luis tearing out a piece of notebook paper to make spitballs, or see Stan creep among the desks to snatch Harold's cap from his back pocket, or notice Angelica abandoning her math problems to snap open her purse in order to brush her hair for the thousandth time.

---

**WITH-IT-NESS**

The teacher's ability to always be perceptually aware of what is going on in the classroom.

---

As a "with-it" teacher, you park your body with your back to the closest wall so that with your peripheral vision you can see as much of the classroom as possible. A good classroom arrangement will facilitate your body positioning. Additionally, you must never get "lost" perceptually in the one student you are helping. If one student is standing before you, you may step back, take him by the shoulder and turn him around so you are able to look at him and, at the same time, over his shoulder at the class. If you are bending down looking at a student's papers on his desk, you must heighten your hearing awareness to take over for your loss of vision, and then periodically bob your head up like radar to make a 270-degree scan of the classroom so you may make quick eye contact with any student who is giving some thought to gambling on a fun off-task behavior. If you have the classroom furniture, especially the desks, arranged properly, and if you park your body with your back to the wall and facing students, you are now in the best position to see what is happening in the classroom.

We use the the term *check it out,* meaning simply that you need to keep broad perceptions running even when you are focused on one student or activity, and you must "surface" regularly to visually scan and check things out.

## Facial Expression

The smiling exchange between two individuals speaks volumes. If one person makes eye contact and the second smiles, this smile is seen through an animal kingdom perspective as a submission response signaling capitulation and "I want to be a friend." The dominant individual smiles back and the communication is "Yes, I wish to return your friendship." When a smile does not occur, there is a power confrontation between two individuals. As a teacher using the TBC's *Looking,* you want to communicate that the classroom is your territory, that you mean business and are in control, and that you will use the eye signal to establish this dominance.

In confronting Martha, Ms. Dumas is struggling to control the fight or flight response, which causes her eyes to widen and her teeth to clench, producing a fight or flight "face." To stop this from occurring, it is suggested that you allow your face to relax and unclench your teeth by becoming slack jawed. While standing and staring, take your tongue and curl it back in your mouth until you can touch the beginning of the soft tissue at the back of the mouth. This opens up the jaw and creates the slack jaw effect, ensuring that in a confrontation you will not grit your teeth as a result of fight or flight reflex.

Now the student, under the heat of eye contact, will do a *"silly" smile*, described as an open-mouth-and-teeth smile with a slight cock of the head and raised eyebrows, much like a baby might smile at his parents. The *smiley face* communicates to the adult from the child, "Look at me, aren't I cute and adorable and don't you just love me!" The teacher is to return the silly smile with a flat facial expression to send a message: "I am not amused" or "I am bored and will wait right here until you comply." At the same time, the teacher maintains eye contact to provide the visual heat.

## Additional Body Cues

When we are using *Looking,* every part of the body communicates and telegraphs, and it is difficult to hide internal tension. You should take a wide foot stance and place your hands, which are normally a give-away for tension, behind your body, clasping them together, simply standing as relaxed as possible. You resemble a baseball umpire at this point!

Ms. Dumas now has the Queen Victoria stance established. She stands, turns, squares off, goes slack-jawed, and says nothing. What is critical in this is that all of these actions are taken at a speed just slightly faster than slow motion. A teacher who wants to "rip Nancy's face off" would march in sudden, quick, and intense actions, which are not actions that communicate confidence and control. *Slower is better. Calmness is strength and communicates power.*[17]

## Relaxing Breaths

Any instruction in how to self-master tension and control your emotional and physical actions—such as relaxation therapy, stress management, and prepared childbirth training—involves learning to breathe properly during a stressful situation. This is done by taking two controlled slow, shallow breaths filling about 20 percent of your lung capacity and letting it out slowly, then resting for a few seconds and repeating the sequence. The slow exhaling is critical, relaxing the body and mind and slowing down the pace of all actions.

The uninitiated may have little appreciation for the value of controlled breathing, or may even find it humorous: "What, I need to be taught how to breathe? Ha!" But controlled breathing is the anchor and central technique on which is based all control in a stressful confrontational discipline situation.

The reader who wishes to put relaxing breathing techniques into practice would be advised to find a person who has had prepared childbirth training and have that person explain, model, and coach you through the process until you feel comfortable and in command of these techniques. The vignette with Ms. Dumas and Nancy shows how the teacher needs to punctuate every new action by first taking two relaxing breaths before moving in a slow, controlled manner.

## SUMMARY

When first beginning a limit-setting action, we begin with the mininium teacher action, from the TBC, as *Looking*. Under this category of behavior (see Figure 3–3), the teacher—in order to confront the off-task or misbehaving student—first "squares off." This means the teacher dramatically slows down his or her responses, attempting not to "go chemical"—instead getting under control. The teacher moves so her body is square-shouldered to the student. She establishes unbroken eye contact with the misbehaving student to prompt the student into an awareness that the teacher wants compliance. In this squared stance, the teacher places her hands behind her back and moves to a wider solid foot stance. The teacher body-telegraphs "I mean business," but not in a scolding or hostile manner.

To maintain self-control, the teacher takes repeated relaxing breaths before initiating any overt teacher behavior. Finally, if need be, the teacher will move from proximity-far, closing space to proximity-near, and then, in some demanding situations, to proximity-intimate.

Let's review these points in using the TBC's *Looking*:

| FIGURE 3–3   **Teacher Behavior Continuum** | | | | |
|---|---|---|---|---|
| *Looking* | Naming | Questioning | Commanding | Acting |
| 1. Square off<br>   a. slow down<br>   b. shoulders to<br>     shoulders<br>   c. broad foot<br>     stance<br>   d. unbroken eye<br>     contact<br>2. Relaxing breaths<br>3. Close space<br>   a. far<br>   b. near<br>   c. intimate | | | | |

- Move slowly (slightly faster than slow motion).

- Take two relaxing breaths before and after each action.

- Maintain unwavering eye contact.

- Escalate your power by closing space but be prepared to stop when compliance is established.

- Do not respond to back talk.

- Prompt if necessary.

- Be prepared to use as much time as needed.

- If you must deal with more than one student, put up a wall and deal with one at a time.

- Exit or move out in a slow, predetermined manner.

- If you expect an assault, drop Limit Setting and begin the Backup System (see Chapter 8).

The limit-setting process of *Looking* uses the least form of power and conserves the teacher's energies. Ideally, simply *Looking* would be the most preferred form of getting a desist from a misbehaving student.

# Endnotes

1. Jones, F. (1987). *Positive Classroom Discipline*. New York: McGraw-Hill.
2. Jones, F. (1993). *Positive Classroom Discipline: Trainee Manual*. St. Cruz, CA: Fred Jones and Associates, Inc., p. 32.
3. Jones, *Positive Classroom Discipline*, p. 57.
4. Ibid.
5. Ibid.
6. Ibid.
7. Ibid.

8. Kounin, J. (1970). *Discipline and Group Management in Classrooms*. New York: Holt, Rinehart and Winston.
9. Jones, *Positive Classroom Discipline*.
10. Dreikurs, R. (1964). *Children: The Challenge*. New York: PLUME.
11. Jones, *Positive Classroom Discipline*.
12. Ibid.
13. Ibid
14. Ibid.
15. Ibid.
16. Dreikurs, *Children: The Challenge*.
17. Jones, *Positive Classroom Discipline*.

# 4

# Naming

## The Relationship-Listening Face

If you are *unsuccessful* in limit setting with the use of *Looking* (Step 1 on the Teacher Behavior Continuum) and its subbehaviors of *closing space*, *proximity*, and various *visual prompts*, you now escalate your power by moving up the TBC to *Step 2: Naming*. In using *Naming*, you begin to use words, as *verbal encoding*, to describe the situation and/or the feelings of the student as you see them. You assume the Relationship-Listening Face and attitude.

## VERBAL ENCODING

Verbal encoding could be used by the teacher in the example of Martha's use of profanity:

> *Martha, the neighbor, now joins Nancy in the confrontation and attempts to gang up on Ms. Dumas, stating, "Yeah, get out of her face. Are you queer or something? F--- off!!"* (back talk: profanity).
> *Ms. Dumas replies, "Martha, those words are telling me that you are angry and there is something very wrong (verbal encoding), and that we need to talk. I need you to return to your math work, and we will meet after lunch to talk more about this."*

Some may see verbal encoding as a very "soft," or minimal power, technique. It has the sole purpose of bringing the child to a conscious awareness of his action, his and others' feelings, and the action's effect on others.

> ## VERBAL ENCODING
>
> Labeling the student's emotions and feelings, both positive and negative, through the use of the teacher's words.

## RELATIONSHIP-LISTENING FACE

The Relationship-Listening position is to view the misbehaving student as a person who has internal emotional turmoil. This inner tension shows itself as "acting out" or misbehavior. Your role as teacher, wearing the Relationship-Listening Face, is not to view this misbehavior (such as Martha's verbal aggression in the form of profanity) as a personal affront, but rather as an attempt to communicate and signal to you that a student is unhappy and needs a nonjudgmental supportive relationship and response. Punishing the child for swearing, for example, would simply increase that anger or inner tension and make the teacher-student relationship even worse.

Using the construct of the triune brain (previously described in Chapter 3), we may say that, for whatever reason, Martha has regressed. Because of an inner *fight or flight response*, she has moved from the rational thinking of the neocortex to the paleocortex ("doggy-horsey" brain ). This is seen by her "snapping and snarling" actions of swearing at the teacher, *"Yeah, get out of her face. Are you queer or something? F--- off!"* Students under great tension can also regress to the reptilian brain (*going brain stemmed*) and become either noncommunicative and passive, or physically aggressive and assaultive.

The objective of the Relationship-Listening Face is to take supportive empathetic actions that maintain the positive relationship with the student in order to help her become more rational and self-directed through the vehicle of language and communication. What separates humans from fight or flight animals is that we have language and a higher order of reasoning—we can rationally and collectively solve our problems.

When we wish to communicate, we must translate and encode our inner thoughts in order to express them to another person in such a manner that real communication occurs. However, when the student is angry and flooded with adrenaline and has regressed to the "doggy-horsey brain" (paleocortex), this encoding and first attempt of communication simply comes out as verbal aggression. "Shut up, get out of my face!" or "I hate you and I hate this school!" may be the student's first attempts to encode inner thoughts and feelings and signal the teacher that something is really upsetting this student emotionally. The central Relationship-Listening technique is the use of *Naming*, which encourages the student to ventilate by "talking it out" while the teacher (attempting to understand the student's communication) uses *active listening* or verbal encoding to reflect back, or mirror, what she thinks she is hearing the student say and feel. The more the student talks, even though it is aggressive, hostile, or negative in tone, the more he is able to ventilate and externalize his inner feelings. After a period of time, he will relax sufficiently for the rational brain (neocortex) to again come into use. At this point, real student and teacher problem solving can begin. Let's see how this may unfold:

> *The class is busy working on math problems. Ms. Dumas is able to pull a chair close to Martha and speak to her in such a manner that her classmates cannot hear.*
>
> ***Ms. Dumas:*** *"When I am told to 'shut up' and called such names* (behavior), *it makes me angry* (feelings), *and I lose respect from the other students* (effect) *and I lose a lot of valuable teaching time"* (I-message).
>
> ***Martha:*** *"I hate this school!"*
>
> ***Ms. Dumas:*** *"School is making you unhappy"* (active listening).
>
> ***Martha:*** *"I'm going back to my old school!"*
>
> ***Ms. Dumas:*** *"You were happy at your other school"* (active listening).
>
> ***Martha:*** *"Yeah, I, ah,—never get picked"* (now sits passively and appears to be thinking deeply).
>
> ***Ms. Dumas:*** *"Would you like to tell me more?"* (door opener).
>
> ***Martha:*** *"It ain't fair—I'm better than half those bitches."*
>
> ***Ms. Dumas:*** *(says nothing, but maintains eye contact and nods in such a manner to indicate to Martha that she is still listening)* (acknowledgment).
>
> ***Martha:*** *"Mrs. Jenkins doesn't like me!"*
>
> ***Ms. Dumas:*** *"Mrs. Jenkins has done something that makes you feel that she doesn't like you"* (active listening).
>
> ***Martha:*** *"Yeah, she cut me! I went to tumbling camp for two weeks this summer and I know more than all the girls she picked. It ain't fair!"*
>
> ***Ms. Dumas:*** *"You worked hard but you were cut from the tumbling squad"* (active listening).
>
> ***Martha:*** *"Well, no, she made me an alternate, but I only get to tumble when someone is sick or can't make it to the meet."*

In this brief exchange, the teacher opened communication with the student with the use of an *I-message* (described next) but did not warn, threaten, or lecture her on her behavior. This would have erected *roadblocks to communication.* Instead, the teacher permitted and encouraged Martha to make attempts at communicating and to talk out her feelings. Martha's first attempts to encode what was bothering her came out as "snapping and snarling," reflective of the "doggy-horsey" brain. The teacher simply listened nonjudgmentally and attempted to hear what Martha was trying to say *(empathic listening)*. Her statements were partial thoughts full of bitterness and aggressive language, but the more Martha externalized, the more it became clear what was really bothering her: She wasn't placed on the starting tumbling squad.

In order to understand if she was hearing Martha correctly, Ms. Dumas played back (mirrored) a summary of what she was hearing through a process of *active listening*. She also used *door openers* in the form of questions ("Would you like to tell me more?") to encourage more externalizing and gave periodic nonverbal *acknowledgments* to show that she was still in tune with Martha. The more Martha talked, the more the inner tensions were expelled and the rational brain came into play. Later, we will see the teacher begin to help Martha do some problem solving to deal with her anger. As noted, the teacher did not use *roadblocks to communication* by lecturing Martha that she should at least be grateful that she is still on the tumbling squad, or pointing out that 30 other girls were completely cut from the squad, or reminding her that she is the only fourth-grader to make a squad dominated by older, more experienced fifth-graders. While Martha is flooded and using the "doggy-horsey" brain, she is not ready for such rational information or facts, and may feel that the teacher "just doesn't understand and doesn't like her, just like Mrs. Jenkins." The teacher's position in using the Relationship-Listening techniques is to be fully available to the student in a nonjudgmental relationship, and to encourage and permit the student to verbalize while the teacher listens (thus the label Relationship-Listening). Let's see other techniques available to the teacher using *Step 2: Naming* with this Relationship-Listening Face.

## The I-Message (Behavior-Effect-Feeling)

An *I-message* is a subbehavior for the teacher under the general category of *Naming* on the Teacher Behavior Continuum. When a student such as Martha, with her profanity and verbal aggression, is acting in such a manner that it disrupts the class and is having a tangible effect on the teacher, the I-message is the least guilt-inducing method (after the TBC's first teacher behavior of *Looking* has failed) to directly express verbally to the student how her actions are affecting the teacher and the entire classroom. Here is an example of an I-message:

---

### I-MESSAGE

A teacher technique of expressing to a child that a behavior is having a negative effect on the teacher. This statement must contain three elements: the child's *behavior*, its *effect* on the teacher, and the teacher's *feeling* as a result of the behavior

---

*"When I am told to 'shut up' and called such names* (behavior),
*it makes me angry* (feelings), *and I lose respect from the other
students* (effect) *and I lose a lot of valuable teaching time."*

The I-message is a way to inform the student of the problem that
*you*, the teacher, are facing. The I-message is not saying "You did something wrong" (the word *you* is not permitted in an I-message) and it is
not saying "Here is how I want you to change." It *is* saying, "Student, *I*
want to let you in on how my world is being affected by your behavior."
This nonjudgmental statement still gives the student the power to cognitively reflect on her actions and come up with her own solutions on
how she will change, and so there is no coercion by the teacher.

---

### EXAMPLES OF POOR AND GOOD I-MESSAGES

*Poor Example*: "I want you to get your feet off that table now!"

This is a you-message implying guilt. It contains a poor definition of the
improper behavior, no example of the effect, and a lack of expression of
the teacher's feelings.

*Good Example*: "When feet are put on the table *(behavior)*, dirt
comes off our shoes and gets on the table. We must rewash the table
before we eat *(effect)*, and I get aggravated *(feeling)* having to do more
work."

*Poor Example*: "When the school books are torn *(behavior)*, I don't
like it!"

This message starts well with a good statement of behavior, but no
effect is given, and "I don't like it" is a value judgment rather than an
expression of the teacher's feelings.

*Good Example*: "When the school books are torn *(behavior)*, other
students cannot use them *(effect)*, and that makes me very concerned for
their care *(feeling)*."

---

### EXAMPLES OF GOOD I-MESSAGES

"When backpacks are left on the floor *(behavior)*, people might trip
over them and fall *(effect)*, and I worry *(feeling)* that someone will get
hurt."

"When tables are not cleaned after lunch *(behavior)*, spilled milk
and other 'gooey stuff' will make it uncomfortable for other groups to eat
there later *(effect)*, and I am afraid *(feelings)* we will have a health problem."

"When I am told to 'shut up' when I am speaking in our class meeting *(behavior)*, I am not able to explain the rules to everyone *(effect)*, and
I worry *(feelings)* that someone will get hurt using this new equipment."

*(continued)*

---

**EXAMPLES OF GOOD I-MESSAGES** *(continued)*

"When students stand on the table *(behavior)*, I am afraid *(feeling)* that they will fall and get hurt *(effect)*."

"When people scream in the hallways *(behavior)*, it hurts my ears *(effect)* and I get uncomfortable *(feelings)*."

"When people write or scribble on the desk tops *(behavior)*, it destroys them *(effect)*, and I am afraid *(feeling)* we soon will have no good writing surfaces."

"When objects are thrown *(behavior)*, there is a real possibility they could hurt someone's eyes *(effect)*, and that scares *(feeling)* me because I am the teacher and I must keep people safe."

"When children climb over the fence and leave the playground *(behavior)*, I can't see them to keep them safe *(effect)*, and that frightens me *(feeling)*."

---

Generally, after you deliver an I-message, the student might respond in one of three ways. First, she might simply stop the misbehavior (Martha returns to her math seatwork), thereby ending the encounter. Second, the student might continue to defy you, prompting an escalation of power along the Teacher Behavior Continuum to the *Questioning* stage of the Confronting-Contracting Face (see Chapter 5). Finally, the student might begin to respond to the teacher with some form of language. This *back talk* language is typically of two types: defensive language (verbal aggression, denial, or attempting to distract the teacher to a side issue) or real verbal communication (how the student may wish to solve a specific dilemma).

Let's see an example of defensive language:

*A first-grade student is stabbing at his classmates with a paintbrush loaded with paint.*

***Teacher:*** *"When friends are stabbed with a wet paintbrush* (behavior), *it soils their clothing and scares other children* (effect). *I need to keep people safe and clean, and it frightens me* (feeling) *when people are stabbed."*

***Student:*** *"I didn't do anything!* (denial) *(the teacher simply looks on). You're a butt-head!* (verbal aggression). *Carol was playing 'sword' and you didn't say anything to her!"* (sidetracking).

In viewing this first-grade painter's defensive verbal response, you must simply see these statements as an immature child's attempt to find some defensive way of handling the situation. You must not view "I didn't do anything" *(denial)* as lying. Instead, you should simply ignore these denials. This may be nothing more than the student's natural tendency to deny reality as he is faced with it. In addition, some students emotionally "flood," causing a fight or flight response of the reptilian brain, and they are quite frightened. These students actually may not remember what they did, even though it occurred just moments before. Figure 4–1 gives some examples of I-messages responding to specific situations.

| FIGURE 4–1    I-Messages | |
|---|---|
| **CHILD'S ACTION** | **TEACHER "I"-MESSAGE** |
| Joe starts to talk during seatwork while the teacher is reading to a small group. He talks loudly enough that it starts to disturb everyone listening to the story. | "When someone talks during seatwork *(behavior)*, I have a hard time reading so everyone can hear *(effect)*, and that makes me feel frustrated *(feeling)*." |
| After getting up from the art table, Joanne leaves her supplies and trash behind. | "When students leave their supplies behind *(behavior)*, I am fearful *(feeling)* that these materials will be lost or broken *(effect)*." |
| Kate finishes eating and departs with her lunch box, leaving behind her trash. | "I get frustrated *(feeling)* when I have to clean up the snack table *(effect)* after trash is left behind *(behavior)*." |
| When the door is opened to go out to the playground, Jeffrey runs through the door and down the stairs. | "When students run down the stairs *(behavior)*, I am fearful *(feeling)* that people will fall and get injured *(effect)*, and my job is to keep people safe." |
| Sara is trying to tie her shoe when she stops, begins to cry, and comes to talk to the teacher through the crying. | "When children cry and talk to me at the same time *(behavior)*, I can't understand what is being said *(effect)*, and I am disappointed *(feeling)* that I can't help." |
| The teacher is talking to a parent when Timmy interrupts and starts talking. | "It makes me sad *(feeling)* when I cannot understand two people who are talking to me at the same time *(behavior)*, and I become confused *(effect)*." |
| Brett deliberately splashes a classmate while they are washing their hands. | "When water is splashed *(behavior)*, people's clothes get wet and the floor gets wet and dangerously slippery *(effect)*, and that frightens me *(feeling)* because I need to keep people safe." |
| Geri and Kendra fight over a book by pulling it back and forth. | "When books are pulled *(behavior)*, I am concerned *(feeling)* that they will get damaged or be destroyed and we won't have them any more *(effect)*." |

---

**FEELING WORDS FOR TEACHERS AND STUDENTS**

At times when using I-messages with young students, your encoding of feelings seems repetitive, such as overusing the phrase "that scares me." At the same time, you are helping students learn to put words and labels to their own feelings. This list of feeling words[1] might help broaden your feeling vocabulary.

| Negative Feelings | | Positive Feelings | |
| --- | --- | --- | --- |
| angry | sad | appreciate | great |
| confused | scared | better | happy |
| disappointed | sorry | enjoy | like |
| frightened | unfair | excited | love |
| hate | unhappy | glad | pleased |
| hurt | want to give up | good | proud |
| left out | worried | | |
| mad | | | |

---

We also must not be frightened, angered, or offended by the "you're a butt-head" comment (or sexual or swear words) or by verbal abuse such as that thrown at Ms. Dumas by Martha. Through the fight or flight construct, we see that verbal agression is a more productive response than a physically aggressive response from the reptilian brain. You might respond, "Martha, when those words are said to me (*behavior*), I hear anger, but I don't know why you're angry (*effect*), and I feel disappointed (*feeling*) that I am not able to help you (*I message*). What words could you use to help me understand what you want?" (*door opener*).

---

**DOOR OPENERS**

When a student is having difficulty expressing something that is troubling him, the teacher uses a question (as a "door opener") to invite him to talk about his concerns.

---

You must not be drawn into a power play by the student's attempt to make you feel guilty ("Carol was playing 'sword' and you didn't say anything to her!"), which could lead you to respond to this assertion by trying to deny the student's criticism or explain your behavior to him. It has been said that the best defense at times is a good offense, so you should just see this as an attempt—and a fairly sophisticated one—to "sidetrack" you down a blind alley and take the focus off the student and his actions. You may simply ignore this sidetracking statement or use some of the following techniques to respond to denial, verbal aggression, or guilt statements used by students to sidetrack you.

---

*Note:* The statement "I don't like it when so-and-so is done!" is not an I-message. It is an expression of the teacher's value judgment or preferences.

---

## Active Listening/Door Openers/Acknowledgments

Students can become emotionally flooded as a result of adults' actions intended to demonstrate to them that their behavior is not appropriate and will need to change. When this happens, their verbal response toward adults might be verbal aggression. Calling the teacher a "butt-head" or shouting out "I hate you!" should simply be viewed as the student's first attempt at using language; he is attempting to communicate with you by taking a step up from the reptilian response of physical aggression. You should not be offended or frightened by this immature behavior, but instead should accept the verbal aggression as an attempt at verbal communication. If you avoid reprimanding the student, and even encourage him to verbalize or speak more, you will see that the hostility feelings will soon leave his language and greater reasoning and verbal problem solving will begin.

Effective communication is a very difficult process among adults, but it is even more difficult for elementary-age students with their limited intellectual experience and verbal ability. Let us attempt to understand how communication would be explained by Thomas Gordon,[2] one of the leaders of the Relationship-Listening school of discipline. Gordon suggests that adults and children constantly maintain one of two internal states: equilibrium or disequilibrium. A child who is full and not hungry, and who is playing happily, is at equilibrium. An hour or two later, the youngster begins to tire and gets inner messages that he is now beginning to get hungry, indicating a growing disequilibrium. When this hunger is very strong, the child attempts to communicate this inner need to his mother. The first surface communication, when heard by the mother, is not always what the child really means.

> ***Child (whining):***   "Mom, when is Dad going to get home from work?"
>
> ***Mother:***   "Ann, you know that Dad always gets home at six o'clock."

The child has failed to communicate her real need, and the mother has failed to hear what was *really* being said—thus, poor communication occurs. What the child really meant to say was, "Mom, I am very hungry and I don't think I can wait until Dad gets home to eat."

---

### ACTIVE LISTENING

The process of mirroring back to a student his or her emotional feelings and the problem being expressed, to the extent the teacher can understand them.

---

When the child has an inner need, she must express it externally, and so she tries *verbally encoding* that need to express her wants.

Now, let's replay the discussion, this time with the mother using *active listening*:

> *Child (whining):*   "Mom, when is Dad going to get home from work?"
>
> *Mother:*   "At six o'clock, but you would like Dad to get home sooner?" *(active listening).*
>
> *Child:*   "Ah, he'll be late again!"
>
> *Mother:*   "You're worried that he might not be on time today" *(active listening).*
>
> *Child:*   "I don't think I can wait for Dad if he's going to be late."
>
> *Mother:*   (looks at child, nods and smiles) *(acknowledgments)*
>
> *Child:*   "I'm starving!"
>
> *Mother:*   "You're very hungry, and you'd like to eat now and not wait for Dad because he might be late?" *(active listening).*
>
> *Child:*   "Yeah. A-a-ah . . . "
>
> *Mother:*   "You would like to tell me more?" *(door opener).*
>
> *Child:*   "Yeah, it rained while I was waiting for the bus this morning, and I forgot to bring my lunch into the shelter. It got wet and was ruined, and all I had to eat for lunch was a banana."
>
> *Mother:*   "Oh, that *does* make a difference. The rule is that we wait for Dad so we can all eat dinner together, but because you missed out on lunch today, why don't you have a glass of milk and two oatmeal cookies to tide you over."

*Active listening* is a technique for improving communication between student and teacher whereby the student is encouraged to "talk out" repeatedly, and your role is to attempt to mirror back to the child the emotional feelings you think you are hearing from the child. If you take first or surface communication statements from the child as fact, especially when the child is flooded, you may not hear what the child is really attempting to communicate. The nonverbal behavior of nodding your head (called *acknowledgments*) and asking questions like "Would you like to tell me more?" *(door openers)* simply serve to encourage the student to continue to talk and attempt to communicate.

---

### ACKNOWLEDGMENTS

A modality behavior, such as making eye contact or nodding your head, to indicate that you are listening to what the child is saying and you are encouraging him to continue.

---

Let's take another teacher-student example, this time involving our young paintbrush-swordsman:

> ***Teacher (using Naming):*** "Jimmy, paints can be scary. That is fun and exciting for you, but other children are frightened by the paintbrush. I need to keep them safe, and I feel frustrated when I have to keep stopping my teaching for this" *(I-message).*
>
> ***Jimmy:*** "I don't like him!" (referring to a classmate who just passed by and was the target of Jimmy's latest attempt to stab with the paint brush).
>
> ***Teacher:*** "You're angry with Walter?" *(active listening).*
>
> ***Jimmy:*** "He's mean!"
>
> ***Teacher:*** "Walter has been mean to you?"
>
> ***Jimmy:*** "Yes, I'm his best friend, and he let Robert sit beside him at snack!"
>
> ***Teacher:*** "You're angry because you were not able to sit by your friend" *(active listening).*
>
> ***Jimmy:*** "Yes, could I sit next to Walter?"

The teacher's efforts to determine the cause of Jimmy's aggression have exposed a deeper problem Jimmy is facing, and now the teacher can begin dealing with it from a new perspective.

## LIMIT SETTING AND RELATIONSHIP-LISTENING TECHNIQUES

Limit setting is a process for taking actions toward a student whose actions are preventing the teacher from teaching, and other classmates from learning, or who is failing to follow required procedures and rules. The tools available to the teacher for limit setting, within the Relationship-Listening techniques, are I-messages, active listening, and, to a lesser extent, door openers and acknowledgments. Verbal statements, such as an I-message, would be delivered to the student while adhering to the Cardinal Rule: "Make a desist as private as possible." This normally requires the teacher to use these techniques in the proximity position of *intimate*, softly whispered in the student's ear.

> *Martha, the neighbor, now joins Nancy's power team and attempts to gang up on Ms. Dumas, stating, "Yeah, get out of her face. Are you queer or something? F--- off!!"* (backtalk: profanity).

The teacher now escalates to the slightly more powerful Relationship-Listening technique of *Step 2: Naming:*

> *"Martha, those words are telling me that you are angry* (active listening) *and there is something very wrong, and that we need to talk. I need you to return to your math work now, and we will meet after lunch to talk more about this."*

As part of the Limit-Setting System, the teacher does not take time to do extensive active listening, door openers, or acknowledgments. The teacher primarily delivers the I-message or, as in this case, an active listening statement. If necessary, she promises to meet later with the student, as part of the Backup System, to discuss it further. Through *Naming*, the student has been given a desist request without guilt or anger.

## SUMMARY

The "face" or attitude of Relationship-Listening takes the position that when students act out in a negative manner, there must be some form of need being blocked, causing an inner emotional disequilibrium. The emotional tension, also called *flooding*, is ineffectively expressed by the youngster's negative behavior. In using the Relationship-Listening techniques, we view the student as a capable person with the inner strength and ability to solve his or her own problems; through solving such problems, with our nonjudgmental help, the child becomes more empowered as an adaptive maturing person. Let the child find the solution for his or her own problems; if you provide the solution, you will make the child dependent and weaken his or her future problem-solving ability.

As you use Relationship-Listening techniques as part of a Limit-Setting System, deal with misbehavior by first using the techniques of *Step 1: Looking*. If this fails to work, you would escalate to *Step 2: Naming*. In carrying out the teacher techniques under *Naming*, as a form of verbal encoding or active listening, you may be required to deliver an *I-message* (behavior-effect-feeling) to consciously make the child aware of his or her actions. If these minimal verbal techniques are not effective in getting a desist from the student, you may need to escalate to other steps or systems as part of the TBC.

If these techniques are effective, the end result will be a child who is free to express inner thoughts and feelings, knowing you will respond in a nonjudgmental manner. In this way, a binding relationship is formed between you and the student. It is through this relationship and the ability to express needs that the student now becomes free to solve his or her own problems and gain greater maturity.

# Endnotes

1. Dinkmeyer, D., McKay, G. D., & Dinkmeyer, J. S. (1989). *Parenting Young Children.* Circle Pines, MN: American Guidance Service.

2. Gordon, T. (1974) *T. E. T: Teacher Effectiveness Training.* New York: David McKay.

# 5

# Questioning

## The Confronting-Contracting Face

We have seen that the Relationship-Listening Face, through a process using the limit-setting techniques of *Looking* and *Naming*, calls for minimal intervention. Relationship-Listening techniques rely on a process of talking it out, facilitated by the teacher in an attempt to encourage the student in the direction of appropriate behavior. When those minimal supportive actions do not achieve the desired results, the teacher escalates across the Teacher Behavior Continuum to the Confronting-Contracting Face by moving to the use of *Step 3: Questions*.

This Confronting-Contracting Face and its accompanying attitude are much more demanding of the student and call for a greater use of power by the teacher. The goal of Confronting-Contracting is to have the student mentally reflect on his or her past behavior and its negative effects, and project the negative future outcome if such misbehavior continues. The student is also confronted and asked to come up with an idea of how to deal with the realities he or she faces and to "live within the rules."

Many misbehaving students fail to take time to evaluate their own behavior, to use their rational capacities to make decisions and control their actions. Instead, they are reactive, being easily triggered to act in an inappropriate manner. The Confronting-Contracting Face draws on and attempts to use the cognitive and rational capacities of the student. The teacher does not solve the problem for the student, but expects him to come up with an acceptable solution himself, thus strengthening the student's problem-solving abilities. The Confronting-Contracting Face utilizes five major steps.

## CONFRONTING-CONTRACTING LIMIT SETTING

The first two steps of this Confronting-Contracting process involve Limit Setting:

- Step 1: "Stop!" statements
- Step 2: "What-how" questions directed at the student (see Figure 5–1)

## CONFRONTING-CONTRACTING BACKUP SYSTEM

The remaining steps, because they take much time and become public, involve the use of a Backup System, which is discussed in detail in Chapter 8, as well as an Incentive System (Chapter 9) and an Encouragement System (Chapter 10). These steps are:

- Step 3: Contracting
- Step 4: Time out (circumstances may call for this step to be employed *before* Step 3)
- Step 5: Notify parents (see Figure 5–1)

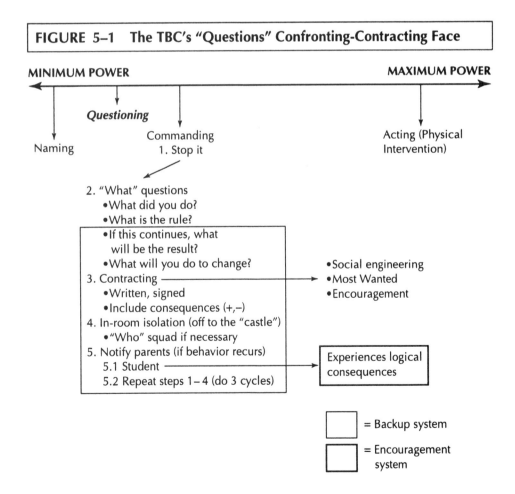

FIGURE 5–1    The TBC's "Questions" Confronting-Contracting Face

MINIMUM POWER

*Questioning*

Naming

Commanding
1. Stop it

Acting (Physical Intervention)

MAXIMUM POWER

2. "What" questions
  •What did you do?
  •What is the rule?
  •If this continues, what will be the result?
  •What will you do to change?
3. Contracting
  •Written, signed
  •Include consequences (+,–)
4. In-room isolation (off to the "castle")
  •"Who" squad if necessary
5. Notify parents (if behavior recurs)
  5.1 Student
  5.2 Repeat steps 1– 4 (do 3 cycles)

•Social engineering
•Most Wanted
•Encouragement

Experiences logical consequences

= Backup system

= Encouragement system

## LIMIT SETTING

Let us now see the limit-setting process unfold. We will use a variation on the missing-hat incident from Chapter 1 that introduces the process of *Questioning*:

> *George, a small quiet student, is frantically looking around and under his desk. Several students around him are watching him, and some are starting to laugh softly. Mr. Leonard moves to George and, speaking softly so others will not be disturbed, asks, "George, what's the matter?" George replies, "Someone swiped my hat!" Kathy, who sits next to George, says, "Mike took it, I saw him!" Mike retorts, "I didn't take it. Check it out, man, I don't have his stupid hat!" Kathy insists, "You do, too!"*
>
> *Mr. Leonard moves closer to Mike* (closing space) *and makes eye contact, and then notices the brim of the hat sticking out from under Mike's seat.* (TBC Step 1: Looking) *The teacher moves in, placing both hands on Mike's desk* (proximity: intimate). *Mr. Leonard waits patiently, taking relaxing breaths, maintaining a Queen Victoria pose, and holding his visual focus. Mike rolls his eyes and gives a slight smile. Mr. Leonard* visually prompts *him by pointing to the brim of the hat and then to George. The gesture is to signal Mike to return George's hat. Again, Mike rolls his eyes as if in disgust, and slumps deeper into his chair. Mr. Leonard waits, permitting the "visual burn" to continue.*
>
> *Other students who were working now begin to detect that something is happening, and they begin to stop their work to watch the action. Mr. Leonard leans over and gives Mike an* ear warning *that others do not hear. "Stop, Mike. This may not continue.* ("Stop!" statement) *When you tease by taking someone's property and disrupt the class so that everyone stops their work, we lose valuable time, and I find that quite annoying."* (TBC Step 2: Naming—I-message) *Mr. Leonard backs out of Mike's "personal space" and gives him several seconds to respond. Mike takes a baseball hat from under his seat, places it on his head, throws his feet up onto his desk, and smiles broadly at Mr. Leonard. Again, Mr. Leonard places his hands on Mike's desk and quietly asks, "What is the rule regarding personal property? What are you going to do to solve this problem, Mike, so that we may all get back to our work?"* (TBC Step 3: Questioning) *Mike responds, "F--- off, asshole!"*

In this "lost-hat" vignette, the entire class is busy doing seatwork until Mike, by his actions, causes a disruption. The first cardinal rule is "Discipline comes before instruction." If Mr. Leonard is busy working one to one with a student, he may become aware that there is a disruption beginning but choose to ignore it in order to finish the teaching he is doing. But if these small disruptions are not dealt with immediately, more and more of them will erupt.[1] The teacher must break off instruction and deal with this incident.

Mr. Leonard must also keep in mind the second cardinal rule: "Make a desist as private as possible." If he shouts directly across the room or moves in a hostile manner toward Mike, it will alert the entire class; the students will stop their work, and as a result the teacher will have become a bigger classroom disruption than Mike's misbehavior had been. Handling the "hat incident" takes skilled intervention as to how much power the teacher should use and how he should respond.

The third cardinal rule says "Use as little power as necessary to get the positive change in the misbehaving student's behavior." We saw Mr. Leonard starting with the first steps on the TBC and then escalating up the continuum. Initially, he attempted to use *Looking* through a process of *closing space* and moving to *intimate proximity,* all the while using teacher self-control activities (*squaring off* and *relaxed breathing*). Next, Mr. Leonard escalated to *Naming* as an *I-message* ("When you tease by taking someone's property and disrupt the class so that everyone stops their work, we lose valuable time, and I find that quite annoying."). He then gave Mike some time to comply and respond. Mike escalated his defiance, flaunting his power by putting the hat on his head and his feet on the desk. In this way, he nonverbally challenged the teacher.

Finally, the teacher escalated to the Confronting-Contracting technique of *Questioning,* using Step 1: "Stop!" statements and Step 2: "What-how" questions. The teacher asked, "What is the rule regarding personal property? What are you going to do to solve this problem, Mike, so that we may all get back to our work?" Notice that the teacher did not tell the student what *not* to do, but simply stated, "Stop." The "What-how" questions related only to what the student did, to the rule, to how this behavior might result in negative outcomes for Mike, and to a challenge for the student to come up with his own ideas of how to change.

---

### CONFRONTING

The teacher responds to misbehavior with a verbal instruction to the student to stop the action.

---

Because of stress in the confronting process and the teacher's recognition of the student's misbehavior, after such a confrontation the student does not necessarily mentally reflect on his entire sequence of behavior (especially when it is emotionally charged, as with Mike's swearing.) The student simply knows he is being confronted by the teacher, and most likely his mind is racing through thoughts of "Will the teacher punish me?" or "How can I get out of this situation and away from the teacher?" or "Will other students feel that I am a coward because of my actions if I don't save face?"

The "What-how" questions ask the student to be mentally reflective. If the student cannot remember what happened—and sometimes he will not, or cannot articulate it—the teacher will tell the student what did occur. However, it would be preferable to have the student verbally state his own actions.

Mike is a "high-stakes player," and when he uses profanity directly at the teacher with classmates as witnesses, the teacher may also feel emotionally flooded and angry and could regress to a "fight or flight" position with an *adrenaline dump*. It is imperative that the teacher use all of the self-controlling activities explained in the previous chapter on *Looking*. He must use controlled breathing, posture, eye contact, and slow movements in an attempt to stop any regression to "fight or flight." If, because of his anger, the teacher begins using the "doggy-horsey" brain, he will lose mental control of this confrontation.

---

### "WHAT-HOW" QUESTIONS

Questioning language that confronts the misbehaving student to intellectually reflect on his past misbehavior or the rules, and to consider how he will change.

---

## CONFRONTING-CONTRACTING ORIENTATION

The Confronting-Contracting Face reflects the attitude that you, as the teacher, are the adult and clearly know what is acceptable and unacceptable behavior. When you see a student misbehaving, you will clearly confront that student to get him to desist and make it clear that you will not permit this to continue. The Confronting-Contracting view is that there is *one* central motivation for all students: the attempt to find ways of socially belonging. If this social acceptance is blocked and the student feels unwanted and left out, the student will begin to disrupt the social situation in your classroom with a host of negative behaviors in an attempt to get excessive attention or to control you and others through power techniques. By his actions, the student enables himself to get attention and show power by misbehaving or challenging you.

It is almost as if the student is saying, "If I can't get recognition for being the best *good* kid, I will get it by being the best *bad* kid!" Being the most difficult student brings him social acknowledgment and recognition, even though it is negative. This misbehavior, motivated by a sense of not belonging, produces a self-defeating cycle in which the teacher and peers begin to have feelings of dislike for this student because of these offensive misbehaviors. The student now feels even more rejection, and may become revengeful or so hurt that he retreats into a shell of passive helplessness.[2]

In short, you can view the misbehaving student as someone who feels unwanted and unaccepted by others and who cannot find social acceptance. Admittedly, this may be very hard to do when you might feel threatened by the student. Your role is to take clear actions to (1) stop the misbehavior, (2) confront the misbehaving student with questions designed to get him to cognitively reflect on the wisdom of such negative behavior, and (3) challenge the student to think of new ways of behaving that are socially acceptable. (Further steps of Confronting-Contracting will be seen in the later discription of the Backup System.)

With such misbehaving students, you are likely to see a repetitive host of misbehaviors and aggressive actions that, on the surface, do not appear to be related to immediate behavior by other students. Such a person may harass other students without any provocation. First feelings of acceptance for all children come from the home setting. If a child feels he was rejected in early family interactions, he will assume he will be similarly rejected in a classroom situation and will set out with negative actions to prove that others do not like him.

The less skilled teacher might bring Mike aside and verbally reprimand and lecture him for his actions, applying large doses of guilt for the behavior or hand out punishment. Worse still, the teacher might issue a very public reprimand in front of the entire class. Such actions might unknowingly cause the teacher to fall into the student's power trap, as these behaviors are precisely what he expects and wants from the teacher in order to make him the center of attention or permit him to show how powerful he can be. Alternatively, if the teacher disciplines him with harsh punishment consequences, the student might regress and become revengeful toward those around him in more subtle ways that the teacher will not see or detect. Instead, this student must become the target for the teacher's positive efforts to help him acquire the social skills that will enable him to find acceptance.

A number of techniques can enable the teacher to be proactive in helping students acquire social skills. Before these are presented, however, it may be helpful to first explain the "outside aggressor" phenomenon.

## THE OUTSIDE AGGRESSOR PHENOMENON

A visitor to a kindergarten playground is asked by a 5-year-old, "What's your name, Mister?" The man responds, "Mr. Wolfe." The student, hearing it as "woof," jumps up and runs screaming to the opposite end of the playground, shouting, "Woof, Woof!" Then each member of his group picks up a light twig. They "stalk" the visitor, walking up behind him on tip-toe and forcefully striking the man in the back with the sticks. They run off, again screaming, "Woof!" We have just witnessed the phenomenon of the *outside aggressor*.

Young students have two large islands of emotional extremes—when they love they love totally and when the hate they hate totally.

Their feelings of rivalry are still very strong, thus they have a difficult time coming together in groups. One of the more primitive and base levels of social interaction, which first develops during the early years, is coming together in a group and finding an outside person, object, or fantasy object against which to project the group members' strong competitive feelings and aggression. This creates an implicit agreement not to take aggressive action against each other and establishes a temporary feeling of belonging. In the previous classroom incident, Mr. Leonard could become the outside aggressor if Mike is able to challenge him publicly in class and cause the class to identify with Mike and against the teacher.

Although the outside aggressor phenomenon begins in early childhood,[3] examples can be seen among older students and adults. Perhaps you can recall an interaction at a dinner party when one person must depart early, leaving everyone else behind to talk about him in a most negative manner. The "leaver" becomes the dinner group's outside aggressor. Members of the group have, by default, informally agreed to project their aggressive criticism at the departed person, and not to speak ill of one another. The game works if almost everyone says something derogatory. Thus, for a short period of time the members of the "dinner gang" have a superior feeling of being above someone else, a feeling of primitive belonging to this "in" group. Politicians throughout history have used this outside aggressor phenomenon to gain control of groups; perhaps the most glaring and frightening example was the way in which Hitler controlled an entire nation by casting one ethic group as the outside aggressor.

Reaction to the outside aggressor is an expectable, normal behavior among school-age students. Every substitute teacher's greatest fear is that the students will make the substitute their outside aggressor—after all, they know each other but do not know him or her. Misbehaving students develop the skill to turn the entire classroom of peers against the teacher by challenging the teacher's power, thereby making the teacher the outside aggressor. Or this student may become the school's outside aggressor, disliked by peers, teachers, school crossing guards, bus drivers, cafeteria workers, and anyone else who has daily contact with him. He has become the "best bad" student in the school. Your role as the teacher who is forced to deal with this kind of misbehaving student, of course, is to engineer ways through which this student can learn to be social in a more healthy manner, and to help him find belonging and acquire social skills. Most of this help will come to the misbehaving student as a part of the Backup System, which will require you to use much more time to counsel the student through private meetings or conferences.

## Limit-Setting Techniques

Let's return to the "hat-taking" vignette and pick it up where Mike hurls his verbal obscenities at the teacher. There are a number of ways Mr. Leonard can now respond, but it is critical that he not fall into a power confrontation with Mike by *going public*. If Mike is motivated by the desire for power, he attempts to demonstrate his power to the teacher and his classmates by controlling the teacher's actions and getting the teacher angry (regressing to *fight or flight*). If this happens, the teacher's voice becomes harsh and shrill, and he begins to issue threats or warnings—he snaps and snarls by using his "doggy-horsey" brain. When the teacher loses his composure it is *"show time"* for Mike and the classmates, and most likely the teacher will demonstrate fear and very unskilled, exasperated behavior. In this way, the teacher could become the outside aggressor.

When a teacher verbally "slam-dunks" a misbehaving student like Mike in front of peers by going public, the *"ripple effect"*[4] punishes not only Mike but all students. Because they have witnessed the teacher snapping and snarling and because they are in a less powerful position, the students feel vulnerable to the teacher's tirade. Even though they might dislike Mike and his behavior, they now identify with him and, through this ripple effect, feel just as verbally punished as Mike. In fact, because they are more socially sensitive, they may feel even more punished than Mike. The immediate goal for the teacher who has just been the object of Mike's verbal aggression is to get himself or Mike out of the immediate situation—which provides the public interaction of the classmates as spectators—and to get back to teaching or learning. The teacher may deescalate to *Naming*, such as, "Mike, that language is not acceptable to me and we must talk. I will need you to stay when class is dismissed." The teacher slowly moves back to helping students doing seatwork or other forms of instruction. If Mike sits passively, even if he is still wearing the hat and his feet are over his desk, he is ignored. The teacher knows that at least Mike is no longer preventing others from learning. Mr. Leonard will retrieve the hat and deal with the swearing later, without the classmates as an audience, through the use of the Backup System.

## Disengaging

Although most teachers will not openly admit it, student misbehavior can be frightening. Suppose Mike bites a classmate, producing an ugly blue toothmark on Gwen's arm. Now suppose Gwen's mother is the most vocal member of the school board or the school's PTO. Under these circumstances, the teacher would feel "under the gun," and of course quite sympathetic to Gwen's plight. When this happens on a frequent basis, the teacher must acknowledge his own feelings. He becomes frightened of Mike, and gradually feels hurt and angry. Teachers are not robots who are emotionless, who never get angry, who always have good feelings toward all students. This is an unrealistic picture and simply does not happen. Some students are appealing and some are very unappealing; the unappealing students generally are the ones who cannot find acceptance in their homes or from fellow classmates. The nonsocially adjusted misbehaving student in the classroom, because of feelings of rejection, begins to seek excessive attention and power, becomes

| | FIGURE 5–2    Nonsocially Adaptive Student | |
|---|---|---|
| **Student's Motivation** | **Behavior Characteristics** | **Teacher's Feelings** |
| Attention Getting | Repetitively does actions to make him the center of attention. When asked to desist, will comply but will start again later. | Annoyed |
| Power | Repetitively does actions to make him the center of attention. When asked to desist, becomes defiant and escalates negative behavior and challenges the adult. | Beaten |
| Revenge | Hurts others for no apparent reason. | Hurt |
| Helplessness | Wishes not to be seen; passive and lethargic; rejects social contact. | Inadequate |

revengeful and, finally, retreats into a passive state of helplessness. If you accept that teachers are human beings with a range of feelings, you can allow that the excessive attention-getting student may produce feelings of annoyance in you, that you may at times feel beaten by the power-needy student, that you may feel hurt by the revengeful student, and that you may feel inadequate in working with the passive-helpless student (see Figure 5–2).

You must acknowledge to yourself that it is possible you will have these feelings toward certain students. Your feelings only become a problem when you begin to regress into becoming revengeful and feeling helpless toward these students. Therefore, you now have a second possible reason to use isolation—that is, in order to get yourself *disengaged*. If you are angry and overcome by your own feelings because of the repetitive demands the problem student is placing on you, you may become emotionally flooded in the middle of an incident. You need to do skilled confronting, yet you are not able to handle this successfully and professionally because your clear thinking has been flooded by emotions. You should place the misbehaving student in isolation—the "relax chair" or time out—for a period of time. As an emotionally flooded individual, you put space between yourself and this student for several minutes, or even an hour, until you have disengaged from your strong emotions. Once you are calm and relaxed, you will have energies to approach the difficult student to begin your steps of confronting. *You cannot do Confronting-Contracting when angered.* You must of course remember to use the self-controlling techniques under the TBC's heading *Looking*, including relaxing breaths, slowed actions, squaring off, physical stance, and others.

The private meeting, as a part of the Backkup System, ends with a contract between the student and the teacher. The student at a future time will find himself in a similar situation and will be faced with the possibility of again acting with such destructive behavior. The question, "What will you do to change?" permits him to actually think out and anticipate these future situations. He has determined and contracted with the teacher how he can act in a more productive manner in future incidents. The contingency contract for change between the teacher and student could be sealed with a simple handshake and smile in the first attempts, but it is advised that you actually put this agreement in writing and have both the teacher and student sign the contract, with each getting a copy. The contingency contract may also contain a logical consequence to be employed if the student fails to live up to this contract.

## SUMMARY

The techniques of the Confronting-Contracting Face require the teacher to face a misbehaving student with a demand to stop and, through "What-how" questions, get the student to reach an awareness of his actions, a clear recognition of the rules, and a plan for solving the problem through change. If the student is "flooded," the teacher uses a "relax chair" or time out as part of the Backup System, until the student feels he is now ready to join the group, and has contracted to do so. Most misbehaving students are motivated by four needs (attention getting, power, revenge, or helplessness) because they lack the social skills to obtain recognition and belonging. If the *Questioning* techniques fail to be effective, following our TBC contruct, the teacher will now move to *Commanding*.

# Related Readings

Dinkmeyer, D., & Dreikurs, R. (1963). *Encouraging Students to Learn: The Encouragement Process*. Englewood Cliffs, NJ: Prentice-Hall.

Dinkmeyer, D., & McKay, G. D. (1983). *Parenting Teenagers: Systematic Training for Effective Parenting of Teens*. Circle Pines, MN: American Guidance Service.

Dinkmeyer, D., & McKay, G. D. (1989). *The Parent's Handbook: Systematic Training for Effective Parenting*. Circle Pines, MN: American Guidance Service.

Dinkmeyer, D., McKay, G. D., & Dinkmeyer, J. S. (1989). *Parenting Young Children*. Circle Pines, MN: American Guidance Service.

Dreikurs, R. (1964). *Children: The Challenge*. New York: Hawthorn/Dutton.

Dreikurs, R. (1968). *Psychology in the Classroom: A Manual for Teachers,* 2nd ed. New York: Harper & Row.

Dreikurs, R., & Cassel, P. (1972). *Discipline Without Tears: What to Do with Children Who Misbehave*. New York: Hawthorn Books.

Dreikurs, R., & Grey, L. (1968). *Logical Consequences*. New York: Meredith Press.

Glasser, W. (1969). *Schools Without Failure*. New York: Harper & Row.

Glasser, W. (1975). *Reality Therapy: A New Approach to Psychiatry*. New York: Harper & Row.

Glasser, W. (1986). *Control Theory in the Classroom*. New York: Harper & Row.

Glasser, W. *Glasser's Approach to Discipline*. Los Angeles: Educator Training Center.

# Endnotes

1. Kounin, J. S. (1970). *Discipline and Group Management in Classrooms*. New York: Holt, Rinehart and Winston.
2. Albert, L. (1989). *Cooperative Discipline*. Circle Pines, MN: American Guidance Service.
3. Isaacs, S. (1972). *Social Development in Young Children*. New York: Schocken Books.
4. Kounin, J. S. (1970). *Discipline and Group Management in Classroom*. New York: Holt, Rinehart and Winston.

# 6

# Commanding

## The Rules and Consequences Face

As we have seen, the Three Faces of Discipline model considers that you, as the teacher, can consciously be aware of and design the actions you take toward a misbehaving student. The Relationship-Listening Face accepts that the misbehaving student is rational and may be made more purposeful and cooperative through a supportive nonjudgmental approach requiring the student to talk out his problem. The Confronting-Contracting Face, primarily through the use of questioning techniques, presents a clear use of power and demands that you use verbal techniques to stop the misbehavior and get the student to become cognitively aware of his action and how it misserves him socially. The student is permitted almost total control in choosing how he or she will change, but you engineer ways to help the student gain social skills.

These two faces should work to deal with the large majority of behavior problems. With some students, however, these techniques will not be enough, and you will be required to escalate to the more powerful techniques of Rules and Consequences.

## RULES AND CONSEQUENCES

The Rules and Consequences Face, and its movement to *Commanding* on the TBC, comes into play when the student is flooded and in a defensive stance and you need to escalate to a greater use of power. Even with your *Questioning* and mediation, the student cannot accurately view his own behavior, nor does he have the ability to change his actions of his own free will. To help such students requires strong intrusion and management techniques that demand that you first be assertive to help the student gain self-control and a reawakening sense of trust.

Let's return to our earlier vignette involving Mike, Mr. Leonard, and the missing hat:

*Other students who were working now begin to detect that something is happening, and they begin to stop their work to watch the action. (Recall that the teacher has already used the nonverbal techniques of proximity and eye contact from TBC's* Looking.*) Mr. Leonard leans over and gives Mike an* ear warning *so that others do not hear: "When you tease by taking someone's property and disrupt the class so that everyone stops their work, we lose valuable time, and I find that quite annoying." (TBC Step 2:* Naming—I-message*) Mr. Leonard backs out of Mike's personal space and gives him several seconds to respond. Mike takes a baseball hat from under his seat, places it on his head, throws his feet up onto his desk, and smiles broadly at Mr. Leonard. Mr. Leonard places his hands on Mike's desk, and quietly asks, "What is the rule regarding personal property? What are you going to do to solve this problem, Mike, so that we may all get back to our work?" (Step 3:* Questioning*) Mike responds, "F--- off, asshole!"*

**Mr. Leonard** *(makes eye contact, stands at the edge of Mike's comfort bubble, squares off, and gestures as a visual prompt): "Mike, place your feet on the floor under your desk. Take the hat off and give it to George"* (Step 4: Command).

**Mike:** *(takes a quick glance at the teacher and at his classmates, and smiles)*

**Mr. Leonard:** *"Mike, place your feet on the floor under your desk, and take off the hat and give it to George!"* (broken record).

**Mike:** *(makes no response)*

**Mr. Leonard:** *"Mike, place your feet on the floor under your desk, and take off the hat and give it to George!"* (broken record).

**Mike:** *(no response)*

**Mr. Leonard:** *"You now have a choice. I want you to stand, walk to the back of the room, and seat yourself in that chair for the remainder of the morning, or I will call in Mr. Jenkins, the principal, and another teacher from across the hall and we will remove you to the principal's office (promises a* follow-through by stating consequences). *Mike, move to the chair now!"* (time out).

In this incident we have seen the teacher first use the Relationship-Listening Face with *Naming*, then escalate to the Confronting-Contracting Face with *Questioning*, and then further escalate to the Rules and Consequences Face with *Commanding*. Through the techniques of the Rules and Consequences Face, the teacher plays a more specific role in demanding appropriate behavior by the student.

How shall we view the interaction between Mike and the teacher? What guides the teacher's behavior and verbal statements while using the Rules and Consequences Face? The teacher *assertively demands*,

---

### BROKEN RECORD

The process by which, after a student fails to act on the teacher's request for a particular behavior, the teacher repeats the command over and over in a controlled manner (as if a "broken record").

---

through a *Command,* that the misbehaviors desist and the student's behavior change to more desired behaviors.

## The Assertive Position

The assertive position, as a part of the Rules and Consequences Face, supports the following message to the teacher: *You are the teacher and this is your classroom; you have a perfect right to get your needs as a teacher met.* You have arrived at this assertive position, as a part of the limit-setting process, by either of two ways: (1) attempting to use the minimum amount of teacher power—*Looking, Naming,* and *Questioning*—but being forced to escalate to these stronger techniques or (2) seeing that the student's action was potentially dangerous to himself or others or could lead to the destruction of property, requiring the use of the *severity clause.* The cardinal rules of "Make a desist as private as possible" and "Use as little power as necessary to get positive changes in the misbehaving student's behavior" must be *dropped when genuine danger or property destruction* are involved and time is of the utmost importance. Implementing the *severity clause* requires the teacher to move straight to directive statements as a *Command* and, if need be, to *Acting* with *Physical Intervention,* also through the use of the Rules and Consequences Face.

The Rules and Consequences Face takes the position that the misbehaving student is taking away your right to teach and other students' right to learn, and thus you must assert your control. You do this by determining the rules and behavior you want in your classroom and making them clear to the students. When a student breaks these rules, you must take assertive action by stating clearly what behavior you want stopped and then demanding compliance from the student. If there is no compliance, you have a plan and are prepared to take actions to decrease misbehavior through the use of time out or by physically intervening.

A *Commanding* teacher, using techniques selected from the writings and practices of noted expert Lee Canter,[1] is one "who clearly and firmly communicates her wants and needs to her students, and is prepared to reinforce her words with appropriate actions. She responds in a manner which maximizes her potential to get her needs met, but in no way violates the best interest of the students."

## The Nonassertive or Hostile Teacher

Adhering to Canter's definition, we can see that many seemingly assertive commands by a teacher are actually nonassertive and generally ineffective. The passive, or flight, response brought on by the teacher's own fear ("Tommy, behave yourself!") merely pleads and begs for students to behave and change their ways. This teacher appears to be unclear as to what behavior she does want and has no plan to obtain that behavior from the students. The hostile, or fight, teacher responds by screaming at the students ("Shut up and sit down, I don't want to hear any more from you today!") or might grab, shake, or even strike the misbehaving student—this teacher has regressed either to the "doggy-horsey" or the "reptilian" brain. The hostile teacher knows what she wants, but her actions in attempting to get that behavior violate the best interest of the student.

## Characteristics of Nonassertive Teachers

### The Passive Teacher

Takes these unproductive actions:

1. Asks the student to achieve an intermediate but nonspecific behavioral goal.
   *Example*: Asks the student to make an effort, as in "Try to be good!"

2. Makes statements to the student about his behavior that do not communicate what she wants the student to do.
   *Example*: "I can't imagine why you are doing that!" or "What is wrong with you?"

3. Says all the right words ("Stop fighting!") but does not back up the words with the necessary consequences to impress the student and influence him to choose to eliminate the improper behavior.

4. Demands the student to stop and threatens to follow through, but fails to do so.
   *Example*: "The next time you do that, you're going to time out!" A few minutes later: "I am warning you—one more time and out you go!"

5. May plainly ignore the behavior as if it never occurred, hoping it will go away.

### The Hostile Teacher

Takes these unproductive actions:

1. Uses a you-statement that conveys a negative "put-down" message, but in no way clearly communicates to the student what the teacher wants, leaving the student simply feeling guilty.
   *Example*: "I am sick of your behavior. How many times am I going to need to tell you?"

2. Expresses her negative value judgment of the student and/or his behavior.
   *Example*: "You are acting like a little monster this morning."

3. Threatens the student in an angry manner, with no evidence of consistent follow-through.
   *Example*: "You just wait. I'll get you for this!"

4. Utilizes follow-through consequences that are overly severe.
   *Example*: "You are going to stay after school for two weeks."

5. Physically responds to a student out of anger.
   *Example*: Pulls the child's hair; squeezes the child's arm; shakes, throws, or hits the student.

## Characteristics of Assertive Teachers

The assertive teacher, using the TBC's *Command*, is one who can state her wants and needs clearly to the student without violating the child's rights, initially done through an assertive command. In the process of delivering an assertive command, the teacher:

1. Moves to the student and makes direct *eye contact*

2. *States the child's name*

3. *Gestures*

4. *Touches* the student (on the shoulder when appropriate)

5. Verbally demands that the student stop (*demands a desist*)

6. *Demands change* for positive behavior by the student (tells the student what to do, rather than what not to do)

7. Promises a *follow-through* consequence.

Note that nearly all modalities are used to communicate with the student in an assertive command: visual (through eye contact and gesture); auditory (by stating the child's name and demanding he desist); and tactile (through touching).

Let's repeat the previous vignette and see how the teacher uses the assertive command.

> *Mike responds, "F--- off, asshole!"*
>
> ***Mr. Leonard*** *(takes two relaxing breaths and moves to prox-imity: intimate):   "Mike (states the child's name, makes direct eye contact, stands at the edge of Mike's comfort bubble, squares off, gestures as a visual prompt, places a hand gently on Mike's shoulder* [touches the student]*), place your feet on the floor under your desk. Take the hat off and give it to George"* (demands a desist, *telling the student what to do rather than what not to do).*
>
> ***Mike:***   *(takes a quick glance at the teacher and at his class-mates, and smiles)*

*Mr. Leonard* (takes two relaxing breaths): *"Mike, place your feet on the floor under your desk, and take off the hat and give it to George!"* (broken record).

*Mike:*   (makes no response)

*Mr. Leonard* (takes two relaxing breaths): *"Mike, place your feet on the floor under your desk, and take off the hat and give it to George!"* (broken record).

*Mike:*   (no response)

*Mr. Leonard* (takes two relaxing breaths): *"Mike, this is your last warning. Follow my instructions, now!"*

*Mike:*   (no response)

*Mr. Leonard* (takes two relaxing breaths):   *"You now have a choice. I want you to stand, walk to the back of the room, and seat yourself in that chair for the remainder of the morning, or I will call in Mr. Jenkins, the principal, and another teacher from across the hall and we will remove you to the principal's office.* (promises a follow-through by stating consequences). *Mike, move to the chair now!"* (time out).

Once the teacher has delivered this assertive *Command*, he does not allow himself to be sidetracked by excuses as back talk or other discussions by the student. He repeats the *Command* two or three times as a *broken record* and then promises a follow-up action—if the student does not comply, he is placed in time out in an out-of-classroom setting (see Figure 6–1).

---

**ASSERTIVE COMMAND**

A command used to communicate to the student the direct behavior that the teacher wants, incorporating the following elements:

- A statement of the child's name
- A gesture, in which the teacher signals through hand movement and/or nodding of her head
- Eye contact, whereby the teacher positions herself in front of the student, close enough to ensure that they are looking into each other's eyes
- Touching, whereby the teacher touches the student to make him aware of her presence and her need for his attention
- A demand that the student desist the improper behavior
- A statement of the consequence, whereby the teacher tells the student what punishing action will occur if the student does not perform the desired appropriate behavior (or continues to perform the inappropriate behavior)

---

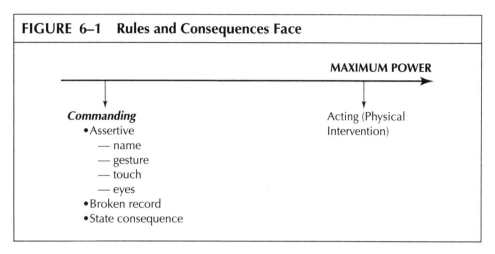

FIGURE 6–1    **Rules and Consequences Face**

This strong assertive *Command,* as a limit-setting technique, is a very powerful intervention technique. It is public and very time consuming, and can quickly lead to very public Backup System steps involving the principal, parents, and other professionals. For these reasons, it should be used only when the other, less powerful limit-setting techniques have not worked over a reasonable period of time or when the student is endangering himself or classmates or taking actions that may lead to property damage. For day-in, day-out classroom management, once having used the assertive *Command,* the teacher may now be forced to use the TBC's *Acting* in the form of physical intervention by isolating the student, physically transporting him out of the classroom, or—in the worst case—physically restraining a student who has become assaultive.

## BACKUP SYSTEM

### Time Out

Limit setting is intended to remove a noncompliant student from the educational environment and quickly return to the learning process so that time is not wasted. When all the limit-setting techniques fail to work, the teacher drops the limit-setting approach and moves to time out, removing the student to some extent from the educational setting and beginning the use of a Backup System. The Backup System makes use of isolation and gradual removal of the student from the classroom, with the eventual involvement of the principal and others. It is used when the Limit-Setting System has failed to be effective.

Time-out procedures deny a student, for a fixed period of time, the opportunity to receive reinforcement. This removal of stimuli is actually time out from positive reinforcement—those activities that serve to reinforce the student's inappropriate behavior. Time out generally is used when the classroom activities reinforce the student and the teacher's application of the limit-setting techniques is ineffective. In the vignette of Mike and the missing hat, the class may unknowingly be reinforcing Mike to continue to act in such a defiant manner by giving him the attention he so dearly seeks. Recall this portion of the vignette:

> ***Mike:*** *(takes a quick glance at the teacher and at his classmates, and smiles)*

The next option for the teacher would be to remove the student from some or all of the reinforcement he is receiving. The teacher may then choose from among four distinct categories of time out: nonseclusionary time out, contingency contracting observation, exclusionary time out, and seclusionary time out. These will be described in detail in Chapter 8, which details the Backup System.

## SUMMARY

The Rules and Consequences Face uses the central technique of assertive *Commands*. The teacher asserts himself with the use of an assertive command that makes it quite clear to the misbehaving student what actions the teacher wants immediately. If the student fails to respond positively to the command, the teacher must move to the TBC's *Acting* as a last step before dropping the Limit-Setting System and moving to the time-consuming Backup System, which uses various forms of isolation or time out.

# Related Readings

Alberto, P. A., & Troutman, A. C. (1990). *Applied Behavior Analysis for Teachers,* 3rd ed. New York: Merrill-Macmillan.

Canter, L. and Canter, M. (1976). *Assertive Discipline: A Take-Charge Approach for* *Today's Educator.* Los Angeles: Lee Canter & Associates.

# Endnote

1. Canter, L., & Canter, M. (1976). *Assertive Discipline: A Take-Charge Approach for* *Today's Educator.* Los Angeles: Lee Canter & Associates.

# 7

# Acting

## The Rules and Consequences Face

Let's revisit the classroom and see Mike's growing defiance and belligerence toward his teacher:

> *Mr. Leonard (takes two relaxing breaths): "Mike, place your feet on the floor under your desk, and take off the hat and give it to George!"* (broken record).
>
> *Mike: "Why should I?"* (defensive response as verbal escalation).
>
> *Mr. Leonard (takes two relaxing breaths): "Feet damage desktops, and teasing by taking someone else's property causes conflict and disrupts my teaching, and that is really frustrating"* (I-message).
>
> *Mike: "But why do I need to take my feet down? My shoes aren't doing any damage"* (back talk and, again, verbal escalation as questioning).
>
> *Mr. Leonard: "Mike, this is your last warning. Follow my instructions now!"*
>
> *Mike: (no response)*
>
> *Mr. Leonard (takes two relaxing breaths): "You now have a choice. I want you to stand, walk to the back of the room, and seat yourself in that chair for the remainder of the morning, or else stand and go to the principal's office. If you do not move, I will call in Mr. Jenkins, the principal, and another teacher from across the hall and we will transport you to the principal's office (promises a follow-through by stating consequences). Mike, move to the chair now!"* (time out).
>
> *Mike (snickers): "I'd like to see you make me! You touch me and you're a.... (unintelligible threats)!"* (verbal escalation as refusal).

During any of the *Commands* for the student to go "off to the castle" or go to any form of time out, we might get from the hostile student a passive or active refusal or even threats, as with the example of Mike and his attitude of, "I'd like to see you make me! You touch me and you're a.... (unintelligible threats)!" This action of refusal and threats takes both the student and the teacher into the high profile and very public techniques and actions. The teacher gives a final private warning, intended to be a promise preparatory to a consequence:

> **Mr. Leonard:** "Mike, stand and go to the chair and seat yourself *(broken record)*. This is the last request, and if you fail to move, I will need to bring another teacher and the assistant principal in here to remove you, and if that is done you'll be in much more serious trouble *(promise of a consequence)*. Let's keep this between us. Now, move!"

## ACTING (PHYSICAL INTERVENTION) AND THE BACKUP SYSTEM

Once the *promise of a consequence*, as part of the limit-setting *Commanding* process, is made, you as the teacher must follow through—the student may become defiant or potentially assaultive. At this point, the Limit-Setting System stops and you must now move to the Backup System. The classroom activities are clearly disrupted, and your educational program cannot continue with the student behaving in the classroom in such a manner. You must call on the help of others, such as the principal and fellow teachers (get backup).

### The Response Team

We have observed Ms. Dumas in her dealings with Martha ("Yeah, get out of her face. Are you queer or something? F--- off!!") and Mr. Leonard in his dealings with Mike ("I'd like to see you make me!"). Each teacher has reached the point of having to move to the Backup System. The teachers have previously prepared three envelopes that they keep in their lesson plan books. When necessary, they take the envelopes out, write the classroom number on each, and give one to each of three students they know to be very dependable and who are seated near the door. These students now run one letter across the hall, a second to the next-door neighboring teacher, and the final letter to the principal or assistant principal. The letter says simply, "Help. I need the Response Team immediately—Room B-17, Ms. Dumas (or Mr. Leonard), Crisis Code A." If a classroom telephone is available, of course, the teacher would simply telephone the administrative office. The principal and teachers (some schools even have resource officers) arrive, asking "Who?" The teacher identifies the student who needs to be removed from the classroom and transported to the office.

The *Response Team* will again follow the cardinal rules concerning the use of power and privacy. These rules are followed as the situation escalates along the Teacher Behavior Continuum from *Looking* to *Naming*, *Questioning*, and *Commanding*, before escalating to the point of nonviolent crisis management through the use of *Acting* (*Physical Intervention*).

The removal of a defiant and potentially "acting-out student" places *both* the teacher and the student in a "fight or flight" stance involving an *adrenaline dump*. It has the highest probability of producing an assault by the student and an overuse of physical power by the adults, potentially leading to an injury or property damage.

Experts have identified four distinct levels of crisis in situations involving confrontation and noncompliance by a student such as Martha or Mike: (1) anxiety, (2) defensive, (3) acting-out student, and (4) tension reduction.[1] Let's see a new example that clearly shows an assaultive behavior by a student and the ensuing levels of crisis and teacher behavior (see Figure 7–1).

| FIGURE 7–1    Levels of Crisis, Student Behavior, and Teacher Techniques | | |
|---|---|---|
| **Crisis Level** | **Student Behavior Characteristics** | **Teacher Goals and Techniques** |
| *1: Anxiety Phase*—Attention getting | As a result of some frustration, possibly as a result of the teacher's limit setting, the student appears as if he is a tightly wound spring, ready to snap. His hands may be clenched into a fist with white knuckles, and he may drop his eyes or glare intently, his gaze either focusing sharply on a peer or teacher or, instead, alternately focusing on his subject and then darting away. He may become physically restrictive, pulling inside himself and turning away, or he may become active, pacing like a caged cat and exhibiting nervous ticks. His actions clearly attract the *attention* of peers and observant adults. | The student, if caught quickly, is still rational enough to respond to the teacher's language. Have the student ventilate representationally through language (talk it out). Redirect the student away from social interaction, giving him his "personal space." If possible, make few or no demands. With the use of language, employ Relationship-Listening techniques (active listening, I-messages, and door openers and promises to problem solve). |
| *2: Defensive Phase*—Power | In order to maintain his *power* over a teacher or peer, the student now verbally escalates up a continuum by (1) *Questioning*— asks manipulative questions of "Why?"; (2) *Refusal*—refuses to cooperate; (3) *Release*—verbally releases pent-up feelings through screaming or shouting verbal aggression in the form of swearing, name calling, and similar verbal outbursts that may help to release or ventilate stored-up tension. The student may also use (4) *Intimidation*—a verbal attempt to intimidate threatening to do harm to the teacher or himself. Finally, if the conflict is able to be contained, there is a (5) *Tension Reduction*—whereby the student lacks energy, feels guilt, and is embarrassed about his behavior. | The teacher positions herself in an alert *supportive stance* and permits the child's ventilation through verbal aggression. If the verbal aggression turns to defiance, the teacher moves to provide a *Command* as the Rules and Consequence techniques (assuring the student of potential consequences) and promises of safety. Give the student time and space to ventilate, and if possible, do not physically intervene. |

*(continued)*

| FIGURE 7–1 | Levels of Crisis, Student Behavior, and Teacher Techniques *(continued)* | |
|---|---|---|
| *3: Acting-Out Student Phase*—Assault/revengeful | The student now becomes totally *revengeful* and nonrational, and cannot control his own actions. He physically strikes out in a direct assault toward peers or the teacher by a *strike*, as a hit or throwing, or a *grab*, such as holding, hair pulling, choking, or biting. | In response to the assault, the teacher defends herself with defensive actions from a position of a supportive stance and accompanies her physical actions with an *command*, sending two messages: a command to desist action in a way the teacher desires, and verbal reassurance through a *promise of safety* and nonaggression toward the student. If the student appears to be attempting to injure himself or others or do major property damage, the teacher may be required to use team restraining techniques to stop and then transport the student. |
| *4: Tension Reduction Phase*—Helplessness | After the violent action, the student is deflated and becomes passive with little energy. He has feelings of guilt and feels *helpless* as to how others might respond to him. | Help cognitively recapitulate the happenings for the student, first by having him verbally talk about it using the Confronting-Contracting techniques, "What-how" questions, and contracting. Reestablish the relationship verbally and by touching (shaking hands, hugging, or other forms if possible). |

## Crisis Level 1: Anxiety Phase

*Mrs. Monroe is supervising the playground area near the school cafeteria when she comes upon James, standing before the school wall and bouncing a golf ball off the bricks. Each time the ball hits the wall, it makes a white circle on the bricks and comes dangerously close to nearby windows.*

**Mrs. Monroe:** *"James (name), stop! (She points to the ball in James's hand [gesture] and moves face to face [eye contact and proximity-near]. The ball is causing damage and may break a window. Put the ball in your pocket" (Command). (Because we have a potential danger to school property, the severity clause comes into play and the teacher moves straight to the Rules and Consequences Face with a Command).*

**James:** *(stands still, holds the golf ball tightly with both hands, glares directly at Mrs. Monroe, and then looks down at the wall, and—in direct defiance—repeats the throwing-and-catching activity)*

**Mrs. Monroe:** *"James (name), stop! (She again points to the ball [gesture], moves face to face [eye contact] and places her-*

*self between James and the wall). Put the ball in your pocket or give it to me"* (broken record).

## Crisis Level 2: Defensive Phase

*James (screams): "You bitch! You bitch! Keep your bitch hands off me! Keep your bitch hands off me! No, let me go— don't touch me!"* (verbal escalation *as release*).

*Mrs. Monroe (lets 45 seconds pass but maintains the unbroken eye contact with James): "James (name), stop, calm down. I am not going to touch you! Put the ball in your pocket or in my hand!"* (broken record). *(Mrs. Monroe waits for a few minutes, giving James an opportunity to think and comply.) "If you cannot, I will need to bring another teacher and the assistant principal here to transport you to the office, and if that is done you'll be in much more serious trouble* (promise of a consequence). *Let's keep this between us. Now, put the ball in your pocket or in my hand !"*(preparatory statement).

*James: "You bitch! You're going down!" (James now pushes through the door toward the music room, and Mrs. Monroe follows.)*

*Mrs. Monroe: (using a walkie-talkie, she calls the administrative office and declares a* Crisis Code A *[for potential assault], indicating that she is near the music room.) (Figure 7–2 explains various codes.)*

## Crisis Level 3: Acting-Out Student Phase (Assault)

*James turns and with both hands—including the one still holding the ball—suddenly and forcefully pushes Mrs. Monroe at shoulder level and strikes her, causing her to fall back three full steps. Mrs. Monroe quickly catches her balance.*

*Mrs. Monroe: "James (name), stop. Calm down!*

*James: "No—f--- off, old lady, you're going down!"*

*James screams at full volume, and again attempts to push Mrs. Monroe with both hands. Mrs. Monroe grasps both his arms at the wrist to restrain him. He drops the ball and attempts to butt her with his head. He now lashes out with his right leg in three quick kicking motions, one of which strikes Mrs. Monroe squarely on the shin, causing her definite pain.[2]*

*The teacher now releases the student to see if he will quiet down. Instead, he runs into the nearby music classroom, knocking over furniture that is in his path. Mrs. Monroe prevents James from leaving by physically blocking the door. He kicks the door, to his discomfort, and runs his arm across a storage shelf holding musical instruments, knocking most of the instruments to the floor with a great crashing noise. He now moves to the window and violently strikes it with his fist; it*

---

**FIGURE 7–2    Suggested Codes**

These are emergency codes that can be communicated to the office or announced over the school public address system. They will communicate to the teachers, staff, and school personnel but will not be understood by the students (who otherwise might panic and become overly concerned.)

**Code W (for Weapon)**
Communicates that a student, or any person, has a weapon and the school resource officer or police need to come to the teacher's assistance. When announced on the school public address system, this could signal all personnel to take classroom and schoolwide actions to protect themselves and the students under their supervision. (*Examples:* Pull all window blinds or curtains; this might stop flying glass. Barricade the classroom door with a heavy object such as a filing cabinet so it cannot be opened. Move the students as a group on the floor and away from windows or doors. Keep students occupied by reading them a story until the all-clear is given.)

**Code A (for Assault)**
Communicates that the teacher is being or is about to be assaulted, and the Response Team must immediately come to assist.

**Code H (for Help)**
Communicates that Response Team help is needed within the next hour, but the teacher is not in a dangerous crisis situation.

**Code R (for Runner)**
Communicates that a student has run out of the classroom and is leaving the campus. The teacher would include the student's name and age and the possible direction of the student when last seen.

Many other codes may be used as needed by the school, but the use of more than five could create a list too long for good memory and communication.

---

*cracks, but the window pane stays intact. This action carries the real potential for James to injure himself, and before a second blow can land, Mrs. Monroe again grasps James's wrists and pulls him away from the window. He now runs out the unblocked door and into the arms of Miss Harrison, who has arrived to assist. James steps back and attempts to punch Miss Harrison, who blocks James's blow with a raised arm and then steps aside.*

*After the full blow has been thrown by James, Miss Harrison quickly steps behind James and grasps his right wrist with her right hand. The second member of the Response Team and the assistant principal, Mr. Kelsay, grasp James's left wrist in a parallel fashion. At the same time, Miss Harrison takes her open left hand and places it on James's right shoulder from behind. Again, Mr. Kelsay parallels Miss Harrison's hand movements. (See Drawing 10, Team Restraint, later in this chapter.) With their arms on James's shoulders, the adults push James's head and shoulders down until his head is below his waistline. From this position, it is impossible for him to pick up his feet to kick. Each teacher places the foot closest to James in front of his body and between his feet, thus preventing him from walking out of the restraining hold. The third member of the team moves in front of James and holds up his shoulders to keep him from falling forward on his face. James is now standing flat-footed, bent over with his head below his waist, and each of his arms is held upward and wrapped around a teacher. He is wedged between the teachers, immobilized, and not able to kick or strike.*

***Miss Harrison*** *(now whispers):* *"James, we are not going to hurt you, and we are not going to let you hurt us. You are safe. We are trying to keep you safe. We will not hurt you* (broken record). *We are teachers; we will not hurt you. James, we are restraining you like this to keep you safe"* (broken record). *(James attempts to struggle free, but the team holds him firmly.) "We are holding you but we are not hurting you* (broken record). *We need to hold you like this until you can relax. Quiet down, James. Relax. Breathe and relax." (James continues to struggle violently but without success. His head is below his waist, but he still screams a list of profanities at the teachers. Miss Harrison, however, continues to speak to him in a whisper.) "We are not going to let you hurt us, and we are not going to hurt you. You are safe. We are the teachers. We are going to hold you like this until you quiet down." (James now begins to cry and slowly stops struggling.)*

*The restraining teachers slowly permit James to straighten himself and stand upright, but as he does, both Miss Harrison and Mr. Kelsay—who still are grasping his wrist—take their nongrasping hands, swing them under James's arms, and grasp their own wrists. They now are holding James in a transporting position. Holding him firmly by each of his wrists and pushing with their shoulders, they quickly turn James around, go out the door, and transport him to the office. The third team member remains in close pursuit and ready to help by restraining James if he physically struggles again.*

---

### RESTRAINING TECHNIQUES

Nonviolent methods of holding students so they will not hurt themselves or others.

---

We have just witnessed one of the most demanding teacher-student interactions—one that involves a clear assault on the teacher and a danger to the student and the potential for destruction of school property.

When you are forced to deal with such a student, your heart is pounding and the adrenaline is rushing through your body, pushing you to a state of hyper-alertness and creating a defensive stance for your own protection and the student's safety. Out of your own understandable fright, you may emotionally flood, thus causing you real difficulty in thinking correctly and acting constructively as these sudden and quick actions unfold.

Experts who have studied such violent actions by students recognize a general level-by-level progression in the behavior and actions of a potentially assaultive student. If these levels of crisis progression are understood, then when the sudden quick developments do occur, they can be better recognized and thus less frightening. Previous mental rehearsal will permit you to respond constructively.

Recall from the earlier discussion of the triune brain construct that under emotional stress the student will regress from the rational neocortex brain (Crisis Level 1: Anxiety Phase) to the paleocortex, or "doggy-horsey" brain, where he snaps and snarls (Crisis Level 2: Defensive Phase). Finally, he will regress to the reptilian brain (Crisis Level 3: Acting-Out Student) with physical assault. Eventually, his thinking will begin the process of returning to rational activity (Crisis Level 4: Tension Reduction).

## CRISIS LEVEL 1: ANXIETY PHASE

When the student is still in the *anxiety phase*, he or she is still rational. The teacher may still be able to appeal to the student's rational abilities to reflect on the situation and use the power of reason to prevent the situation from escalating to a more serious confrontation.

## CRISIS LEVEL 2: DEFENSIVE PHASE

At any time that the student regresses to the *defensive phase* by shouting, swearing, and clenching his fist at the teacher, the teacher would shift her feet from a *square position* to a *supportive stance*, and begin statements toward the student intended to assure him of safety. "We will not hurt you (*promise of safety*). We need you to quiet down and move to the door, and go to the office." If you permit the student to ventilate by shouting and swearing, he will just be wearing himself out. Then, if necessary, you can move to verbal desist through the Rules and Consequences Face.

---

### SUPPORTIVE STANCE

When a child is about to be violent, the teacher approaches to calm him down. The teacher faces the student at a 45-degree angle and, without gesturing, attempts to communicate that she is not going to physically confront or assault the student.

---

FIGURE 7–3   Crisis Development

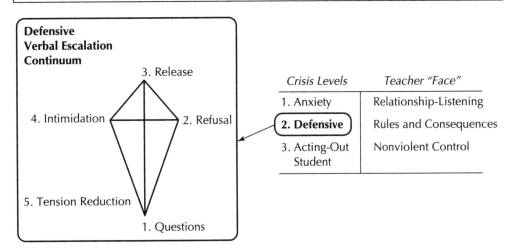

This defiant verbal behavior by the student, as it gets more and more out of control, may also progress through escalation stages that can be recognized and displayed on a Verbal Escalation Continuum, as follows (see Figure 7–3):

1. *Questioning*
   The first stage, Questioning, is where the student asks "Why" questions when he already knows the answer. This is a subtle defiance ploy by the student.
   *Intervention*: First give a real answer to the question, and then repeat the command; if necessary, repeat the command again as a *broken record* response.

2. *Refusal*
   A further verbal escalation sees the student move to verbal defiance: "No, I won't do it, and you can't make me!" The student at the Refusal stage is losing rational ability.
   *Intervention*: Your response is to assure the student that you will not attempt to "make him" and that the student can be powerful. Then repeat the Command. If the refusal continues, move to a promise of a consequence, but always said in such a manner as to give the student a clear choice. "Mike, you can either do so-and-so, or I will need to call Mr. Hopkins, the principal, and we will do so-and-so! Take your choice."

3. *Release*
   Still escalating further, the student performs a verbal release by screaming, shouting profanities, and appearing to become generally hysterical. Giving the student information and talking to him is useless because he has regressed to the "doggy-horsey" brain, is "snapping and snarling" and is clearly not rational.
   *Intervention*: Your response is to do nothing; simply hold tight in a supportive stance. The student, by the verbal release, is just eating

up his energy, and in two or three minutes he will tire and may become quiet.

4. *Intimidation*
In this form of verbal escalation, the student makes threatening statements in an attempt to intimidate. These threats may be to do injury to you or your property, or even a threat to hurt himself. You must accept these threats as real and take clear action.
*Intervention*: You must now take all necessary actions to get assistance through school policies and regular training practices. The school should have in place a severity Crisis Code system understood by all teachers, administrators, and staff. When it receives a call or note from a teacher with the Crisis Code A, for example, the administration knows that a teacher is in danger of being assaulted, and a Response Team will come to the teacher's assistance immediately.

5. *Tension Reduction*
After any of these verbal outbursts or an acting-out behavior, the student normally will retreat to a stage called Tension Reduction. He may feel a large amount of remorse or guilt for his previous verbal outburst or physical aggression.
*Intervention*: In dealing with the student in the middle of Tension Reduction, first wear your Relationship-Listening Face before moving to your Confronting-Contracting Face. The previously violent or verbally threatening student is deflated. He appears introverted, quiet, and flat in his facial expression and will have difficulty speaking. He becomes withdrawn, with little energy. He may have feelings of guilt and helplessness as to how others might respond to him—especially the teacher he may have assaulted or verbally abused or threatened.

Some students will begin self-abusive activities such as pulling out their hair, biting themselves, or some similar act of inwardly directed physical abuse. Since the student is more relaxed and is now rational, your wish is to help him cognitively recall what has happened, for he may not actually remember what started the crisis incident or what transpired once it began. There are two goals in Tension Reduction: (1) enabling the student to cognitively reflect on what occurred and challenging him to consider or contract how he might act differently in the future and (2) reestablishing equilibrium in the relationship between the student and you. Seeing your actions, the student must realize that his negative behavior is unacceptable but that you still accept him as a worthy person. These two goals are achieved through a private meeting, which clearly moves us into the Backup System (see Chapter 8).

## Private Meeting (Semi-Private)

It is recommended that during the Tension Reduction process, you and the student be eye to eye in a very close proximity-near setting. This can

---

**TENSION REDUCTION**

After a violent act, the child feels guilty and remorseful, and the teacher approaches the child to reestablish friendly relations and dispel those negative feelings.

---

be done by seating the student and yourself on chairs, ideally without a table or any other object between you.

During this stage, it is important that the student be able to state cognitively—or for you to describe—the events that have occurred in a way that imparts no guilt, and for the relationship between you and the student to reach a new emotional equilibrium free of hostility. This reunion is important for both the student and you.

Be very cautious about forcing a verbal apology that requires the child to say "I'm sorry." This verbal statement may be something the teacher needs, but if it is forced, the student will begin to have feelings of guilt and start a new crisis. If the Tension Reduction process goes well, the student will have feelings of remorse and will wish to apologize, but he may express it to you in a nonverbal form. There is a feeling of warmth and the student may wish to hug you, or he may meet your eyes, saying nothing but smiling affectionately; feel free to authentically return the smile. You must also learn to nonverbally express your "forgiveness" back to the child through similar cuddling and smiling, but you must also convey these feelings in the form of verbal expression as a statement of a *promise of safety*.

As a general rule, after a significant isolation or assaultive event, a *private meeting* should occur between the teacher and the student (the principal and others may also be included if appropriate).

*Minutes later, the bell rings and the students depart, passing Ms. Dumas as she stands at the door. When Martha arrives, the teacher signals her to move to a nearby desk, then closes the door to the now empty classroom.* (private meeting) *It is time for Ms. Dumas to deal with Martha regarding her use of profanity.* (Don't go public!) *Ms. Dumas has not forgotten Martha's words, "Yeah, get out of her face. Are you queer or something? F--- off!" (This swearing and behavior would be classified as Crisis Level 2: Defensive Phase, and seen as Intimidation on the Verbal Escalation Continuum.)*

*(A meeting between Mr. Leonard and Mike, or Mrs. Monroe and James, would follow similar teacher techniques.)*

Again, the teacher has the decision as to what "face" to wear and the parallel techniques to use in carrying out this meeting. The cardinal rule is to use the least powerful technique necessary, so at first the teacher might try a private meeting using Relationship-Listening techniques. If there are later incidents involving isolation and future private meetings, the teacher may escalate to Confronting-Contracting meeting techniques, and then finally to a Rules and Consequences approach.

## The Relationship-Listening Meeting

The teacher assumes a Relationship-Listening Face. Because the techniques are taken from a counseling model, this face is ideally suited for one-to-one interaction between student and teacher. Go slowly, continuing to use such *Looking* techniques as eye contact and relaxing breaths. You and the student are seated so that you are knee to knee, which places you at the edge of the student's *comfort bubble*.

The Relationship-Listening teacher (see Figure 7–4) might open with an *I-message:* "Martha, when a student swears at me like you did (*behavior*), such harsh words stop me from talking and working with a student (*effect*). It also causes me to lose the respect of your classmates (*effect*), and I feel first frustrated and then angry (*feelings*). We need to talk about this." (*door opener*) In dealing with James, you might use a *door opener:* "James, we have had a terrible experience in the band room, and I feel a need to talk about it with you."

You are now free to use:

- Acknowledgments

- Verbal encoding of the student's feelings through critical listening

- Door openers

- The Six Steps to Problem Solving (see Chapter 8)

For a short private meeting, you may use no-lose *plus/delta techniques* by simply having you and the student write out a list of all the items that are going well and all those that are not. This can be done on tablet paper where both may see. Through no-lose problem solving, you

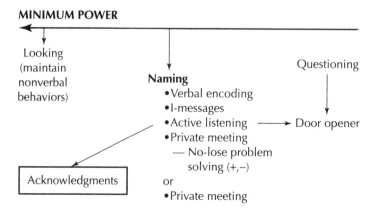

**FIGURE 7–4   Relationship-Listening Face**

ask the student how you both can move the minuses into the plus column. "What actions can we take to work this out so that we are both comfortable and both get our needs met, and so we will not have to face such a situation in the future?"

The objective in using the Relationship-Listening Face is to attempt to maintain the relationship with the misbehaving student and work things out in a nonpunitive no-lose manner. The attitude, or "face," is one that allows your actions to say, "I will nonjudgmentally express to you *(I-message)* how your actions may be taking away my rights and impacting on me as a teacher. I am here to listen to you empathetically and uncritically. I will help by listening and attempting to get clarity, through *active listening*, and when you wish, I can help through my guidance to permit you to solve your own problems. I will not do this for you."

Sometimes issues may arise out of the private meeting that do not have a concrete effect on you or the school. The student wishes to share these issues or seek your guidance in matters related to values that will translate to later student behavior, so you may use the preceding techniques to have the student think out clearly about these important issues.

## The Confronting-Contracting Meeting

The Confronting-Contracting private meeting begins with a series of "What" questions (see Figure 5–1). "Martha (or Mike, or James), this must stop. This shall not continue to go on! What are you doing? What is the rule? I want you to think about this behavior; is it helping you?" Again, go slowly, continue to use nonverbal limit-setting behaviors such as eye contact and relaxing breaths, and have both the student and yourself seated so that you are knee to knee or at the edge of the student's *comfort bubble*. The Confronting-Contracting attitude is to give the student time, with your counseling, to reflect cognitively on what he is doing—requiring the brain's neocortex to be engaged. If the student is in a state of fight or flight, you might need to take some time to have him relax, so that real thinking can take place. This is not a meeting to scold the student, but to have him *think*.

Finally, ask, "What will you do to change?" and then push for a contract. The student likely will be faced with another opportunity in the future to act in a similar misbehaving manner. Now is the time to use rational thinking to have the student come up with his own appropriate strategy so he will know how to behave the next time this incident occurs. The contract may be informal and sealed with a handshake if it is done in a mini-meeting within the classroom. When contracting is done in an after-class meeting, the contract is written and signed by both the student and teacher, and may include a logical consequence if the contract is broken. The original contract is given to the student and a copy is stored in the teacher's grade book or student filing system for later retrieval if necessary.

## CRISIS LEVEL 3: ACTING-OUT STUDENT

Let us return to a fuller discussion of the *acting-out student*, and techniques for the proper way to approach such a potentially out-of-control student. This may include, when necessary, transporting the assaultive student. Once the student is so flooded emotionally that he is on the very edge (acting out), he has regressed through the "doggy-horsey" brain to the "reptilian" brain and is an irrational reflexive being. He normally cannot hear your words (commands) or cognitively process your verbal communication. Instead, he is on a sensory defensive alert, and is now receiving 90 percent of his incoming messages by what he sees and interprets from your body posture and motion or from your voice tone, volume, and cadence. The manner in which you approach this irrational student will assist you in calming him down, or, on the negative side, trigger him to act out.

### The Supportive Stance

In controlling your own body actions and wishing to communicate a non-hostile position, you use the *supportive stance*, which attempts to calm the student. In doing a supportive stance, you turn your body at an angle to the student, with your preferred foot pointed toward the student and the other foot at a 45-degree angle. You must not place yourself square shoulder to shoulder (described in the previous chapter) for two reasons. For one, the squared-off stance communicates a power challenge and will likely be viewed as hostile by the irrational student and may trigger him to act out. Additionally, if you were to be grabbed or receive a blow, such as being kicked, from the irrational student while in this squared-off power stance, you would expose all of the vulnerable parts of your body—face, neck, stomach, and groin—to the blow. The angled supportive stance (see Drawing 1) is interpreted by the irrational student as nonhostile. Also, if you are assaulted, any blow would be against the side of your body (shoulder, hip, or leg). Taking an unexpected blow against the side of your body may hurt, but these body parts are less sensitive and less prone to injury. The supportive stance also gives you the best footing to block and move to deflect any action by the acting-out student and to remove yourself from the situation—to escape. The squared-off stance, on the other hand, leaves you flat-footed and exposes you to any quick blows (see Figure 7–5).

In further carrying out the supportive stance, place both hands in front of you and face the student in a palms-up position, but still be ready to use your hands to block an assault. Be careful not to gesture or make any threatening moves with your hands, such as wagging your finger or similar hostile gestures. It is also important not to conceal your hands by placing them behind your back, which the irrational student may interpret as a sign that you may be holding something dangerous behind you. Also, do not put your hands on your hips, clench your fist, or point. Move in a slow manner, moving to the edge of the student's comfort bubble, about one leg length away from the student, but be careful not to invade this "bubble" space.

**DRAWING 1    The Angled Supportive Stance**

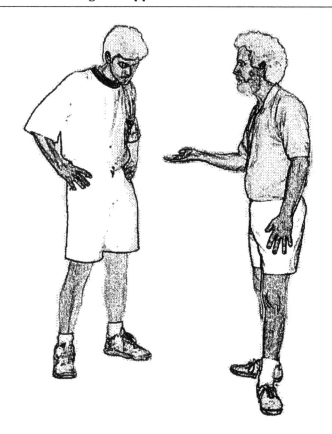

**FIGURE 7–5    A Comparison of the Body Stances**

| "Squared Off" Power Stance | Supportive Stance |
|---|---|
| *Purpose:* Communicates and maintains power | *Purpose:* Communicates support and nonhostile attitude |
| • Shoulder squared off<br>• Eye contact (visual burn)<br>• Hands behind the back<br>• Face is flat and expressionless (slack jaw)<br>• Say nothing<br>• "Close space" | • Feet positioned as in an "L"<br>• Open hand, palms up in front<br>• Nonglaring eye contact<br>• Control of voice (tone, volume, cadence)<br>• Promise of safety<br>• Give command and promise of consequence<br>• Repeat as "broken record"<br>• Stand at the edge of privacy bubble (proximity-near) |

While employing the supportive stance, make eye contact, promise the student safety, and state a command, repeating it two or three times (*broken record*) attempting to get the emotionally flooded student to hear you. If you do not get a change in the student's behavior, clearly state a preparatory statement for possible consequences. "James, I am not going to hurt you or touch you! I want you to calm down, take a couple of breaths, and relax. (*promise of safety*) James, lower your voice, put the ball in your pocket, and go to the cafeteria *(Command).* Lower your voice, put the ball in your pocket, and go to the cafeteria. (*broken record*) (A few seconds pass.) If you do not, I will need to call Assistant Principal Kelsay and two other teachers and we will escort you to the office. Take your choice."

---

### PROMISE OF SAFETY

When the student has been violent, the teacher repeatedly tells him that she is not going to return that violence (hit) and the child is safe with the teacher.

---

In response to a student's assault, the teacher will defend herself by using blocking and release techniques. If the student is endangering himself or others or doing severe damage to property, use the restraining techniques described below (with the help of a second or third adult if one is nearby to form a Response Team). You should accompany your physical actions with a *Command* sending two messages: a directive to desist the unwanted action, and a promise of safety and nonaggression toward the student.

## Assault

Experts have studied the nature of assault in order to design ways that the teacher may act to keep herself safe and in turn not injure the student— called *Nonviolent Crisis Intervention.*[3] They have discovered that there are typically two ways that a student may assault: a strike or a grab. Each is described here, along with some suggested teacher actions.

### A Strike

A strike occurs when a weapon (foot, fist, object) comes in contact with a target (the teacher's body).[4] The general techniques for defending against a strike are to block and move.

**Assault by Kicking**   From a supportive stance with your feet at a 45-degree angle, lift your foot that is pointing toward the student, balancing on the other foot. While holding your foot up as a barrier, attempt to block the kick with the back of your foot or shoe and deflect to the side and behind you. If this kicking continues, you may need to get help, and a restraining hold may be required (see Drawing 2).

---

**DRAWING 2   Kick Block**

---

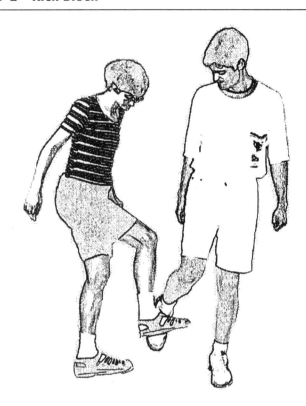

**Assault by Hitting and Throwing**   The three-foot spacing at the edge of the student's privacy bubble in the *supportive stance* may provide the teacher with some room to anticipate a punch that is delivered by the student. You would block and deflect this punch with the backside of your arm by holding it across your body. When a student throws a blow with his fist, he has a forward momentum, and once you deflect the blow you may grab the back of the student's arm and pull him past you with the aid of his forward momentum. You may then exit to get help, or may choose to position yourself with your back to an exit door permitting an escape, return to the supportive stance, and command the student to desist.

When the student is throwing something at you, there are two ways of handling an incoming object that has the potential to do you bodily harm. You can either move out of its path and dodge, or block and deflect. If you have time you may pick up an object—a book, or perhaps a small chair you can hold like a lion tamer—and use it to block and deflect the blow or thrown object.

## A Grab

Besides being assaulted by a strike, you may also experience a grab, which is defined as a strike that clings to a target. Under this definition, every grab begins as a strike, and continues in the form of choking, biting or grabbing.

**Assault by Choking**[5]    When a student assaults you by a front choking—placing his hands around your throat and squeezing—you respond by standing erect, thrusting both arms upright above your head, taking one step back to put the student off balance, and turning suddenly to the right or left so the student's hands will be pulled. Do not try to grab the child's hands and pull them off your throat; this will simply be inefficient or ineffective, and the student might dig his fingernails into your throat (see Drawings 3 and 4). Accompany the quick movement with a psychological response by shouting or screaming, startling the assaultive student and throwing him slightly off balance, permitting you a short second to get free.

**DRAWING 3    Front Choke Release**

**DRAWING 4    Rear Choke Release**

**Assault by Biting**   If the student has caught you off guard and has sunk his teeth into you (most likely an arm), you can free yourself from the biting hold by putting the edge of your flat hand under the child's nose and against his upper lip and quickly vibrating your hand up and down with sufficient force to free yourself without injuring the student. Do not pull away from the bite but rather lean into it. If you pull, you may cause more damage by tearing than the bite itself. If the student has turned in such a manner that you cannot immediately get to his upper lip area, take the fingertips of your flat hand and push them firmly into his cheek, finding the teeth between the upper and lower jaw and again vibrating your hand in an up-and-down motion to free yourself (see Drawing 5). You would also accompany the release attempt with a psychological response such as a shout.

**Assault by Grabbing**   An assault by grabbing will usually come in the form of the student doing a one- or two-handed grab of either your arms or your hair.

## One- and Two-Hand Grabbing Release

When the student uses either one or two hands to grab your arm, there is a weak link in the grab between the student's thumb and forefinger. Simply take your free hand, bring it over the top of the student's grab, lock the fingers of your two hands, and pull directly up. (see Drawings 6 and 7). Again, accompany this release with a shout.

## One- and Two-Hand Hair-Pulling Release

If the student grabs your hair, either with one hand or two, clasp his hand and push it into or against your head as a platform, while at the

---

**DRAWING 5   Bite Release**

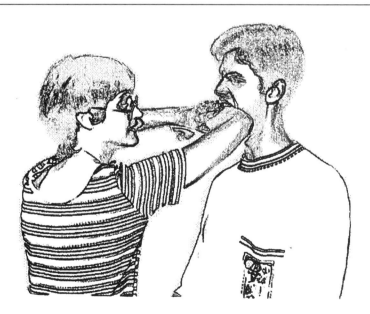

| DRAWING 6   One-Hand Grab Release |
| --- |

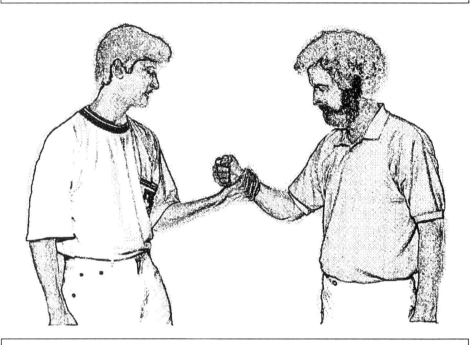

| DRAWING 7   Two-Hand Grab Release |
| --- |

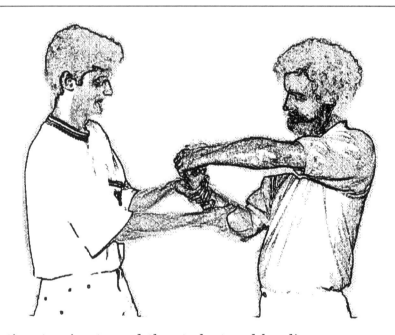

same time turning toward the student and bending your upper body down in a 45-degree angle. The student's wrist is bent backwards, causing a loss of strength in his hands and enabling you to break free and physically move away (see Drawings 8 and 9).

If, after an incident of choking, biting, kicking, grabbing, or hitting/throwing, the student retreats and moves to a protective corner or space out of the way of classroom activities, presenting no danger to himself or others, you should simply leave him alone. You may consider him to have moved to Tension Reduction. However, if the student is still endangering others, property, or himself, you must now use nonviolent restraining techniques to stop his dangerous actions.

**DRAWING 8    One-Hand Hair Grab Release**

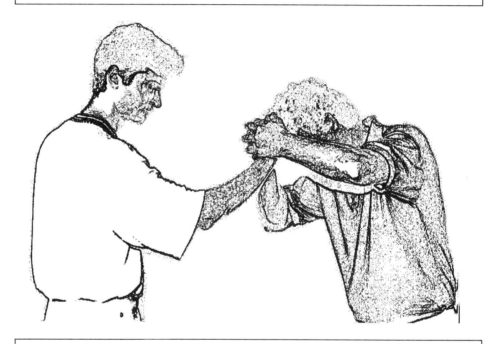

**DRAWING 9    Two-Hand Hair Grab Release**

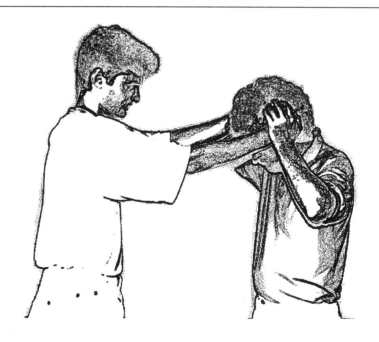

## Nonviolent Restraining

### Basket-Weave Hold Restraint[6]

If the student is small enough and you have a strength advantage, you may choose to use the basket-weave hold. This is a preferable restraining technique for a small student. This hold is accomplished by getting behind the assaulting student and putting your arms around him, grasping his right wrist with your left hand and his left wrist with your right hand, and pulling toward you in a way that causes the student's arms to cross over the front of his body (see Drawing 10). As you stand, move your body sideways to the student with your feet at a 45-degree angle. This places the student's back on your right hip, and you then pull his arms back toward you and lift up. This causes the child's heels to come slightly off the floor, forcing him to stand on his tip-toes with his weight supported by your thigh. You also may hold or restrain the student in a seated position. Remember to use only the minimum amount of force needed, so that no injury is done to the student.

*Note:* The basket-weave restraint is the most powerful hold suggested for a small student, where the teacher has a substantial physical strength advantage. If the child is too big and strong, you may be required to use a team restraint.

---

**DRAWING 10    Basket-Weave Restraint**

## Team Restraint

Once a full blow has been thrown by the assaulting student, and two other members of the Response Team are there to help you, you quickly step behind the student and grasp his right wrist with your right hand, with the thumb side of your hand facing down and in. At the same time, take your open left hand and place it on the student's right shoulder from behind. The thumb of your left hand should be positioned in the "V" formed by the student's arm and rib cage (see Drawing 11). Also take your left foot and place it in front of the student's body and between his two feet, thus preventing the child from walking out of the restraining hold. Now push down with your left hand on the child's shoulder, while gently turning the child's wrist clockwise with your right hand. Be careful to apply only the needed pressure in order not to hurt the child—these are to be nonviolent restraining techniques. The second member of the Response Team parallels your actions with the student—her left hand on the student's left wrist, her right hand on the student's left shoulder, and her right foot parallel to your foot in front of the student. Again, this is all coordinated, and the two members grab, move their feet, push down, and hold in one smooth action. The student is pushed head-down until his head is below his waistline. From this position, it is impossible for him to pick up his feet to kick. The third Response Team member moves in front of the student, places his hand palms-up under the student's shoulder and holds him to prevent him from falling forward. The acting-out student is told to calm down and advised that he may get up when he assures the Response Team that he will not resist or act out. Once the team members are assured that the student is calmed, he is now permitted slowly to stand erect, but the first two teachers maintain their hold on his wrists and move into a transporting hold.

## Transporting Techniques

If the child does stop struggling and you now have him in an upright position, quickly take the hand that had been holding his shoulder and move it under his arm. Being careful not to release the child's wrist, use your free hand to grasp the inside of the elbow of his other arm (see Drawing 12). Now walk quickly, bringing the child with you at the fastest manageable pace, applying a forward pressure with your inside shoulder that touches the student. A second Response Team member can get behind the child, place both hands on the student's shoulder blades and push (see Drawing 13). If at any time during the transporting process the child excessively struggles to get free, simply reapply the team restraint described above. Never transport a student who is struggling and acting out.

*Important:* Accompany your physical restraining with parallel language of *supportive command*, *preparatory directive statement*, and *promise of safety*.

As we have seen, there generally are four levels of crisis development leading to possible violent acts by the student: Level 1: Anxiety

DRAWING 11    Team Restraint

DRAWING 12    Single Transport

DRAWING 13   Two Person Transport

Phase; Level 2: Defensive Phase; Level 3: Acting-Out Student Phase; and finally, Level 4: Tension Reduction Phase.

It is important to point out that during this crisis management, as with the removal of Martha, Mike, or James, the classroom teacher will be the Response Team leader and will use verbal mediation to attempt to calm the acting-out student. The classroom teacher plays the lead role for the following reasons:

1. The assistant principal and the Response Team members do not have a relationship with the student and know very little background as to what has happened to precipitate the event.

2. Giving up the power to an administrator or another teacher weakens the classroom teacher's power with the student and her authority in the eyes of the classmates.

3. With the classroom teacher maintaining the leadership, there is continuity of action during escalation and deescalation of power through the Three Faces of Discipline techniques.

4. Power does not involve physical strength, and the yielding of the leadership to a physically larger male faculty member or administrator (which historically has been the practice) suggests that this is a physical power confrontation.

A potentially assaultive student's behavior with a weapon (knife, gun, explosives) may also be viewed through the crisis construct (Figure 7–1). However, disarming such a student is clearly outside your role and skill as a teacher—don't attempt to be a hero. If possible, evacuate all students *and yourself.* Get out of the classroom or the area, and call the police. It is mandatory that the school administration have predetermined steps and procedures to deal with a student carrying a weapon, with all teachers and staff drilled in the procedures and Emergency Codes.

If the armed student is restricting your departure through threats, and an evacuation cannot be carried out, you are then forced to deal with that student through this *defensive-phase* level. These guidelines will help if you are caught in such a situation:

- Do not challenge with eye contact.

- Do not *close space* or invade the student's *comfort bubble.*

- Use repeated relaxing breaths to keep yourself under control so that you do not experience an *adrenaline dump.*

- Do not *square off* with the student, but place yourself in a *supportive stance* (feet placed in an "L" position).

- Do not cross your arms over your chest or make any gestures; simply put your hands behind your back.

- Send for help if at all possible.

If the student wishes to talk, this usually is an encouraging sign. Use Relationship-Listening *door openers* and *active listening* to encourage ventilation. If the student appears to be attempting to rationally think through his actions, you might use *"What" questions* from the Confronting-Contracting techniques. When in doubt in dealing with an armed student when evacuation is impossible, the best action is to do nothing.[7]

What has been described here is how you may deal with the Level 3: Acting-Out Student by gradually escalating your power with the use of the TBC, from *Looking* (eye contact and proximity) to *Naming* (Relationship-Listening), *Questioning* (Confronting-Contracting), *Commanding* (Rules and Consequences with assertive commands), and, ultimately, *Acting (Physical Intervention)* (nonviolent crisis management). The use of outside help from a Response Team involves very *public* techniques. Return repeatedly to a controlled use of verbal limit setting, with its minimal use of power, escalating only gradually from Relationship-Listening to Confronting-Contracting, and, when warranted, Rules and Consequences.

## CRISIS LEVEL 4: TENSION REDUCTION

After the violent act, the student feels deflated and becomes withdrawn, with little energy. He has feelings of guilt and feels *helpless* as to how others might respond to him, especially the teacher he may have assaulted. The teacher techniques for handling the student during Tension Reduction were discribed in the previous discussion of Verbal Escalation; the reader may wish to reread that section.

## Classmates as Onlookers to the Assault

When possible, the teacher should take steps to remove onlooking classmates by having the other students move to another room, by sectioning an area off from the view of other students, or (if possible) moving the misbehaving student to another room. Witnessing the irrational, flooded student can be very frightening for classmates, and seeing your restraining actions on the assaulting child may appear to young students as if you are hurting this child.

It is quite important to deal with the classmates who were onlookers to an assault by the revengeful student. Witnessing such aggression can cause an individual child or an entire group of children to move to Level 1: Anxiety, whereby they become highly anxious with accompanying behavior that might escalate through the crisis levels. You may deal with this by doing the ventilating techniques previously suggested in working with Level 1: Anxiety children. After these violent incidents, you now view the entire class as being in Level 1: Anxiety, so you want them to "talk it out." This "talking it out" involves holding one or more class problem-solving meetings, using the Relationship-Listening techniques.

## Class Meetings (Verbal Ventilation)

The entire class is seated in a circle. The formerly assaulting student is included in the meeting, and should be seated if possible. Just as the Confronting-Contracting techniques were used for Level 4: Tension Reduction to enable the teacher to establish an emotional equilibrium with the previously assaulting child, this tension reduction will also need to be reestablished with the student's classmates. They have seen or heard the frightening event, and have identified themselves as a part of the action. Through verbal ventilating in the class meeting, an attempt is made to reach the point where the teacher and students have gotten rid of any feelings of hostility. If you do not do this, the classmates—out of their fear of the acting-out child—will begin to make the misbehaving student the *outside aggressor*.

Let's watch such a meeting unfold. Notice that the meeting begins with the teacher wearing a Relationship-Listening Face with its accompanying techniques, before moving to Confronting-Contracting:

> **Teacher** *(opens the meeting): "Friends, I would like to talk about some scary and frightening things that happened this morning"* (door opener).
>
> **Children:** *(no one speaks for several moments, but then a discussion begins)*
>
> **Harriet:** *"James was psyched!"*

*Paul:*   *"He hit the teacher."*

*Teacher:*   *"James was very angry. And when he gets angry, he hits"* (active listening).

*Diana:*   *"Keep him away from me!"*

*Teacher:*   *"When people hit, it is hard to like them."*

*Paul:*   *"You hurt James's arm."*

*Teacher:*   *"When I held James, you thought I was hurting him"* (active listening).

*John:*   *"You didn't hit James."*

*Teacher:*   *"What else did you see and feel?"* (door opener).

*Nancy:*   *"I saw James hit you and kick you. He cried and screamed swear words."*

*(This verbal ventilation may continue for 5 to 10 minutes with the teacher maintaining a Relationship-Listening Face and its techniques. Now the teacher moves to Confronting-Contracting and does not hesitate to deal with the realities of the situation and explain misinformation.)*

*Teacher:*   *"What happened first.... Harriet?"* ("What" questions).

*Harriet:*   *"James bounced the ball against the school—he wasn't following the rule."*

*Teacher:*   *"What happened next?"* ("What" questions).

*John:*   *"You told James to stop, and he pushed you and hit you."*

*Teacher:*   *"What happened next?"* (Confronting: "What" questions).

*Diana:*   *"James screamed and hit, and you held him. And there was a big crash."*

*Teacher:*   *"What happened next?"* ("What" questions).

*Paul:*   *"You hurt James's arm."*

*Teacher:*   *"No. Because James got so mad that he could hurt me, and he could hurt others, and he could hurt himself, I needed to hold him tightly to keep him safe. I am the teacher and boss but I do not hurt students. I am a friend, but when students get very angry, I need to hold them tight to keep them safe"* (a reality explanation and promise of safety).

*Paul:*   *"You hurt James's arm."*

*Teacher:*   *"No, Paul. I was holding his arm and hands tightly so that his hands would not hurt me. I did not hurt James; I was keeping him safe. Come up here, Paul. (Paul stands before the teacher.) Let me show you how safely I was holding James." (The teacher now demonstrates the basket-weave restraint on Paul and two other children. Paul giggles as if it is a game, and now a number of other children want a chance. The teacher demonstrates the basket-weave restraint on all children who have requested it—including James, who wants to be a part of this new game.)*

***Teacher:*** *"When students get very angry, they sometimes try to hurt other people. I am the teacher, and I keep people safe. And no matter how mean people are, I will not hit them, I will not hurt them, I will not kick them, and I will not bite them. I am the teacher and I hold students to keep them safe (reality explanation and* promise of safety*). Now we need to make some promises—we need to have an agreement. What should we do when others make us angry?"*

***Nearly the entire class, in unison:*** *"Use words."*

***Teacher:*** *"Yes, when others make us angry, the rule is, 'We do not hit, but we tell that person with words,' and we can come to the teacher to get help. Hitting, biting, kicking, and spitting are against the rules. Also, how can we help James when he gets mad?"*

***Diana:*** *"We can share with him."*

***John:*** *"We can let him play with us."*

***Teacher:*** *"Does everyone agree with this? Good! We all now have an agreement. We are going to use words when we are angry, and we are going to invite James to be our friend and play with us"* (contracting).

This vignette, of course, is for purposes of modeling teacher techniques, and is certainly rather artificial. This ventilation process and the confronting and contracting might take many minutes, or even many meetings, and may need to occur throughout the year if aggression is high in the classroom. But the techniques to be used, and the general attitude and processes to be employed, should develop in a direction much as the one demonstrated here.

This class meeting will serve a number of purposes: (1) it ventilates any pent-up anxiety and feelings that any child might have after witnessing the aggression; (2) it helps the assaultive student and his classmates reestablish an emotional equilibrium through tension reduction, potentially preventing the assaultive student from becoming the *outside aggressor;* (3) it helps students understand that if they, too, should become angry (and they may), the teacher will not take aggressive action against them but instead will help; and (4) it dispels any misinformation and misperceptions the children may have ("You hurt James's arm.").

## SUMMARY

There will be times that some students emotionally flood, creating a crisis that may lead to an assault by the student against the teacher or others. This behavior represents four levels: Anxiety Phase, Defensive Phase, Acting-Out Student Phase, and Tension Reduction Phase. If you understand the behavior and these levels, you are more empowered to know how to act and how to intervene with such out-of-control students. Generally, a teacher can employ TBC techniques, first with the techniques of controlling her own behavior and using proximity, eye contact, and the supportive stance. If the teacher needs to escalate, she would again use as little power as necessary, moving from the *Naming* techniques of the Relationship-Listening Face to *Questioning* and its accompanying Confronting-Contracting techniques. If necessary, the teacher can move to *Commanding* and the Rules and Consequences Face. Also, if it is unavoidable, the teacher may be required to *Physically Intervene (Acting)* by first protecting herself from the student's assaults and then restraining the student and transporting him to areas were he may be isolated. Finally, once the student is calmed down, the teacher may reestablish the teacher-student relationship through a progression of discussion techniques.

# Endnotes

1. McMurrain, T. (1975). *Intervention in Human Crisis*. Atlanta: Humanics Press. *Nonviolent Crisis Intervention for the Educator: Volume III—The Assaultive Student.* Brookfield, WI: National Crisis Prevention Institute, Inc.

2. *Note*: After reading the full explanation that follows, you will see that the teacher in this example made a number of mistakes in handling this incident and dealing with a revengeful child. She should have used *supportive demand and stance* rather than *assertive demand and stance* (explained later). But if the teacher has had little past experience and does not know the history of this child, she might judge his actions as an attempt to grab attention or power, and then might find herself handling the revengeful incident as best she can once it begins.

3. National Crisis Prevention Institute, Inc.

4. Ibid.

5. Ibid.

6. Ibid.

7. Jones, F. (1987). *Positive Classroom Discipline*. New York: McGraw-Hill.

# The Backup System

## PROFESSIONAL-ADMINISTRATIVE BACKUP SYSTEM

When all your limit-setting methods and techniques have failed to stop the student's misbehavior and his actions continue to disrupt the classroom learning environment, it may be time to call for help from others. The first step in moving to the Professional-Adminstrative Backup System is recognizing that this student's actions and behaviors are beyond your skills and abilities—in short, you need help.

This will force you to go public with your actions toward the misbehaving student, who has resisted your attempts to resolve the problem in private. The student may then need to be isolated, or you may need to seek help from other professionals outside your classroom (other teachers, the school counselor or psychologist, perhaps even mental health organizations and law enforcement.)

The Professional-Adminstrative Backup System involves two parts: a Professional Sphere, with specific procedures designed to resolve the problem within an academic setting, and an Adminstrative-Legal Sphere, for problems that go beyond the realm of the educational setting (see Figure III–1).

Among the procedures used as part of a Backup System are isolation/time out, private conferencing, contracting, professional staffing, and a technique called The Six Steps to Problem Solving. These concepts will be explained in detail in subsequent chapters.

The Backup System, as part of the Three Faces of Discipline philosophy, draws on the series of techniques previously learned in the three categories of Relationship-Listening, Confronting-Contracting, and Rules and Consequences. Techniques for managing violent and assaultive student behavior are also included.

**FIGURE III–1   Professional and Administrative Spheres of Responsibility**

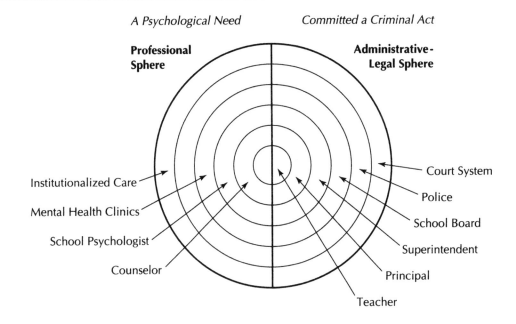

# The Backup System

# 8

When you have used all your limit-setting techniques (described previously) and the student's behavior is still disrupting the classroom learning climate, you may need to declare that this student's actions and behavior are beyond your skills and abilities. In such a case, you would turn to a Backup System, using isolation or time out, private meetings, and contracting with the student, before seeking professional help from others outside your classroom—thereby making the discipline action public. Such professional help might involve the other teachers, the school counselor, a school psychologist, and various mental health organizations or—in the most extreme cases—even institutionalized care for the student. The actions of the student could also involve criminal acts, which might necessitate the involvement of the administration, school board, police, juvenile authorities, and the court system.

The Professional-Administrative Backup System involves two parts. The first entails a Professional Sphere, with clearly delineated steps and procedures designed to permit you, as the primary deliverer of educational services, to gain professional consultation, through staffing, from colleagues. The objective is to enable you to increase your skill and become more effective with a particular very difficult student.

The second part utilizes an Administrative-Legal Sphere involving a yielding of primary responsibility for the management and restraint of the student's behavior. This would occur because of the severity of the student's actions, which may be criminal or at the least threaten your safety and well-being or that of your class—or even the disruptive student himself. Understandable and clearly defined steps and procedures must be established to dictate when such crisis students should be referred to the administrative authorities or legal system.

## DOCUMENTATION OF THE BACKUP STEPS
## (THE BACKUP SYSTEM CHECKLIST)

To guide the teacher through suggested backup steps, a Backup System Checklist is provided (see Figure 8–1). By writing in dates and checking appropriate boxes, the teacher can easily document his or her own actions. The checklist, when followed, helps in these ways:

1. It provides a pathway for the teacher to follow.

2. Because it records the date of actions and techniques, a time line of events can later be created to document the attempts that the teacher has made to help this misbehaving student.

3. It provides legal and professional documentation for
   • the administrator
   • the professional (school psychologist, counselor, etc.)
   • legal authorities who may question any of the procedures
   • parents

4. The Checklist, with its boxes to be checked and its spaces for dates, means less paperwork for the teacher, who otherwise would have to write this documentation in anecdotal records.

### Procedures

The teacher begins using the Backup System Checklist by taking the checklist form (Figure 8–1), dating it, giving the student's grade level or home room, and including the student's and teacher's names. The Checklist is kept in the teacher's lesson plan book within easy reach of the teacher. The Checklist contains boxes to be marked whenever the teacher has performed one of the actions, and a line for dating its completion.

Generally, the teacher begins with step 1 under the left column (Relationship-Listening techniques) and progresses down the column and across the Checklist following a plan of action. The Relationship-Listening column (Figure 8–2) would guide the teacher to progress through a sequence of three private (knee-to-knee) conferences. The student has been so disruptive (that is, preventing the teacher from teaching) that the teacher needs to call the student aside for a private conference. At each of the conferences the teacher would use procedures of

1. I-messages

2. Active listening

3. Door openers

4. No-lose problem solving

A box is provided so the teacher may place a check to document her actions. The teacher also writes the date of each private conference.

# FIGURE 8–1 Backup System Checklist

Date (beginning) _____  
Grade _____

Student's Name _____  
Teacher's Name _____

| | Relationship-Listening | Confronting-Contracting | Rules and Consequences |
|---|---|---|---|
| **Limit Setting** | • I-Message<br>• Active Listening<br>(Proxemics—far, near, intimate) | • Stop ("this may not continue!")<br>• "What" questions ("…will be the consequences?")<br>(Proxemics—far, near, intimate) | • Assertive Command (tell what to do!)<br>• Promise a Consequence<br>(Proxemics—far, near, intimate) |

Severity Clause →→→→→→→→→→→→→→→→→→→→→→→→→→→→→→→→→→→→→→→→→→→→→→→→→→→→→→→

| | Relationship-Listening | Confronting-Contracting | Rules and Consequences |
|---|---|---|---|
| **Backup System** | **1. 1st Knee-to-Knee Conference**<br>☐ a. I-Message<br>☐ b. Active Listening<br>☐ c. Door Openers (acknowledgments, critical listening)<br>☐ d. No-Lose Problem Solving<br>_____ Date<br><br>**2. 2nd Knee-to-Knee Conference**<br>☐ (Repeat a, b, c, d)<br>_____ Date<br><br>**3. 3rd Knee-to-Knee Conference**<br>☐ (Repeat a, b, c, d)<br>_____ Date | **1. 1st Conference**<br>1.1 "What" question<br>☐ "What did you do?"<br>☐ "What is the rule?"<br>☐ "What is the consequence?"<br>☐ "How will you change?"<br>_____ Date<br>1.2 Contract<br>☐ handshake<br>☐ written<br>_____ Date<br>☐ 1.3 (if broken) Logical Consequences<br>_____ Date<br>• *Level 1 Time Out*<br>(Mediate afterwards with R-L or C-C)<br>• *Level 2 Time Out (In Room)*<br><br>**2. 1st In-Room Time Out/Conference**<br>☐ 2.1 "What" questions<br>☐ 2.2 Contract (written-enclose)<br>_____ Date<br>☐ 2.3 (if broken) Logical Consequences<br>_____ Date<br><br>**3. 2nd In-Room Time Out/Conference**<br>☐ 3.1 Repeat 1 and 2 (above)<br>_____ Date<br>☐ 3.2 (if broken) Logical Consequences<br>_____ Date<br>• *Level 3 Time Out (Out-of-Room)*<br><br>**4. 3rd In-Room Time Out/ Conference**<br>☐ Repeat 1 and 2 (above)<br>_____ Date<br>☐ 3.2 (if broken) Logical Consequences<br>_____ Date | **5. ☐ Telephone Parents**<br>_____ Date<br>5.1 (Begin Encouragement System)<br>_____ Date<br>• *Level 3 Time Out (Out-of-Room)*<br><br>**6. ☐ 1st Out-of-Room Time Out**<br>(Repeat 1, 2, and 3, enclose Time Out Form)<br>_____ Date<br><br>**7. ☐ 2nd Out-of-Room Time Out**<br>(Repeat 1, 2, and 3, enclose Time Out Form)<br>_____ Date<br><br>**8. ☐ Telephone/ In Writing**<br>(Enclose/copy to principal/Parents)<br>_____ Date<br>• *Level 4 Time Out (Principal)*<br><br>**9. ☐ Office**<br>(Repeat 1, 2, and 3)<br>_____ Date<br>(Repeat 1, 2, and 3)<br>_____ Date<br><br>**10. ☐ Conference with Parents**<br>(Repeat 1, 2, and 3)<br>_____ Date<br><br>**11. ☐ Staffing (members)**<br>_____<br>_____ Date | **11.1 "Who" squad**<br>☐ _____ Date<br>Members: _____<br>_____<br>Severity Code Called<br>☐ Weapon _____ Date<br>☐ <u>A</u>ssault, _____ Date<br>☐ <u>C</u>risis _____ Date<br>☐ <u>R</u>unner _____ Date<br>☐ Transporting (performed)<br>_____ Date<br>(enclose form)<br>_____ Date<br>(enclose form)<br>_____ Date<br>(enclose form)<br>_____ Date<br>☐ Restraint (performed)<br>_____ Date<br>(enclose form)<br><br>**11.2 Out-of-School Time Out**<br>_____ Date<br>or<br>**11.2 Mental Health Referral**<br>_____ Date<br>or<br>**11.2 Legal Referral (HRS/Police)**<br>_____ Date |

121

---

**FIGURE 8–2    Relationship-Listening**

1. 1st Private Conference
❑ a. I-Message
❑ b. Active Listening
❑ c. Door Openers (acknowledgments, critical listening)
❑ d. No-Lose Problem Solving
_____ Date

2. 2nd Private Conference
❑ (Repeat a, b, c, d)
_____ Date

3. 3rd Private Conference
❑ (Repeat a, b, c, d)
_____ Date

---

## Private Conferences

In handling a Backup System private meeting with a student such as Mike (in the lost-hat incident), the teacher meets with Mike after class and again begins to escalate up the TBC, first using the Relationship-Listening techniques. (*Reminder*: The Relationship-Listening Face, during these techniques, is one that views the student as (1) logical and rational, (2) able to control himself , (3) able to be trusted, (4) able to solve his own problems, and (5) having a right to express strong feeling/ anger.)

---

**PRIVATE CONFERENCING**

A meeting—either planned as part of the Backup System or spontaneous—held between the student and teacher to work out either the child's or teacher's problem and how behavior might be changed accordingly.

---

### *Looking* (Relationship-Listening Face)

Both Mike and the teacher should be seated in chairs, *squared off*, with the teacher's knees at the edge of Mike's *comfort bubble* (*proximity: near*). Mr. Leonard maintains unswerving eye contact with Mike but is not hostile, aggressive, or unpleasant to him in any manner (such as finger pointing and gesturing). The teacher's face takes on the Queen Victoria look that says, "I am bored"; he periodically takes two *controlled breaths*. Mr. Leonard may wish to permit a little time to go by as he maintains his eye contact and says nothing—he doesn't rush this, as a minute used now may save hours later.

### *Naming* (Relationship-Listening Face)

Mr. Leonard says calmly, "Mike, we had a very unpleasant morning." (*active listening*) The teacher now says nothing, and lets the heat of the relationship simmer to see if Mike will begin to speak first. In this first step on the TBC, Mr. Leonard is returning to his Relationship-Listening Face and wishes Mike to talk it out and externalize what is bothering him so that real problem solving may occur. The teacher may choose to stay in the Relationship-Listening Face and use *door openers* ("Let's talk about the happenings in the class this morning"), *acknowledgments, I-messages* ("When I am told to 'f--- off' and that I am an 'asshole' (*behavior*), it hurts our relationship (*effect*), and I feel frustrated (*feelings*) because this cuts off our communication"), and *active listening* ("I could tell that something was bothering you this morning"). Mr. Leonard may also use the Six Steps to Problem Solving process to settle any difficulties in his relationship with Mike.

If the student remained disruptive after the first private conference and the use of the Relationship-Listening techniques, the teacher would continue to use Relationship-Listening techniques for two more private meetings carried out in a similar manner (Steps 2 and 3). If the teacher believes this is not effective and feels the need for more power, he may turn to *Questioning* in private meetings.

## SIX STEPS TO PROBLEM SOLVING

To help students learn to think through a problem logically, the teacher might lead the student through a six-step process while using the Relationship-Listening techniques to carry out these private meetings.

The example that follows is a meeting using the Six Steps to Problem Solving. This time, we'll return to the example of Martha, who has been offensive to the teacher.

> **Ms. Dumas:** *"Mrs. Jenkins has done something that makes you feel she doesn't like you"* (active listening).
>
> **Martha:** *"Yeah, she cut me! I went to tumbling camp for two weeks this summer and I know more than all of the girls she picked. It ain't fair!"*
>
> **Ms. Dumas:** *"You worked hard but you were cut from the tumbling team"* (active listening).
>
> **Martha:** *"Well, no, she made me an alternate, but I only get to perform when someone is sick or can't make the meet."*
>
> **Ms. Dumas:** *"You wish you would be on the first-string team."*
>
> **Martha:** *"Yeah! But, I'll probably fail this stupid math."*
>
> **Ms. Dumas:** *"Failing math would make you ineligible to be on the tumbling team."*
>
> **Martha:** *"Yeah, I don't understand this stuff!"*

**Ms. Dumas:** *"Ah, I see. You have a problem here—and that is passing math so you can remain on the tumbling team (Step 1: Defining the Problem). Let's work together to think of ways you might solve this problem. What are your ideas?"* (Step 2: Generating Solutions).

**Martha:** *"I was trying to get Janet to help me with the homework."*

**Ms. Dumas:** *"That may work—getting a person to tutor you. But let's think of a lot of other ways, too"*(door opener).

**Martha:** *"Well, my dad's pretty good at this stuff."*

**Ms. Dumas:** *"OK, we have two solutions: getting another student to tutor you, or getting your father to help. What else can you think of?"* (door opener).

**Martha:** *"Well, I could take math in summer school."*

**Ms. Dumas:** *(nods head as an* acknowledgment)

**Martha:** *"Janet and I have free time together before school ends each day. Could I get her to help me with the problems then?"*

**Ms. Dumas:** *"It sounds like you have generated a number of solutions: getting a tutor, getting help from your father, taking math in summer school, or getting Janet to help you at the end of the school day. Which of your ideas would be best?"* (Step 3: Evaluating the Solutions).

**Martha:** *"Getting Janet to help at the end of the day. And sometimes getting Dad to help when I'm at home."*

**Ms. Dumas:** *"Do you want to evaluate your other possibilities?"* (door openers).

**Martha:** *"Well, if I took math in summer school, I would miss junior cheerleading camp! And I don't know any tutors or have any other time to meet with a tutor."*

**Ms. Dumas:** *"So getting Janet to help you at the end of the day and getting help from Dad . . . is that what you will do?"* (Step 4: Deciding on a Solution).

**Martha:** *"Yes."*

*For the next two weeks, the teacher notices that Martha's homework is completed, she has scored well on two quizzes, and her off-task behavior in class has stopped* (Step 5: Implementing the Solution). *After class, the teacher talks to Martha.*

**Ms. Dumas:** *"Was your solution to your problem a good one?"* (Step 6: Evaluating the Solution).

**Martha:** *"Yes, it was* great, *and I figured it out all by myself! You know, my Dad is a whiz at this math stuff."*

**Six Steps to Problem Solving**

1. *Defining the Problem*
   Before any discussion may occur in a conference, a clear statement of the problem must be given by the teacher or the student.

2. *Generating Solutions*
   All parties—teachers and students—are encouraged to come up with a creative list of solutions, no matter how unrealistic the solutions may be, without evaluating the merits of the suggestions.

3. *Evaluating the Solutions*
   All solutions are openly evaluated for the "goodness" or "badness" of the solutions.

4. *Deciding on a Solution*
   All parties—teacher and student or the students as a group—must decide on a solution that is acceptable to everyone.

5. *Implementing the Solution*
   All parties must decide what their role is in carrying out the solution and commit themselves to the actions required. They must agree on when a later evaluation of the effectiveness of the solution will occur.

6. *Evaluating the Solution*
   A later follow-up meeting will occur to see if the solution was effective and what other actions might now be needed.

The teacher has used the Six Steps to Problem Solving to help Martha through a process of on-the-spot *conferencing* or *private meeting* as a part of the Backup System. First, we saw Martha as an off-task and verbally hostile student. Then, through *active listening,* we discovered that Martha had an inner disequilibrium, or "blocked" need—she wanted to be a first-string member of the tumbling team, which required her to pass math to remain eligible for the squad. The teacher did not solve this problem for her, but was willing to take the time to listen, as part of the Backup System, and encourage Martha to communicate (speak out) about this problem until a solution was developed. The communication was guided by a rather simple sequence of procedures: (1) help in *Defining the Problem*; (2) trying to stimulate creativity toward *Generating Solutions* but without evaluating them; (3) *Evaluating the Solutions*; and then (4) *Deciding on a Solution.* The teacher also observed Martha (5) *Implementing the Solution,* and later (6) *Evaluating the Solution.*

## PROBLEM OWNERSHIP

Notice that with Martha, who wanted to be on the tumbling team and pass math, the teacher did not take ownership of these problems, nor did the teacher use roadblocks to communication by lecturing, giving solutions, or issuing warnings. Martha owned the problem, and the teacher facilitated her thinking through the problem solving and then encouraged her to act. Teachers are solidly motivated to nurture and help children. They may be super-teachers who see their role as being the person who solves all problems in the classroom. If they do that, however, they rob the student of the authentic experience of clashing with others and objects. This clashing allows the students to acquire skills for solving their own daily problems and becoming autonomous. In order to classify the problems that are seen involving the students in the classroom, the teacher must determine whether the *student* owns the problem or the *teacher* owns the problem. These questions will help:

1. Do the student's actions or problems take away the teacher's or classmates' rights?
   (The student has taken two staplers in art class while others have had only one, and she is moving to take a third one. This requires teacher intervention.)

2. Is the safety of the materials, the classmates, the teacher, or the child involved?
   (The student has brought a real bullet, but no gun, to the class and is grinding down the lead tip of the bullet in the electric pencil sharpener. This requires teacher intervention.)

3. Is the child too young and incapable of "owning" or solving this problem?
   (The child is trying to get the lid off the nail storage can in the carpentry corner, which takes more strength than the 7-year-old has. This requires teacher intervention.)

If the answer to any of these questions is yes, the teacher owns the problem and must respond. Response techniques will be I-messages, active listening, door openers, acknowledgments, and possibly the Six Steps to Problem Solving.

The concept of problem ownership clearly tells teachers to inhibit their "rescuer" tendencies, however.

*Child:*   "Teacher, Michael took my baseball cap!"
*Teacher:*   "What are you going to do to get your cap back?" (door opener)

From 80 to 90 percent of all problems faced by students in the classroom belong to them. The guidelines for problem ownership suggest that teachers must not allow their need to help or their fear of chaos to prompt them to move too quickly and without thinking, thus robbing the students of the experience of solving their own problems.

## QUESTIONS (CONFRONTING-CONTRACTING FACE)

If three private conferences using the Relationship-Listening techniques have been conducted and the student's behavior has not improved or is getting more destructive, the pathway of teacher action suggested by the Checklist now requires the teacher to move to the Confronting-Contracting Face (see Figure 8–3). Again, another series of conferences between the teacher and student will be held but this time it will be carried out in a very different manner. If this first conference fails to be successful, the teacher holds a second and then a third conference, repeating the suggested techniques of a, b, c, and d.

---

**FIGURE 8–3   Confronting-Contracting Face**

**1. 1st Conference**
1.1 "What" question
❏ "What did you do?"
❏ "What is the rule?"
❏ "What is the consequence?"
❏ "How will you change?"
1.2 Contract
❏ handshake
❏ written
_____ Date
❏ 1.3 (if broken) Logical Consequences
_____ Date

• *Level 1 Time Out*
(Mediate afterwards with R-L or C-C)

• *Level 2 Time Out (In Room)*

**2. 1st In-Room Time Out/Conference**
❏ 2.1 "What" questions
❏ 2.2 Contract (written-enclose)
_____ Date

❏ 2.3 (if broken) Logical Consequences
_____ Date

**3. 2nd In-Room Time Out/Conference**
❏ 3.1 Repeat 1 and 2 (above)
_____ Date

❏ 3.2 (if broken) Logical Consequences
_____ Date

• *Level 3 Time Out (Out-of-Room)*

**4. 3rd In-Room Time Out/Conference**
❏ Repeat 1 and 2 (above)
_____ Date
❏ 3.2 (if broken) Logical Consequences
_____ Date

---

The Confronting-Contracting Face attempts to maintain an adult relationship with a misbehaving student, by requesting the student to stop and change. The solution for how the student will change remains in his or her own hands. During the first conference, the student and teacher are seated facing each other, literally "knee to knee" (*proximity-near*):

- The teacher maintains eye contact.

- The teacher's face or attitude changes to Confronting-Contracting.

- The teacher wants the student to cognitively think about past behavior:
  a. What is the rule?
  b. What will be the negative results if the student continues such negative behavior?
  c. The student will commit himself or herself to a rational response if similar incidents occur in the future.
  d. The student will commit to a contract or agreement (a contract form is provided as Figure 8–4).

In the conference discussion the teacher uses "What-how" questions and contracting, and suggests possible logical consequences. In addition, isolation and forms of time out may be used, with the degree of separation increasing with each incident of isolation.

Steps 1 through 4 (in Figure 8–3) suggest three "in-room" isolations followed by questioning and contracting. If the student does not live up to the contract, he would experience the logical consequence of his actions. (*Reminder:* The Confronting-Contracting Face, during these techniques, is one that says to the student:

---

**FIGURE 8–4  Contract**

Date _____    Period _____    Semester _____

Location _____

Behavior _____

_____

I will _____

_____

Signature _____    Time Out

Signature _____    Total time: _____Minutes

Signature _____    Type (level):

Signature _____    __1.  __2.  __3.  __4.  __5.  __6.

1. You are "over the line" and must be stopped.

2. Your behavior must change.

3. Control is still in your hands.

4. You must be aware of what you are doing.

5. You must think about the future [*cause-effect*].

6. You may need time away to think [*isolation: time out*].

7. You and I must agree on future behaviors.)

Let's see such interaction unfold:

*Mr. Leonard:* "Mike, what are you doing?" ("What-how" questioning).

*Mike:* "Huh?"

*Mr. Leonard:* "Mike, what are you doing?" ("What-how" questioning).

*Mike:* "I dunno!"

*Mr. Leonard:* "Well, you took another student's property, and you swore at me. I want you to think about your behavior, and decide whether you really want to act this way and what will be the future consequences if this behavior continues. How is this behavior helping you?" ("What-how" questioning).

At this point, the teacher will attempt to get an open discussion with the student about his behavior. Mike will use many examples of back talk (denial, statements of helplessness, blaming, accusing the teacher, insults, profanity, crying, and tangential statements [see Chapter 3 on Looking]). The teacher does not get caught up in a debate over back talk or allow himself to be sidetracked, but uses "fogging" techniques by agreeing in general.

*Mike:* "You're always picking on me. Get off my f---ing back" (backtalk).

*Mr. Leonard:* "My actions may be seen by you as 'picking on you' (fogging—agreeing in general), but what were you doing?"

The teacher keeps repeating, as a *broken record*, the questioning of: "What did you do? What is the rule? How is this helping you? What will be the result of your action if you continue acting this way? What will you do to change?"

The teacher does not stop the confronting process when the student responds by crying (sometimes humorously called "water power") or throwing a temper tantrum. Some students have discovered that such strong expressions of emotion can serve as a power technique to get the adult "off their back" and for them to avoid facing up to their behavior.

The teacher responds to this emotional flooding by returning the student to a time out or relax chair or an isolated space for the sole purpose of permitting him to calm down and get relaxed. The teacher reassures the student that this is a safe space and no one will bother him. This is not a punishment, for when the student is ready to *contingency contract* and rationally discuss the incident, he is free to return. The teacher's voice inflection and nonverbal expressions (*paraverbals*) are not ones of guilt, but take a rather matter-of-fact problem-solving attitude toward the student. The teacher is not sidetracked by the student's claims of unfairness or denial, or by another emotional outburst or crying. Instead, the teacher remains focused on the student's behavior in this particular incident, attempting to limit any implication of guilt. The teacher's approach in using the Confronting-Contracting Face toward the student is: "Look, this is not appropriate behavior here. We are faced with a problem, and I want to work with you to understand the problem and your behavior. I want to give you the power to change. I want you to commit yourself to this change through a contract or agreement. And finally, I want you to understand the consequences of failing to live up to this contract or continuing to behave in such a negative manner."

If the student is defiant, still angry, and still using the "doggy-horsey" brain, and will not talk and *contingency contract*, it would be advisable to permit the student to remain in isolation until he is ready to do so. This may involve keeping him "in the castle" at the back of the room (third grade or older) for an entire day—eating his lunch there and missing out-of-classroom activities. He may have his books and may study, and he is also in a position to hear lectures and other educational classroom activities. The isolation, as *nonseclusionary time out*, is not for the purpose of punishment when used in the Confronting-Contracting Face. The teacher withdraws all social activities from him, and places him in a nonthreatening and nonstimulating situation to permit him to become reflective, to think it over. When he is ready to work it out, the teacher returns to the "What-how" questioning: "What did you do?" "What is the rule?" and so on, and then to contracting.

## UNDERSTANDING TIME OUT

The teacher has escalated across the TBC using up all the limit-setting techniques, and the student's actions have not changed—the student is stopping the teacher from teaching and fellow students from learning. As a result, the teacher has dropped the Limit-Setting System. He has begun the Backup System, where he must move to isolating the student in some form—thus the teacher's actions become public. The degrees of isolation will escalate, as seen in the Checklist, following these time-out definitions.

### Types of Time Outs

Time outs consist of four types: nonseclusionary, contingency contracting observation, exculsionary, and seclusionary (see Figure 8–5).

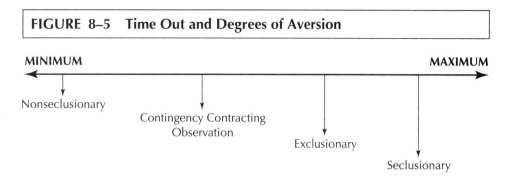

FIGURE 8–5    Time Out and Degrees of Aversion

## Nonseclusionary Time Out

To deal with a minor disturbance, the teacher performs some action (physical intervention) to deny the student reinforcement by removing the materials that are being used inappropriately (paint brushes in art class that are being used destructively, balls or similar physical education equipment used inappropriately, a personal item during seatwork that is disturbing the classroom environment, etc.) or an item that the student treasures. This time out is called *nonseclusionary* because the misbehaving student is not removed from the classroom or immediate environment. The object, rather than the student, is removed.

> *After a visit by a local police officer, a police hat is presented in the first-grade classroom. Paul, a most difficult student, clearly desires to wear the hat. Paul is given a second police hat with his name taped in it, and the teacher tells him, "Police officers are bosses, and if you want to wear the police officer's hat you must be the boss of your own behavior. If you hit, destroy, or disrupt the activities of other students, then you will lose your hat" (if-then statement: "If you do X behavior, then Y consequence will happen").*
>
> *In the first two or three days, when Paul forgets and is disruptive, the teacher takes away his police hat, places it within his view on a hook too high for him to reach, and sets a timer for three to five minutes. When the bell rings, the hat is returned to him. On the first day, Paul loses the hat (nonseclusionary time out) on six occasions; on the second day, it drops to two occasions; and in the remaining three days of the week, the hat is removed only once.*

## Contingency Contracting Observation

Another form of time out is *contingency contracting observation*. The student is removed to the edge of an activity or at the back of the classroom ("off to the castle"). He can still observe the other students being reinforced and is only allowed to return contingent on his obeying the rules.

> *The school has narrow steps with painted arrows pointing the direction in which the students are to walk* (visual prompt).

*The arrows guide the students so they will not collide with each other by going in opposite directions. The rule has been explained and taught to Harold, but he repeatedly seems to enjoy going in the opposite direction and colliding with play-mates, who then complain in the strongest of terms. The teacher brings Harold to the school steps and requires him to sit passively and watch others obeying the rule. The teacher reinforces the other students (models) as they correctly obey the direction rule. After four minutes, she asks Harold, "Do you now see how our rule works, and can you walk following the direction of the arrows?" If he says yes, he is permitted to return; if he says defiantly no, he stays on the steps (the* time out*) for another two minutes and is again asked whether he is ready to comply. If Harold's response of no means that he simply does not truly understand the rule, the teacher would again teach it to him in the three-step directive lesson of say, show, and check, as explained later in Chapter 12.*

---

### MODELING

The demonstration by teacher or peer of a behavior or group of behaviors that the teacher wishes the targeted student to imitate.

---

The contingency contracting observation is nonseclusionary because the student is not removed totally from the environment, such as being required to go inside the school or leave the section of the playground. Instead, he is placed at the edge of the activity so he may observe others being reinforced. Here are some other examples of employing contingency contracting observation:

- Brian is splashing others while he is supposed to be washing his hands. He is removed to the side to watch others washing. When the line of students is complete, he is now allowed to wash his hands after agreeing (*contingency contract*) to do so without splashing.

- Allison is disrupting her peers at the cafeteria table by throwing small pieces of food for the purpose of getting her tablemates to respond. She and her chair are pulled away to approximately four feet from the table and out of reach of her food. After four minutes and following contingency contracting with the teacher, she is able to return to lunch and move her chair up to the table.

- Christopher is being reckless on the tire swing (or slide, or any other playground equipment). He is removed from the apparatus and asked to sit nearby and watch. After four minutes, he is allowed to return, always after a verbal contract.

• While seated on the floor at circle time, Maria repeatedly disturbs others seated nearby. She is removed from the circle and seated on a chair. After three minutes and agreeing to obey the rule, she is allowed to return.

*Note*: The criterion for returning or being released from the contingency contracting observation nonseclusionary time out, as in the preceeding situations, is contingent on the student maintaining nondisruptive behavior for a minimum time requirement. Normally, the student is asked, "Do you know and understand the rule and will you obey it when you return?"

When the techniques of nonseclusionary time out have been tried but have failed, the teacher may recognize that the child's behavior is so serious that it demands a stronger form of response. Two other forms of time out are available in such a situation: exculsionary and seclusionary.

## Exclusionary Time Out

This involves the removal of the student from an activity as a means of denying access to reinforcement but generally not access to the classroom. While the contingency contracting observation and modeling were used in the nonseclusionary time out, *none* of these procedures is used in exclusionary time out. The student may be placed near a corner facing the wall, or in an area of the classroom that is screened off from the room activities so the child's view is restricted—he or she is excluded.

## Seclusionary Time Out

This is the complete removal of the student from the classroom or environment to a time-out room or the principal's office because of the child's misbehavior (usually aggression or noncompliance). This denies the student access to any reinforcement from the classroom, including peers, adults, objects, or activities.

*Note*: The justification for the use of any of the forms of time out is *not* for purposes of retribution as a morality form of punishment (based on the idea that the student has failed morally or has not lived up to the adult's values and expectations). The justification is that the environment and social context are so strongly reinforcing the student to continue his misbehaviors, and the objective is to remove that reinforcement, that the only way to accomplish this is to use one or more forms of time out.

Time out and time-out rooms have historically been misused or mismanaged by teachers, causing great distrust of this technique among parents and the general public. A time-out record form documenting the procedure (giving witness names, circumstances, times, and dates), such as the one in Figure 8–6 should be required for each staff member who uses time out. This Time-Out Record should be attached to the Backup System Checklist.

| FIGURE 8–6    Time-Out Record | | | |
|---|---|---|---|
| Student's Name: | Date: | Time of Day: | Total Time in Time Out: _____ Minutes |
| Teacher's Name:<br><br><br>Other Adult Witness: | | | Type of Time Out (check one):<br>___ Contingency Observation<br>___ Exclusionary<br>___ Seclusionary |
| Description of the Situation: | | State Behavioral Change Wanted: | |

## Levels of Exclusion and Time Out

The teacher will follow a pathway of increased levels or degrees of isolation or time out, as explained in Figure 8–7, which is a guide to follow in escalating the use of time out. The teacher starts in the classroom with minor nonseclusionary time out (levels 1 and 2). If the student does not change his behavior, the teacher gradually escalates to in-classroom isolation (level 3), calls the student's parents, and then moves to out-of-classroom isolation (levels 4 and 5), finally leading to a professional staffing. After most of these time outs, the teacher holds a private meeting with the student and uses techniques that involve a movement from Relationship-Listening to Confronting-Contracting, including experiencing logical consequences, and then moves to the use of the assertive techniques of Rules and Consequences. At levels 3, 4, and 5, the teacher moves through three cycles of time out.

A *cycle* is defined as a form of isolation that entails using the TBC for a private meeting and contracting, and then permitting the student to return with a clean slate. If the contract is broken, the student experiences the logical consequence of his actions. It is recommended that this be done three times, but the teacher and principal would have the flexibility to determine the number of reasonable cycles. Copies of the student-teacher or student-teacher-principal contract would be kept on file for documentation purposes.

## DISENGAGING

As discussed in Chapter 5, a misbehaving student can be frightening. Teachers are not robots who are emotionless, who never get angry, who always have good feelings toward all students. This is an unrealistic picture and simply does not happen. Some students are appealing and some are very unappealing; the unappealing students generally are the

| FIGURE 8–7 | Level of Time-Out Methods and Procedures | | | |
|---|---|---|---|---|
| **Level or Degrees of Isolation** | **Type of Isolation** | **Method** | **Parties Involved** | **Follow-Up Meetings** |
| Level #1 | **Nonseclusionary time out** | Remove toy or object or move seat 3 feet from table. | Teacher and student | May involve no discussion or private meeting by the teacher. |
| Level #2 | **Contingency contracting observation** | Isolate student at edge of classroom to observe (off to the castle). | Teacher and student | *Private Meeting* using R-L, then escalate to C-C, and/or R and C (normally a verbal contract is established). Experience the *logical consequence.* |
| Level #3 (recommend doing three cycles of this form of isolation) | **Exclusionary time out** | Isolate in the classroom, behind a barrier or turned toward a wall. | Teacher and student | *Private Meeting* using R-L, then escalate to C-C, and/or R and C (normally a verbal contract is established). Experience the *logical consequence.* |
| **Notify Parents** After three cycles of Level 3 time out, private meetings and contracting, call parents before doing an out-of-classroom isolation. The methods for handling this parent telephone call are presented in Chapter 5. | | | | |
| Level #4 (recommend doing three cycles of this form of isolation) | **Seclusionary time out** | Isolate in a time-out room or in another classroom across the hall. | Teacher, student, and supervisor of time-out room or teacher across the hall | *Private Meeting* using R-L, then escalate to C-C, and/or R and C (normally a verbal contract is established). Experience the *logical consequence.* |
| **Parent Conference** After three cycles of Level 4 time out, private meetings and contract, hold a parent conference. The methods for handling this parent conference call will follow. | | | | |
| Level #5 (recommend doing three cycles of this form of isolation) | **Seclusionary time out** | Isolate in principal's office. | Teacher, student, and principal | *Private Meeting* using R-L, then escalate to C-C, and/or R and C (normally a verbal contract is established). Experience the *logical consequence.* |
| **Professional Staffing** A staffing session involving the teacher, school psychologist and/or counselor, teachers, administrators, and possibly the student and parent is held. See methods and techniques to follow. | | | | |

ones who cannot find acceptance in their homes and from fellow classmates. We have stated that the nonsocially adjusted misbehaving student, because of feelings of rejection, begins to seek excessive attention and power, becomes revengeful and, finally, retreats into a passive state of helplessness. If you as a teacher acknowledge that you are a human

**FIGURE 8–8   Nonsocially Adaptive Students**

| Student's Motivation | Behavior Characteristics | Teacher's Feelings |
|---|---|---|
| Attention Getting | Repetitively does actions to make him the center of attention. When asked to desist, will comply but will start again later. | Annoyed |
| Power | Repetitively does actions to make him the center of attention. When asked to desist, he becomes defiant and escalates his negative behavior and challenges the adult. | Beaten |
| Revenge | Hurts others for no apparent reason. | Hurt |
| Helplessness | Wishes not to be seen, passive and lethargic, rejects social contact. | Inadequate |

For further reading, see *A Teacher's Guide to Cooperative Discipline: How to Manage Your Classroom and Promote Self-Esteem* by L. Albert, 1989, Circle Pines, MN: American Guidance Service.

being with a range of feelings, you will allow that the excessive attention-getting student produces feelings of *annoyance* in you, that you feel at times *beaten* by the power-needy student, that you feel hurt by the *revengeful* student, and that you feel *inadequate* in working with the passive-helpless student (see Figure 8–8).

It is important to acknowledge to yourself that you have these feelings toward these students. Your feelings only become a problem when you yourself begin to regress into becoming revengeful (*fight response*) or feeling helpless (*flight response*) toward these students. Therefore, you now have a second reason to possibly use isolation as described under Confronting-Contracting—that is, in order to get yourself *disengaged*. If you are angry and overcome by your own feelings because of the repeated demands that the problem student is presenting, you may become emotionally flooded in the middle of a teachable moment and go "brain stemmed." You need to do skilled confronting, yet you are unable to handle this successfully and professionally because your clear thinking has been flooded by emotions. You then may place the misbehaving student in isolation—the "relax chair" or time out—for a period of time. As an emotionally flooded individual, you must spatially move away from this student for many minutes or even an hour until you have disengaged from these strong emotions. Jones states that it takes at least 20 minutes for a teacher's body to clear the adrenaline from its system after he or she has become angry or frightened as a result of a clash with a student.[1] Once you are calm and relaxed, you will have the energy to approach the difficult student to begin your steps of confronting. *You cannot do Confronting-Contracting when angered.* You must, of course, remember to use many of the self-control techniques under the TBC's *Looking*, including relaxing breaths, slowing down your actions, squaring off, using the proper physical stance, and the host of related techniques described in previous chapters.

---

### CONTINGENCY CONTRACTING

A form of time out in which the student is removed to the edge of an activity or at the back of the classroom so he can still observe the other students being reinforced and acting in an appropriate manner. The teacher demands from the misbehaving student that he reflect on his past behavior and come up with a way he will change to ensure that it does not occur again. The student must now commit himself to this as an agreement or contract, contingent on his reentering the classroom and verbally sealed by shaking hands or in writing.

---

## SEALING THE CONTRACT

The private meeting ends with a contract between the student and the teacher. The student will at a future time find himself in a similar situation and will be faced with a possible repeat of his behavior. The question "What will you do to change?" permits the student to actually think out and anticipate these future situations, knowing he has determined and contracted with the teacher regarding how to act in a more productive manner in future incidents. The contingency contract for change between the teacher and student can be sealed simply with a handshake and a smile, at first attempts, but it is advised to actually put this agreement in writing and to have both the teacher and student sign the contract, with each getting a copy. The contingency contract may also contain a logical consequence if the student fails to live up to this contract.

### Common Questions Regarding Confronting-Contracting

*What do we do if the student does not come up with a solution?* If the student is not simply being defiant, but really cannot think of a change in behavior, you may make two to three suggestions and ask him to pick one and commit to it. If he agrees to your suggestion, be sure he knows the *"motor rule"*[2] or response to which he has committed, by teaching him his choice in a Directive Lesson of Say-Show-Check (explained in Chapter 12).

*What if the student refuses to contract?* Permit the student to continue staying in the "relax chair" until he is ready to negotiate. His refusal indicates he is still angry or flooded.

*What if the student's action endangers himself, others, or valuable property?* Endangerment of any type calls into effect the "severity clause," and you immediately move to *Acting* (*Physical Intervention*). The accompanying verbal response could be Step 1: "Stop" followed by Steps 2, 3, and 4, or an *assertive command* (explained in Chapter 6).

## REPEATING PREVIOUS STEPS

In living within the Confronting-Contracting Face, your interaction with the student after an incident of misbehavior is confined to these four steps: "Stop!"statement; "What-how" questioning; contracting with a statement of logical consequences; and, if needed, isolation. After a contingency contract is established between you and the student, the student is to return to the classroom with a *clean slate,* meaning that you must maintain an attitude of optimism. You must believe—and show by your actions that you believe—that the student can and will change his behavior. If you are angry with the student because of his actions and communicate this anger nonverbally, he and his classmates will sense this, and he most likely will live up to your *nonbelief in his ability to change—the power of expectations.*[3]

It is inevitable that some contracts by a student will be broken. When this does occur the student will have to experience the logical consequence of his actions. After the student experiences this logical consequence, you should repeat previous steps in a similar manner: "Stop it! What did you do? What is the rule? What will you do to change?" Again, you will ask for a contract with consequences, and isolation will be used if needed. The student will again return with a "clean slate," and you will be optimistic.

---

### "CLEAN SLATE"

After the teacher and student complete the step of contingency contracting, the student returns to the classroom activity as if nothing has occurred. The student has a "clean slate" whereby the teacher does not continually remind him of past misbehavior and is optimistic that the misbehavior will not be repeated.

---

If the student's behavior still does not become more positive, or even regresses to more destructive behaviors, you would use the sequence of "Stop!" statement, "What-how" questioning, contracting, and time-out for at least three cycles. After *three cycles of these Confronting-Contracting steps,* you may make the judgment to escalate along the Teacher Behavior Continuum to Rules and Consequences techniques (or deescalate to Relationship-Listening techniques if the student's behavior becomes more positive). But before you move to the Rules and Consequences techniques, which may involve removing the

---

**FIGURE 8–9    Confronting-Contracting**

---

5. **Telephone Parents**
   _____ Date
   5.1  (Begin Encouragement System)
   _____ Date

   *Level 3 Time Out (Out-of-Room)*

6. **1st Out-of-Room Time Out**
   (Repeat 1, 2, and 3, enclose Time Out Form)
   _____ Date

7. **2nd Out-of-Room Time Out**
   (Repeat 1, 2, and 3, enclose Time Out Form)
   _____ Date

8. **Telephone/ In Writing**
   (Enclose copy to principal/Parents
   _____ Date

   *Level 4 Time Out (Principal)*

9. **Office**
   (Repeat 1, 2, and 3)
   _____ Date
   (Repeat 1, 2, and 3)
   _____ Date

10. **Conference with Parents**
    (Repeat 1, 2, and 3)
    _____ Date

11. **Staffing (Members)**

    _____
    _____
    _____
    _____
    _____ Date

---

student from the classroom, you notify the student's parents of your difficulties and the actions you are taking (see Figure 8–9).

## Notify Parents

After completing three rounds of in-room time out/conference, the teacher turns to Step 5, Telephone Parents, calling the parents to inform them of the behavior of their child. This telephone conversation is conducted in a manner to inform the parents of the details and facts regarding the student's behavior and the teacher's attempts to work with the student. The teacher is not prescriptive, telling the parents what actions they should take at home. If the parents respond to the teacher with, "Well what do you want me to do about it?" the teacher would state, "I am calling you to keep you informed."

Let's see this unfold, using a hypothetical telephone call by Mike's teacher. Notice the facts and specificity that the teacher provides.

> ***Teacher:*** "Hello, Mrs. Jones. I am Mike's teacher, Mr. Leonard. I felt a need to call you and keep you informed as to my attempts at working with Mike. On four occasions he has disrupted class by taking another student's property, pushing and striking other classmates, making disruptive remarks in class, and swearing at a classmate. When I confronted him, he has on three occasions told me to go f--- myself and referred to me as an asshole. I have counseled him, attempted to contract with him to change his behavior, and isolated him at the back of the classroom on three occasions. I am still optimistic that I can find a way to work with Mike, but I felt that at this point it was important to inform you and your husband as to his recent behavior and my actions."

In using the Confronting-Contracting Face and attitude, you are factual and very reality oriented, both with students and with parents. Do not mask or soft-sell your description of the student's behavior. Describe it in very clear terms with specific examples, but do not express value judgments and imply any guilt or anger. Your position in notifying parents at this point is factual, so that they are informed. Do not ask the parents for a conference until you have escalated to the Rules and Consequences Face, but if they request a conference, you will of course agree, preferably meeting with both the parents and the student.

When parents receive such a call, they are likely to respond in one of three ways. They may accept the descriptions and offer to help; they may respond with a fight or flight response, failing to hear what you are saying (flight) or becoming verbally hostile (fight); or they may begin to use back talk (verbal aggression, denial, or attempting to distract the teacher to a side issue, accusing the teacher of professional incompetence.) Back talk in the form of verbal aggression is to be expected because these parents have just done an "adrenaline dump" and are "snapping and snarling." The teacher's response in dealing with such angry parents is the same as with students.

Begin by retreating to Relationship-Listening techniques using the TBC's *Looking* and *Naming*. Take two controlled breaths and simply say nothing, permitting the parents to ventilate. You have already given, in detail, all the information you wish to give to the parents, and so you should not be drawn into a heated debate regarding any issue. If you wish, you may move to nondirective techniques of active listening, I-messages, door openers, and acknowledgments. If you begin to hear the parents slowly becoming more rational, and they begin to ask, "How can I help?" you may begin to move through the Six Steps to Problem Solving. When using the Relationship-Listening Face and even the Confronting-Contracting Face with students and parents, you are not prescriptive. You do not tell the parents what you want them to do, because in doing so you would now own the problem. By your process of problem solving, lead them through a discussion that enables them to come up with ways through which they think they can help. Teacher to parent, you might say, "What have you found that has worked with your child in the past?"

When you are prescriptive by saying to the parents, "Here is what actions I want you to do...," you might hear from the parents, weeks later, "Well, we did what you said and it still didn't work." Such a statement suggests a lack of real ownership by the parents, and you have been trapped into giving prescriptive solutions and then "slam-dunked" for those suggestions later by having them thrown in your face. If the parents truly insist that they are incapable of dealing with their child, you may suggest that they seek advice from school or private counseling services or a psychologist.

To summarize, notify parents after you have done three cycles of in-classroom isolation (time out) and private meetings, with written contingency contracts and the use of logical consequences. If there is no improvement in the student's behavior or it has gotten worse, you are now compelled to notify parents through a factual telephone call with a clear list of the student's and your past actions. If you hear that parents wish to help, use the Relationship-Listening technique of Six Steps to Problem Solving. On the other hand, if you hear the parent become hostile to your information, you must first get control of your own behavioral response and, if need be, use the Relationship-Listening techniques to allow the parent to ventilate.

After phoning parents, you should begin an Encouragement System, which will be discussed in Chapter 10. Note again that boxes for check marks and lines for dates are provided to document your actions (in Figure 8–9).

In Steps 6 and 7, Out-of-Room Time Out, the student is removed to a separate room in the school for disruptive students or, by prior arrangement, is seated at the back of the classroom across the hall. Notice that before the student is returned to full participation in the classroom, you would repeat "What-how" questions, contracting, and logical consequences if appropriate. A time-out documentation is done for each of these out-of-room isolations using the box on the bottom right corner of the Contract Form (Figure 8–4). This box requires the teacher to indicate the date and time, the number of minutes the student was isolated, and the form of isolation used.

In Step 8, Telephone/In Writing, the teacher acts after the second out-of-room isolation to notify the parents for the second time by telephone. A follow-up letter would also be sent and a copy attached to the Backup System Checklist.

Next, the Backup System would escalate to Step 9, Office (Isolation in the Principal's Office), and Step 10, Conference with Parents. These utilize many of the techniques previously described.

## Meetings and Conferencing—Public

When it is necessary to escalate to Steps 9 and 10, the Backup System becomes very *public* and time consuming because the principal, other professionals, and parents are now involved. For this meeting, it is essential to have total privacy and adequate time for a real discussion to occur. Don't rush this process. Time spent in conferencing now can save much more time later and prevent the necessity of going to the much more time-consuming high-profile corrections processes. In carrying out this meeting, the teacher still maintains his or her power. The teacher is in charge and should not hand over the power for chairing the meeting to an administrator or other professional.

The teacher chooses which "face" to wear and which parallel techniques to utilize in carrying out this meeting. Remember the cardinal rule to use the least powerful techniques or "face" necessary. This would suggest that, at first, the teacher attempt to conduct the meeting with Relationship-Listening techniques, before escalating to Confronting-Contracting and, if necessary, Rules and Consequences.

## The Relationship-Listening Meeting

Because its techniques are taken from a counseling model, the Relationship-Listening Face is ideally suited for one-to-one teacher-student interaction, even with the setting of a meeting attended by parents and others. Go slowly, continue to use the nonverbal behaviors of limit setting (such as eye contact and relaxing breaths), and have all participants—the teacher, student, parent, and principal—seated so that they are knee to knee, or at the edge of each person's "comfort bubble."

The Relationship-Listening teacher might start off with an I-message ("Mike, when I am told to f--- off (*behavior*) such harsh words stop me from working with a student (*effect*), and cause me to lose respect from your classmates (*effect*), and I feel first frustrated and then angry (*feelings*). We need to talk about this." (*door opener*).) The teacher is now free to use (1) acknowledgment, (2) verbal encoding of the student's feeling through critical listening, (3) door openers, and (4) active listening.

For this meeting, the teacher may use the plus/minus method or may simply, with the student, list on a sheet of paper all items that are going well and those that are not. This, of course, is being witnessed by the principal and/or parent. Through No-Lose Problem Solving, the teacher asks the student how they can move the minuses to the plus column. In essence, the teacher asks, "What actions can be taken to work this out so we are both comfortable and both get our needs met?"

If the student's behavior or the problems he is expressing are quite serious, it would be wise to take time to guide the student through the Six Steps to Problem Solving:

1. Define the problem.
2. Generate solutions.
3. Evaluate the solutions.
4. Decide on a solution.
5. Implement the solution.
6. Reevaluate.

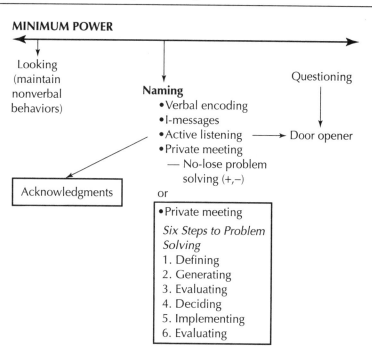

FIGURE 8–10    Relationship-Listening Face

By following this six-step structure, you can help teach the student how to think out future problems, and thus be able to be an independent thinker leading to self-discipline.

The objective in using the Relationship-Listening Face is to attempt to maintain the relationship with your student, and work things out in a nonpunitive no-lose manner. The attitude, or face, is one that through your actions says, "I will nonjudgmentally express to you (I-message) how your actions may be taking away my rights and impacting on me as a teacher. I am here to listen to you empathically and uncritically. I will help by listening and attempting to get clarity, through active listening. And when you wish, I can help through my guidance (Six Steps to Problem Solving) to permit you to solve your own problems. I will not do this for you." See Figure 8–10.

## The Confronting-Contracting Meeting

The teacher is free to choose which face or techniques to use during this public meeting. It is advisable to follow the rule of using the least power necessary, so the Relationship-Listening techniques should be used first before escalating to more powerful faces and techniques. Some teachers may feel uncomfortable and insincere with Relationship-Listening techniques or cannot (or will not) use the amount of time necessary to carry out a Relationship-Listening meeting. These teachers, therefore, may choose not to begin with a Relationship-Listening meeting but decide instead to employ Confronting-Contracting or Rules and Consequences. Although the teacher has the freedom of choice to determine which of the methodologies from these three faces to start out with, the teacher who chooses one of the more powerful "faces" has already narrowed the range of techniques available. If the stronger techniques of Rules and Consequences fail, the teacher will be left with no choice but to move to the time-consuming and less constructive punishment techniques. Again, it is advisable to start the meeting using minimum power and then, only if necessary, gradually escalate to a Confronting-Contracting meeting or a Rules and Consequences meeting. Once the teacher is forced to spend time doing high-profile actions, the likelihood of success is diminished and the process is dramatically more costly in terms of the teacher's time.

The Confronting-Contracting private meeting begins with a series of "What" questions. "Mike, this must stop. This shall not continue to go on! What are you doing? What is the rule? I want you to think about this behavior. How is it helping you?" Again, go slowly, continue to use the nonverbal behaviors of limit setting (such as eye contact and relaxing breaths), and have both the student and yourself seated so you are knee to knee and you are at the edge of the student's "comfort bubble." The Confronting-Contracting approach is to give the student time, with your counseling, to cognitively reflect on what he is doing—requiring the neo-cortex of the brain to be in gear. If the student is in a state of fight or flight you might need to take some time to have him relax so the real thinking can take place. This is not a meeting to scold the student, but to have him *think*.

Finally, you ask, "What will you do to change?" and then push for a contract. The student is likely to be faced with a similar opportunity to act in a similar misbehaving manner in the future. Now is the time to have the student, who is using rational thinking, come up with his own appropriate strategy so he will know how to behave the next time a similar incident occurs. The contract you reach may be informal if it is done in a mini-meeting in the classroom, sealed simply with a hand-shake. If the contracting is done in a meeting after class, a written contract should be signed by both the student and the teacher—and even the principal and parent—and may include a logical consequence if the contract is broken. Copies of the contract are given to the student, teacher, principal, and parent, and a copy is stored in the teacher's grade book or student filing system for later retrieval if necessary.

To repeat: If the behavior of the student still does not improve, the teacher moves to Step 10, Conference with Parents. This conference is carried out with the student, the parents, and possibly the principal in attendance. The teacher goes through items 1, 2, and 3 as she confronts the student and writes the contract. All members in attendance, including the parents, sign the contract.

Finally, the last step in Confronting-Contracting is Step 11, Staffing. This is a meeting in which the teacher asks the school counselor, school psychologist, principal, fellow teachers, and any other teachers and professionals who may be able to contribute to provide information or help in designing a program to change this student's behavior.

## Professional Staffing

Simply put, many minds working together are better than one. Historically, teaching has been a rather solitary profession—one teacher closed in by four walls and a closed door. When the teacher's limit setting fails to be effective with a misbehaving student, she or he often feels like a failure.

Such misbehaving students can be like small grenades—beyond your ability to know when something or someone may pull their "pins" and they explode as small aggressive power forces that destroy the climate for learning and destroy the group's ability to live and work together as a healthy classroom of sharing people. Some teachers depend on being the conductor who can orchestrate this shared space through a Limit-Setting System; if your classroom does not work, you are ineffective and will experience the accompanying feelings of utter helplessness. As a teacher in such a situation, you may feel you are not in control and have no outlet for getting help. In fact, you might be frightened to admit—especially to those in authority over you—that you are having this disciplinary difficulty, for fear that you may be judged as ineffectual and later evaluated negatively at the end of the school year.

The way to get the help you need is by creating a collegial team professional working process. Rarely do other professions expect a professional to live and work in a four-walled island cut off from colleagues. *Doing it alone should not be a virtue that defines your worthiness as a teacher.* Students have changed in the modern world, and the knowledge base of psychology and education has exploded far beyond the ability of a day-in, day-out practicing teacher to keep pace. It is extremely difficult, if not impossible, for the classroom teacher to maintain constantly updated knowledge on the many problems faced by students and new methods of educational discipline practice. The collegial meeting of professional minds takes the form of a Professional-Administrative Backup System leading to a staffing, or brainstorming, session that focuses on one student and that particular child's problems, as well as how this professional (the classroom teacher) might become more effective in meeting this problem child's needs to get a positive change in behavior. Such staffing sessions must become a standard practice. This concept of a staffing team as a collection of problem-solving professionals is a structure to guide the collective minds, so that thinking is orderly and creative and includes everyone on the team. In all meetings that will follow—private and public meetings, and staffing sessions—the teacher will maintain her authority and power as the leader.

In order to overcome roadblocks to good collective problem solving, a clear orderly process will be proposed based on the Six Steps to Problem Solving:[4] (1) defining the problem, (2) generating a possible solution, (3) evaluating, (4) deciding on a solution, (5) implementing, and (6) evaluating the solution. In order to maximize the use of time, a clear *staffing agenda* procedure is proposed for the purpose of collectively working as a team to use the host of techniques drawn from Chapters 1 and 2, the concept of Levels of Crisis, and the development of an Individualized Discipline Plan for intervening with and helping the difficult student. The team approach utilizes a creative application of techniques and procedures to fit the needs of a particular school and a particular teacher working with one of his or her very difficult students.

## Staffing Agenda: Steps and Procedures

Once you have used the full range of time out and held a conference with the parents without any real change in the student's misbehavior, you now turn to a Professional Staffing Process. Team members might include any or all of the following people: teacher, assistant teacher, teacher aides, special education teacher, school principal, school counselor and/or psychologist, social worker or home and family visitor, or any other person having direct contact with the student on a daily basis (including cafeteria or playground supervisors, bus driver, and office staff). On some occasions, it would be helpful to have the student's parents as members of this team. As the child's teacher, you will decide—in consultation with the school administrator—just who is invited. One thing to avoid in team staffing is the notion of rank (defined as administrative rank [principal] or expertise rank [psychologist]). If formally or informally asserted in the team staffing, rank is inhibiting to creative problem solving because those members feeling less "in authority" will hesitate to speak up or challenge a position of some member in a position of "higher rank." The attitude or "face" of the staffing meeting is that roles are clearly defined but not necessarily according to rank. The meeting is for the benefit of *you*, the person who has daily responsibility for the difficult student. All members are there to serve as your consultants and advisors with a direct focus on what you and they can do to help this particular student. It is preferable for meetings to be held at a round table, where all members can see each other face to face, suggesting an equal power relationship among team members, rather than at a rectangular table with a power figure seated at one end. A wall chart or chalkboard should be nearby and in clear view of all team members.

It is helpful at the beginning of a staffing meeting for you, as the teacher being advised, to appoint a timekeeper and a secretary. The timekeeper serves as a type of moderator, announcing before each step begins the purpose of that step, who may speak, the amount of time to

---

**TIMEKEEPER**

A team member appointed by the difficult child's teacher, assigned responsibility for monitoring the time and keeping the staffing steps on task.

| FIGURE 8–11 | Six Steps to Team Staffing Agenda | | |
|---|---|---|---|
| **Purpose** | **Speaker** | **Time** | **Actions** |
| **Stating the Problem** | | | |
| a. Background Information (Teacher) | Teacher | 5 mins. | State general description of the child's behavior problems and desired changes. Present background information using collected data (see Figure 8–12, Student Background Information Form). |
| b. Background Information (Team) | Team Members | 10 mins. | Present information from other team members who may have observed the student under various situations and time periods. |
| c. Clarifying Information | Team Members | 6 mins. | Team members question other team members on data presented and the final changes in desired student behavior. |
| **Generating Solutions** (in writing) | Team Members | 3 mins. | Each team member writes a list of solutions independently of all other members. |
| (oral) | Team Members | 10 mins. | Each member quickly reads her solution list without comment; the secretary writes each solution on a wall chart or chalkboard. |
| **Evaluating Solutions** | Team Members | 10 mins. | Members state their objections (in the form of an I-message) to a suggestion; if there is general agreement to these objections, the suggestion is removed. The secretary strikes out rejected suggestions. |
| **Deciding on Solutions** | Team Members | 5 mins. | Decide on a group plan with roles and each member's responsibility defined. Using the Individualized Discipline Plan (see Figure 8–13), the secretary writes solution agreements and completes the IDP form. |
| **Implementing (a commitment)** | Team Members | 1 min. | All members sign plan as a commitment to the strategies. |
| **Reevaluating Scheduled** | Teacher | 10 mins. | A time is established for a follow-up meeting, normally two to three weeks later, to reevaluate the success of the plan. |

*Source:* From *Solving Discipline Problems: Strategies for Classroom Teachers* by C. Wolfgang and C. D. Glickman, 1980, Boston: Allyn and Bacon. Reprinted by permission.

be spent on that step, and the actions and results needed to be accomplished. A copy of Figure 8–11 should be mounted on the meeting room wall or included in a handout in front of each member for easy reference. The secretary handles writing activities such as keeping notes, writing suggestions on wall charts, and writing the final plan. These duties should be rotated among the team members for each new meeting. The

**FIGURE 8–12    Student Background Information Form**

| Child's Name: | | | | Date: | |
|---|---|---|---|---|---|

| Team Members: | | | | | |
|---|---|---|---|---|---|

| Student's Misbehavior(s): | | | | | |
|---|---|---|---|---|---|

| 1. Describe misbehavior(s) | 2. What activities was the student engaged in at the time? | 3. In what physical surroundings? | 4. How frequent is each type of misbehavior? | 5. What time of day? | 6. What peers/ adults were involved? |
|---|---|---|---|---|---|
| a. | | | | | |
| b. | | | | | |
| c. | | | | | |

**FIGURE 8–13    Individualized Discipline Plan**

| Child's Name: | Summary of Present Behavior: |
|---|---|
| School: | |
| Date of Staffing: | |
| Long-Term Behavioral Changes Desired | (1) |
| (2) | (3) |
| (4) | (5) |

| Short-Term Behavioral Change | Specific Teacher Techniques | Person Responsible | % of Time | Approx. Date of Completion | Reevaluation Date |
|---|---|---|---|---|---|
| | | | | | |

---

**SECRETARY**

One team member appointed by the difficult child's teacher, assigned responsibility for carrying out the writing duties during the staffing process.

---

timekeeper will channel the discussion to conform to the stated goals, and will signal when time periods are up. If the team is well disciplined, the entire Team Staffing activity can be accomplished in 60 minutes.

## Step 1: Stating the Problem (Overview of the Student's Behavior)

### a. Background Information—Teacher

**Purpose:**  The teacher clearly states to the team members a general description of the student's behavior and states clearly those behavioral changes she would like to see in the student.

**Time:**  5 minutes

**Actions:**  The teacher, having direct responsibility for the difficult student, begins the reporting by providing the team with a general description of the child's past behavioral problems. She also summarizes the data on her Student Background Information form (Figure 8–12) and gives a few vignettes to place this behavior in context. Each team member should have copies of these forms, previously completed by each member, during the reporting. Finally, the teacher states clearly the behavior changes she would like to see in the child's daily behavior. For example, "Brian will, in the cafeteria, stop throwing food at snack time and biting other students; and he will follow my directions and requests when I give them to him."

   After completing three  rounds of in-room time out/conference, the teacher turns to Step 5, Telephone Parents, calling the parents to inform them of the behavior of their child. This telephone conversation is conducted in a manner to inform the parents of the details and facts regarding the student's behavior and the teacher's attempts to work with the student. The teacher is not prescriptive, telling the parents what actions they should take at home. If the parents respond to the teacher with, "Well what do you want me to do about it?" the teacher would state, "I am calling you to keep you informed."

### b. Background Information—Team Members

**Purpose:**  Each team member adds any information not previously mentioned by the child's teacher.

**Time:**  10 minutes

**Actions:**  The team members report their data by summarizing their copy of the Student Background Information form (Figure 8–12), moving clockwise around the table in a businesslike manner. It is important to get all data out and "on the table," and it is recommended that members refrain from asking questions of clarification until this is accomplished.

### c. Clarifying Background Information

**Purpose:**   All members may now ask clarifying questions concerning background information previously presented.

**Time:**   6 minutes

**Actions:**   All members of the team have the right to question the teacher or any team member who presented information in order to discuss the child in greater detail. This is also time to identify and explore what techniques have previously been tried. Team members should also question the behavior change goals that the teacher stated in Step 1, and a discussion should occur to get a team agreement on the stated behavior changes desired. Once the goals are agreed on, the secretary will write these goals on the IDP form.

## Step 2: Generating Solutions

### a. Solutions (Written)

**Purpose:**   All members write down their proposed solutions or suggestions as to what actions may be taken to help this difficult child.

**Time:**   3 minutes

**Actions:**   All staff members write down their proposed solutions, listing the actions they and anyone else could take to help the child. During this process, each member should mentally review the teacher-child interaction models of the Three Faces of Discipline. This mental review will help the members decide what teacher methods and techniques would be most helpful and how these actions can be organized systematically. Writing these possible solutions creates active involvement by all members and establishes their active commitment to the problem-solving process.

### b. Solutions (Oral)

**Purpose:**   Each team member verbally presents his or her written ideas to the other members without evaluation or feedback.

**Time:**   10 minutes

**Actions:**   Each member presents his or her ideas orally to the group. The discussion of these ideas is reserved for a later step, in order not to inhibit the free flow of each member's ideas. The attitude in this discussion is that there is no "crazy" idea—no matter how "off the wall" it might initially sound, it is nonetheless put on the table for consideration. Even the seemingly "crazy" idea might later trigger an idea from a team member as to how this idea can be turned into a practical and very real creative solution. Criticism in any manner during this step will stifle creative ideas and keep them from surfacing. While the members are reading their ideas out loud, the secretary writes them on a wall chart (or chalkboard) as a visual display of these ideas.

## Step 3: Evaluating Solutions

**Purpose:**  To have all members verbally explore, in a "brainstorming" format, how each of the ideas presented in Step 2 can be interrelated and developed into a comprehensive, collectively agreed upon plan of action, to achieve both the short-term and long-term behavioral changes or other results desired.

**Time:**  10 minutes

**Actions:**  This step begins with the team taking a quick vote to score the suggestions on the wall chart. One simple but effective method employs a "thumbs up-thumbs down" approach. The secretary writes a plus sign (+) before the number of a proposed solution if *all* team members vote "thumbs up." A question mark (?) is placed before the solution if the members' responses are mixed negative and positive. Finally, a minus sign (–) is added and a line drawn through the suggested solution if *all* members vote "thumbs down." This quick vote provides an immediate, overt display of the group's feelings about each suggestion, and members are now ready for meaningful discussion. However, even when a solution has been scratched out, any member may bring it back for further discussion.

---

### QUICK VOTE

A nonbinding process to quickly gauge support for the list of proposed solutions in Step 3: Evaluating Solutions. The solutions are ranked according to those the group likes (+), dislikes (-), or is not sure of (?).

---

Interaction among the members, which has been controlled and limited in previous steps, now becomes of primary importance as the members fully discuss how their ideas are interrelated or have some commonalties. The team might ask itself: Do our solutions cluster into one "face" of discipline? Do these suggestions indicate the amount of power at which we wish to begin our intervention? Do we need to make educational changes beyond the disciplinary actions?

It is important that the teacher and team members recognize in this step that they have progressed beyond the "personal wisdom" kind of speculative thinking in which the teacher attempts to solve problems by "stabbing in the dark." The constructs, methods, and procedures provided for the teachers and school staffs here have brought the professional out of the darkness in which she functions as a limited technician, and provide a framework for the scientific problem solving that is characteristic of a true professional.

## Step 4: Deciding on Solutions (A Final Written Plan)

**Purpose:** To decide on an orderly plan of action and to put that plan into writing.

**Time:** 5 minutes

**Actions:** The members agree on a plan of action, including their own responsibility for carrying out the various segments of this plan. The secretary writes out this Individualized Discipline Plan, or IDP (see Figure 8–13), with a designation of each person's responsibilities. (All members should receive a copy.)

## Step 5: Implementing the Solution (A Commitment)

**Purpose:** To have the members commit themselves to implementing the plan's procedures.

**Time:** 1 minute

**Actions:** Each staff member is asked to sign or initial the IDP, and by doing so agrees to actively carry out the procedures and return for a follow-up reevaluation. A time for a follow-up reevaluation future meeting should be established at a time convenient for all members.

---

### INDIVIDUALIZED DISCIPLINE PLAN (IDP)

A written plan, created at the end of a staffing process, that details the specific techniques to be utilized in dealing with a difficult student and that identifies those who will be responsible for carrying out the techniques.

---

## Step 6: Reevaluation Meeting

**Purpose:** To have the members return for a meeting to evaluate the plan's effectiveness and call for any changes that might be necessary.

**Time:** 10 minutes (may vary)

**Actions:**  This last step is to meet again to assess the progress of the IDP and determine the effectiveness of the techniques proposed and the changes needed. The reevaluation meeting might simply require a short discussion, but if the teacher is still unsuccessful, the group might need to repeat the six-steps process described previously.

---

### STAFFING AGENDA

The established six-step process (stating the problem, generating solutions, evaluating solutions, deciding on a solution, implementing the solution, and reevaluating) that defines team members' roles, the purposes of each step, the amount of time to be used, and the actions needed to be accomplished.

---

The structured agenda with established procedures is a systematic process loosely based on a six-step problem-solving process, but it can be modified to accommodate team members' own unique working styles. However, it is important to have an agreed-upon structure for such staffing meetings. The solutions generated by the staffing process can be built out of an understanding of the techniques found in Chapters 1 and 2 and augmented by the individual and collective ideas of the team members.

## SUMMARY

The teacher drops  the Limit-Setting  System and moves to the  use of a Backup System when limit-setting techniques prove ineffective with a misbehaving student who continues to disrupt the educational setting. The teacher gradually escalates the use of isolation or time out, private meetings (teacher and student only) and public meetings (teacher, student, principal, and possibly others), and contracting (informal or written), and notifies the parents in a timely manner before removing the student to out-of-classroom isolation. In all conferences or meetings, the teacher maintains the leadership role and escalates up the TBC from the use of Relationship-Listening techniques, to Confronting-Contracting, and then, finally, to Rules and Consequences. If, at the end of all of the Backup System steps, the teacher is still ineffective at finding ways to help the misbehaving student move to more positive behavior, the teacher seeks the help of school staff by holding a staffing meeting, in order to benefit from the professional experience and insights of his or her colleagues.

# Related Readings

Alberto, P. A., & Troutman, A. C. (1990). *Applied Behavior Analysis for Teachers*, 3rd ed. New York: Merrill-Macmillan.

Engelmann, S., & Carnine, D. (1982). *Theory of Instruction: Principles and Application.* New York: Irvington.

Madsen, C. H., & Madsen, C. K. (1981). *Teaching/Discipline: A Positive Approach for Educational Development.* Raleigh, NC: Contemporary Publishing.

# Endnotes

1. Jones, F. (1987). *Positive Classroom Discipline*. New York: McGraw-Hill.
2. A child gets up from the cafeteria table and begins to walk away. Suddenly he stops and, looking back, sees his chair sticking out in the aisle. He returns and automatically uses his lower body to push the chair in under the table. This is an example of one of the hundreds of small rules governing behavior that we follow without thinking each day. It is called a *motor rule,* and is explained in more detail in Section VI, The Management System.
3. Dinkmeyer, D., McKay, G. D., & Dinkmeyer, J. S. (1989). *Parenting Young Children.* Circle Pines, MN: American Guidance Service.
4. Gordon, T. (1974). *T.E.T.: Teacher Effectiveness Training.* New York: David McKay.

# The Incentive System

Dealing with misbehavior is an important element in any classroom, but stopping negative behavior is only half the equation for a well-run classroom. The other half lies in getting students to demonstrate positive behaviors and performance routinely. That's where the Incentive System comes in.

The Limit-Setting System provides techniques for quietly getting students to stop their misbehavior so ongoing teaching is not disrupted, and the Backup System addresses significant disruptions that require more public responses. The Incentive System, on the other hand, is a classroom process for motivating the students to increase the speed of their work and positive behaviors, or to acquire new behaviors not already in their repertoire. The Incentive System, for example, can be used to get students to do their homework or to care for school property, and is a key element in establishing a healthy classroom environment.

# 9

# The Rights and Responsibility Game

What motivates students? What is it that children want to do, and will do excessively and with great passion? The answer, which will differ with age, lies hidden deep within an understanding of the child's psychological developmental. If we understand these developmental "passions," we, as teachers, may harness this motivational steam to stimulate students to do the work we want them to do in our classrooms. We would thus have discovered an Incentive System—a process that will motivate our students to work with great gusto, and even with passion.

A school-age child will not clean his room at home or take out the trash, but will spend hours running up and down a basketball court with a group of like-minded peers to put a ball through a hoop, or assembling a model airplane, or playing endlessly with a video game—he or she is motivated to do these activities passionately. If aliens came from another planet and saw this competitive activity with its massive output of energy, they could easily conclude that the activity is utter nonsense. It isn't work; it doesn't produce a product or provide a service to anyone; and on the surface it simply appears to be a use of excessive energy. Yet the child is passionate about these activities.

Developmentally, the young child (from ages 2 to 7) is characterized by a fantasy belief that parents can make the sun rise and set and control all natural happenings. This represents the *romantic family* period, with its "My daddy is better than your daddy" attitude. The young child, because of his or her dependence, is motivated to work for the approval of parents. It is around the age of 7 that the elementary school child breaks from the childish belief that his or her mom and dad are godlike. With their new cognitive abilities (Piaget, 1965), children near the age of 7 suddenly understand that mom and dad are, after all, mortals. At the same time, the children are pushed out of the "nest" to the first real societal institution—school. Thus, the child now begins to acquire new developmental interests that motivate him or her toward peers.

Beginning at age 7, the elementary school-age child turns to peers. The child seeks out group membership with peers, normally of the same sex, to challenge himself, testing and redefining his identity. These beginning elementary school years are the *club period* (Boy Scouts, Girl Scouts, and similar interest groups) and *games period* (board games such as checkers or Monopoly, card games, and team sports such as baseball, football, and soccer) of development. Give any elementary school-age child a few free minutes and he or she will seek out peers to create teams and begin competitive games. The motivation for children of this age is "being a worthy group member," meaning that others will accept him or her into the group and accept his or her talents *and limitations.*

Most of the club activities and games are heavily controlled by rules not created by adults but generally handed down from an older generation of children to the next generation. These time-tested rules are adapted by the newly formed children's groups on the spot, before any competitive activity can begin. Without adult interference, elementary school children can even argue the rules for 15 minutes and play the game for 5 minutes.

When a child learns a new task that is basic to his or her psychological and physical development, the child can appear "drunk" with enthusiasm to practice that new skill. The 12-month old who learns to walk for the first time is "drunk" with passion and gusto to master this walking; when parents put the child to bed at night, those legs are still pumping with a need to practice—the child is "passionate" about walking. The elementary school-age child is developmentally preoccupied with learning to understand and obey rules and social relationships and to master his or her competitive nature. This shows itself in the passionate desire for playing games that have rules (see Figure 9–1).

In considering the moral concepts of right, wrong, and rules, the beginning elementary school child developmentally has a harsh conscience with a "black and white" sense of right and wrong. The common phrase of "It's not fair" dominates the child's language. Rules are safety devices for creating a collective reality—the game—that, for short periods of time, provides an equal arena for each child to demonstrate his or her skills and to challenge himself or herself safely against others. If the

---

**FIGURE 9–1   The Value of Games with Rules**

1. Morality (rules) is practiced at a motor/practice level without undue harm.

2. One must know and enact a role.

3. One must obey rules that define a role (playing first base) and the larger game (double-dribble in basketball).

4. There is a massive expenditure of energy within the confines of rules and boundaries of the game (channelled aggression).

5. One must follow a leader.

6. Teams are made up of members with varying skills (less-skilled children are still accepted).

games and activities are *not* controlled or organized by adults, winning is only a minor goal of a child participating in these activities. More important is the elementary student's passion for obeying socially agreed upon rules and group membership. Teams will accept unskilled players, but they must "fairly" divide the skilled and unskilled players among the teams so they are balanced in ability. Then the game can begin.

The classroom Incentive System helps the students acquire new behaviors, maintain already learned behaviors, and increase the rate of their work activities. The motivation for doing such actions must be built on the developmental interest in group membership and identity, rules, "gaming," and competition for rewards that are real or symbolic. During the elementary school age, the child's acceptance of authority gradually moves from family authority to peer authority (see Figure 9–2). Elementary-age children now become highly self-critical. They would prefer to suffer any punishment initiated by adults—including the teacher—than to do something that might lower their prestige among their peer group and thus endanger their group membership. The preschool-age child is fearful of losing mother and father's approval, but the elementary school child will risk the loss of parent or teacher approval in order to win peer loyalty. The age of 7 is also, developmentally, the period when the child learns to practice rules through "games-with-rules" play with peers. Just as the toddler needed to practice walking and became "drunk" with this activity, the elementary-age child practices group membership and rules, providing the developmental and psychological impetus for his passion for games with rules.

## TEAM COMPETITION

*The fourth-grade teacher, Mr. Hansen, is teaching a social studies lesson about how corn grows in Kansas, when it becomes apparent that Earl and Rod are not paying attention.*

FIGURE 9–2    Developmental Nature of the Elementary-Aged Child

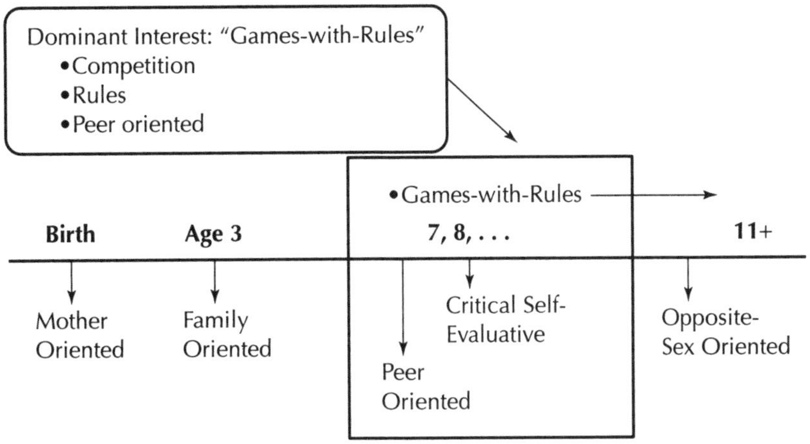

*The boys are off task and are talking so loudly that they are disturbing their neighbors and disrupting Mr. Hansen's lesson. Mr. Hansen does not use a high-profile correction (Kounin, 1970) by stopping his lessons and reprimanding the two boys; instead, while maintaining the rhythm and continuity of his lesson, he walks to one side of the chalkboard, where a mounted score chart represents four teams: red, blue, green, and yellow. The teacher places a check mark under red, blue, and yellow, but does not put a mark under the green team—of which Earl and Rod are members. The boys look up to see what is happening, and realize that they have caused the other three classroom teams to score a point. They quickly return to the lesson, and Mr. Hansen has lost no time or momentum.*

---

### HIGH-PROFILE CORRECTION

An intrusive process whereby the teacher stops his or her teaching to spotlight an off-task student, and in turn disrupts the ongoing activities and thought process. This interrupts ongoing activities and imposes guilt on the student, making all students feel reprimanded. High-profile correction is highly correlated with poor academic gains and ineffective classroom management (Kounin, 1970).

---

*Later, the students have lined up to leave the classroom for special outside activities. Just before they depart, Mr. Hansen, along with most of the students, looks out over the empty room to find it neat and orderly—except for Jason's desk. On and under his desk are scraps of paper, library books, and similar items that were not put away. Mr. Hansen goes to the team score chart and places a check mark under the columns for the red, green, and yellow teams, but does not place one under the column of Jason's blue team. This elicits a small groan of disappointment from the other blue team members. The red, green, and yellow teams are dismissed to the special activity area, while the teacher and the blue team members wait and watch as Jason cleans up his desk area.*

*Later in the day, after the students have returned to their classroom and taken their seats after arriving back from lunch and the playground, Mr. Hansen reaches into a small mailbox mounted near the door and takes out two 3-by-5 pink cards, which were put there by the teacher supervising the cafeteria that day. The teacher holds up the pink cards and announces that they are cafeteria score cards. He reads two names: Rod Burlington and Jason Johnson—"fighting on the playground." He goes to the team score chart and places a check mark for the red and yellow teams, but none for Rod's green team or Jason's blue team.*

At some subsequent preestablished time, we will see Mr. Hansen adding up the check marks for each team; the three highest-scoring teams receive some form of reward as "the winners." Following this, a new game is started.

Let's attempt to understand the rationale and dynamics of such a team competition process as a classroom Incentive System. We can anticipate that the children on all teams, but especially the blue team, will quickly prompt those misbehaving or off-task students such as Jason to "get with the program" because he is causing their team to not "win." The socialization is coming from peer to peer instead of coming unilaterally from an authoritarian teacher to the student. The traditional classroom has generally worked with the premise of the teacher as the authority handing out rewards and, more likely, many more forms of punishment.

Today, a large number of students are growing up with minimal or no family supervision, living much of their lives among their peers—either in poor-quality daycare situations or on the streets. More than at any other time, the modern child's emotional investment is in peer relationships and membership. Adult authority, in the forms of punishment, reprimands, or even rewards, increasingly has little or no effect on such children. Many misbehaving students will challenge the authority of the teacher, while those same students cannot stand against peers, both because of today's form of early socialization occurring with the modern child and because of the developmental interest and needs of the school-age child. The peer group holds the power. And if we understand this dynamic, we can use peer interest to form our Incentive System. Ultimately, this will prove more effective than attempting to hold to an adult authoritarian system, which the difficult student will challenge in an attempt to make the teacher the outside aggressor.

---

### OUTSIDE AGGRESSOR

Groups of students—out of fear, rivalry, or dislike—project their hate (their outside aggression) toward a fellow student or teacher who is not a member of the group.

---

## THE IMMATURE AND MATURE MORAL POSITIONS

The team competition Incentive System called the *Rights and Responsibility Game* is based on the levels of a child's moral development. The child's first developmental moral reasoning is the *immature moral stage*, where she obeys rules out of love and fear of powerful adults, often beginning with her mother and then advancing to her mother and father. The *mature moral* position begins to develop during the elementary school-age period, when right and wrong are defined by the motive of the person and there is an understanding of empathy and reciprocity for others. The elementary school-age child will learn through the Rights and Responsibility Game how her actions can take away the rights of others and, in turn, feel what it is like to have others take away her rights, requiring her to speak up to defend her rights. If the classroom discipline system, during these ages of 7 to 11, is autocratic and based on punishment and fear, then the child's moral reasoning will be retarded. The Rights and Responsibility Game is a transitional process that gives the misbehaving student real day-in and day-out practical experiences of how her rule-breaking actions cause fellow classmates, as a mini-society, to lose. When these peers are given the opportunity to express their dissatisfaction with the classmate's misbehavior, they begin to socialize the misbehaving student and provide an effective feeling for social interactions.

Of course, because there is a reward in the Rights and Responsibility Game, there is still an external *locus of control*. However, when carrying out this Incentive System, the teacher will fade the reward process until the feelings of belonging and being a part of the democratic group become the reward—the locus of control will gradually move internally.

For young children, the nearly total dependence on parents produces the first moral position in which they view adults as god-like or all-powerful. This produces an authoritarian view of what is right or wrong. What is right or wrong is determined by what parents allow or forbid, rather than by an evaluation of the motives of the person and whether the person intended to do a negative act—or even whether the person understands how his or her actions affect others (Piaget, 1965). Thus, the young student obeys rules because of an external locus of control related to the love, as well as the fear of loss of love, from parents and adults such as teachers.

---

### LOCUS OF CONTROL

When students make decisions is it because *they* decided (internal locus of control) or because *someone else* (external locus of control) is insisting or coercing them to perform such action.

---

The *mature moral position* does not fully develop until near the end of the elementary school years. This more mature moral position enables the older student to understand his behavior and actions and how they effect others. The student has developed an empathy for the feelings and rights of others. The child in this mature position understands that rules are collectively created and may be changed, and that the unilateral imposition of rules by someone holding more power (authoritarian) does not make these rules fair or right. The higher cognitive understanding of a mature moral position now enables the locus of control to be internal, based on the student's evaluation of concepts of right and wrong and not just because external authorities state it must be so.

The playing of games with rules that dominates children age 7 and older is a facet of human development, or nature's "built-in" process, that provides experience involving competition and rule-governed behavior and facilitates the movement to this more mature moral position. Just as the toddler was "drunk" with practicing the physical skill of walking, the elementary school-age child developmentally learns to "obey" social rules by practicing through playing games with rules. In the Incentive System, as the Rights and Responsibility Game, teachers build on this developmental interest and—through the incentive game—assist the student toward more socially mature understandings.

Simply defined, the Rights and Responsibility Game is a process through which the teacher places students, by design, into four to six classroom teams, balancing each team with well-behaving and misbehaving students as well as students of different sexes, ethnic backgrounds, and so on. As with any sports team, the groups accept a mascot-symbol (tigers, lions, etc.) and/or a color (red, blue, green, and yellow) with which they can be identified. This game is played daily for a period of six weeks, with acts of misbehavior causing the other team to win points. This permits the teacher to always make a positive act, by rewarding teams and students who are behaving. Much like a sports referee, the teacher makes tally marks on a score sheet mounted on the classroom wall. Misbehaviors outside the classroom, such as in the cafeteria, playground, or special-area activities such as art, music, and physical education, as well as on the school bus, are also counted as a part of the game.

After a period of time, the teams that "win" receive some form of reward, such as food treats, stickers, desired trinkets, or special time for activities that they like to do (called *preferred activity time*, or *PATs*). Over a period of six weeks, these reinforcers are faded out and the rewards gradually disappear, thus enabling the student to move from an external locus (the reward) to an internal locus of control in the form of self-discipline.

The socialization occurs when well-behaving peers express their displeasure, in teacher-supervised problem-solving team meetings, toward a team member who is causing them to lose. These meetings, full of intense discussion, can help counsel the misbehaving student, and can get commitments from all students to work more effectively together. The misbehaving student learns that he lives interdependently among others, that his misbehavior takes away the rights of others and that the all-powerful teacher is not the only one who can punish. In contrast, the team members who are losing out because of their misbehaving team member must learn, as in a democratic society, to speak out and stand against misbehaviors that disrupt the social order. In this way, both the misbehaving student *and* his well-behaving classmates learn through the Rights and Responsibility Game. The Rights and Responsibility Game provides a bridge that leads students out of the immature moral position—the childish fear of authority and feelings of "I behave only because I might get punished"—to the more mature moral position of reciprocity, empathy for others, and an understanding of how their behavior affects the rights of others.

## ESTABLISHING TEAMS

On the first day of school, when the students are unfamiliar to the teacher, the students may arbitrarily be assigned to a team, by directly balancing team membership for sex, race, or other similar outwardly apparent variables, and then seating team members together such as in the Double E classroom seating arrangement (See Chapter 12). The desks or tables at which the students are seated are color coded so that a simple glance at the classroom makes it obvious where members of the red team, blue team, and so on, are seated. During the first several weeks of school, each student will wear a felt piece of material, the color of his or her team, pinned to his or shirt or blouse. (One teacher, seeking an alternative to colored felt pieces, had a local business donate attractive colored baseball caps for all class members, and the students gleefully wore them during the Rights and Responsibility Game.)

Team members should not be all girls or all boys, nor all of the same race or ethnic group. Similarly, all the misbehaving students should not be on the same team. This balancing of team membership deliberately builds on the elementary child's sense of fairness and engineers experiences that require each student to interact with peers who are very different from himself or herself. This results in learning experiences with others of diverse backgrounds.

Quickly, during the first few days of school, the teacher will discover which students are going to have difficulty behaving within the demands of a classroom. She can then reassign students to new teams with the "misbehaving" or target students being evenly divided among the teams. If you watch elementary school-age children picking teams for a softball game, you will see their sense of fairness, whereby players who are highly skilled and those who are unskilled are evenly distributed between the teams so the teams are balanced before the game begins. If too many star players or unskilled players play on one team, the children view this as unfair and they won't participate. The classroom teacher must be sensitive to this same fairness phenomenon, balancing all teams so they have a relatively equal chance of "winning."

When one team has a very difficult misbehaving member and keeps losing points because of that one member, the teacher must first use this tension to do plus/delta meetings (counseling sessions) with the team. However, this one team eventually may feel so burdened that the team members feel they may never win; if this happens, they respond with "It isn't fair," and the whole team will become a discipline problem. Before this occurs, the team's membership will need to be reassigned, with the misbehaving student being moved to a new team. Ideally, the best balance is to have the misbehaving student on a team with one or two peers who are very verbal and are not afraid to speak up to the misbehaving student. These well-behaving team members must have a clear sense of right and wrong, including a sense of fairness, and must be liked and highly respected by all class members. These well-behaved students can help set a positive moral tone for the classroom.

Some teachers may see the Rights and Responsibility Game as manipulative and as placing undue pressures on both the misbehaving student and the well-behaved team members. The Rights and Responsibility Game may be defended, as an Incentive System, with the following justification.

In modern society, the "kid" culture, supported by TV programs and TV marketing, has already obtained great control over the moral and value development of this country's children. Watch closely the way teachers, parents, and adults are portrayed on popular children's programs. Adults are seen as "geeks," ineffective, and "uncool." Certain "star" child actors are seen as "hip," sophisticated, and "really cool," and the children watching would like to emulate them. Increasingly, there is very little "looking up to adults" and wanting to "be like adults"; in fact, the opposite is true, with many adults wanting to wear the status clothing of youth and wanting to act as children do.

This control by the peer group can become excessive, as can be seen in the violent street gangs that wear mascot symbols and colors of membership. The Rights and Responsibility Game understands the motivation of group-peer membership and accepts it as one central motivation, if not the most powerful motivation, of today's youth. Educators now understand this phenomenon and must use it to promote positive, healthy, and mature ways of acting and belonging with others. The Incentive System picks up today's student where he or she is socially and developmentally, and bridges to a more mature position of social responsibility. This classroom practice, through the Rights and Responsibility Game under the guidance and supervision of the teacher, can prepare large numbers of students, when they are outside adult supervision, to speak up and stand up against destructive control of the peer group. We must remember that not only is the misbehaving student learning from the Rules and Responsibility Game, but the well-behaved peers and team members are also learning to stand against destructive behavior rather than to emulate or ignore it.

The teenager who telephones her parents to be taken home from the teen party two hours early because drugs and alcohol have appeared is the child who has learned to make her own decisions and can stand against the peer group when it is wrong. Where do children get practice in making such critical decisions? Ideally, the parent can teach this to the child, but the teacher has a classroom laboratory full of peers for practicing these skills in a real-life manner. The Rights and Responsibility Game and other similar games-with-rules play have the potential for teaching children a host of much-need skills (see Figure 9–3).

## INCENTIVE REINFORCERS

The teams may "win" reinforcers of three types: edibles, tangibles, and preferred activity times (PATs). (See Figure 9–4 for examples of

---

**FIGURE 9–3** **Basic Life Abilities/Skills Practiced in Games with Rules (GWR)**

Think about all the following that can be learned in a GWR activity! Are these abilities missing in the skills of the misbehaving student?

Listening, having a conversation by planning, joining in, giving instructions, following instructions, forms of apologizing, convincing others, controlling and expressing feelings, understanding others, dealing with someone else's anger, expressing affection, dealing with fear, rewarding yourself, asking permission, sharing, helping others, negotiating, using self-control, standing up for your rights, responding to teasing, avoiding trouble with others, keeping out of fights, making a complaint, answering a complaint, sportsmanship after the game, dealing with embarrassment, dealing with being left out, standing up for a friend, responding to persuasion, responding to failure, dealing with contradictory messages, dealing with an accusation, getting ready for a difficult conversation, dealing with group pressure, deciding on what to do, deciding what caused a problem, setting a goal, deciding on your abilities, gathering information, arranging problems by importance, making a decision, concentrating on a task

---

Adapted from *Skill-Streaming the Adolescent: A Structured Learning Approach to Teaching Prosocial Skills* by A. P. Goldstein, R. P. Sprafkin, N. J. Gershaw, and P. Klein, 1981, Champaign, IL: Research Press.

reinforcers.) The type 1 reinforcer (edible) is highly desired by the students but is a less desired reinforcer for the classroom setting. It will be used first, but is then faded to a type 2 (tangibles) and finally faded to type 3 PATs.

The classroom teacher should be aware that after a number of edibles, the child can become saturated and no longer interested. Additionally, edibles can be cumbersome, time consuming, and difficult to administer. Edibles, as a type 1 reinforcer, also appear more like bribes. They are initially very powerful and motivational to large numbers of children, but their use should be phased out over a six-week period.

**FIGURE 9–4** **Incentive Reinforcers**

| Type | Category | Examples |
|---|---|---|
| 1 | Edibles | Foods and liquids (e.g., pieces of cracker, sips of juice, pudding, juice, popsicles, sugarless candies) |
| 2 | Tangibles | Certificates, badges, stickers, balloons, small toys, novelties, and other status or desired items (see U.S. Toy, 1995) |
| 3 | Preferred Activity Time (PAT) | Play and game activities (see example in Jones, 1987) |

## Preferred Activity Time (PAT)

PATs should provide not only socialization benefits but also academic practice. See Figure 9–5 for a detailed example of one form of PAT, called Academic Baseball. Other forms of PAT may include variations of such popular games as Jeopardy, Family Feud, College Bowl, Tic Tac Toe, or Bingo, as well as any other activities that the students favor, such a viewing favorite videos.

Preferred activity time is not "kicking back" time designed to permit students to chat with each other and do nothing. If students are given the freedom to do nothing, that is exactly what they will do. Jones (1987) would clearly admit that the use of PAT with students is really a "shell game." Such activities as a popcorn party would be permitted as a PAT, but would be considered a poor or weak use of PAT. Under Jones's definition, PATs are fun activities that hold high interest for students but have embedded in them a routine of drill and practice, or even content review of the subject matter. In short, they are process activities involving elements of learning. The PAT of watching a video such as *Old Yeller* would involve a book the students will read this semester; seeing the video is a motivating, high-interest activity that the teacher simply turned into a PAT—thus the "shell game."

The book *Positive Discipline* written by Jones (1987) contains a host of starter games to get teachers going at all age levels. The suggested PATs involve:

1. Team competitions: games with line-ups (classroom game of baseball, requiring knowledge of the material being taught)

2. Team competitions: games without line-ups (classroom baseball, volleyball, or College Bowl, which modifies the game so there is no line-up)

3. Team competition with complex work (math teams and cut-throat)

4. Path games (spelling, typing, Bingo)

5. Enrichment activities (permitting the students to break from the tradition and try advanced applications of the subject area)

6. Fun and games (simple party time, which the teacher will rely on the least as the students gradually learn to use the academically mixed games above)

Particularly for today's students, such games might be seen as "not cool." Teachers should permit much feedback from students in choosing and modifying the activities for their own interest. Historically, games with rules are passed down from one generation of children, beginning in the upper-elementary grades, to the younger generation of children. They normally are not taught by adults, but are strictly dependent on the child culture (remember Red Light-Green Light and Red Rover?). Because of television, mall arcades, and the general marketing of childhood leisure activities, these traditional games are being lost and not

**FIGURE 9–5   An Example of a Preferred Activity Time (PAT): Academic Baseball (Grades 2+)**

**Subject Area**
Math, History, Foreign Language, Science, Vocabulary Development, Spelling, etc.

**Objective**
Test review

**Materials and Preparation**
- The teacher or students prepare questions in four degrees of difficulty: single, double, triple, home run.

- Two baseball diamonds will be needed in order to use a ping pong game format (described below). Mark the bases on the floor.

**Student Grouping**
Two teams.

**The Play**
1. The batter is asked by the pitcher to pick the level of difficulty for the question (single, double, triple, or home run).

2. The pitcher selects and asks a question from the single, double, triple, or home run stack. If, however, the teacher is "pitcher" and does not have stacks of questions already prepared, the teacher just asks the questions "off the top of her head."

3. If the student answers correctly, the student walks to the appropriate base and other runners advance the same number of bases.

4. If the question is answered incorrectly, a "flyball" is called, and the question goes to a player of the team that is "in the field."

   - When the teacher says "flyball, " she should wait before calling on a student so that everyone in the field must dig for the answer.

   - If the player in the field answers the question correctly, the flyball has been caught and the batter is out.

   - If the outfielder misses the question, the flyball has been dropped, and the batter goes to first base on an error. All runners advance one base on an error.

5. When using the ping pong game format, the questions alternate between teams. So, the second question goes to the team that was in the field (i.e., playing defense) during the previous question. The ping pong format guarantees that both teams get to bat an equal number of times, that everybody plays all of the time and that both teams are continually engaged in scoring runs.

6. The "ping pong" format does away with innings. In order to make outs meaningful, the final score is computed as *runs minus outs.*

---

**FIGURE 9–5** An Example of a Preferred Activity Time (PAT): Academic Baseball (Grades 2+) *(continued)*

Team #1                                                    Team #2

Score:                                                      Score:
Runs _____                                                  Runs _____
Outs _____                                                  Outs _____
Total _____                                                 Total _____

**Fine Points**

• Most four-level games follow a ping pong format with the question going to the opposite team if missed. It is best to play such games open book. The teacher will find the players on defense digging for the answer as soon as the question is asked. Since kids hate doing nothing, the rest of the students on the team that is "at bat" can usually be found digging for the answer as well.

• Football is similar except that the defense can "sack the quarterback" for a 10-yard loss when the student picks a 10-yard question, or they can intercept a 20-, 30-, or 40-yard pass play.

• If the teacher has any question about rules, it can be turned over to the students. They will make sure the rules are fair. And, speaking of keeping things fair, a perennial preoccupation with teenagers is how to choose teams fairly. Four students of roughly equal scholastic ability can be chosen as captains. They do not need to be fast students; in fact, this is a nice chance for the teacher to honor some of the slower students. The teacher should give the captains a class list and say: "I want you to take this class list to the table in the back of the room and make equal teams for me. Horse-trade until they are equal because you will have to live with them." If the teacher wishes to add a further guarantee of fair play, the students can be told: "It is your job to choose and trade until the teams are equal. After you give me equal teams, you will draw lots to see which team you will captain."

---

passed down by many children today. The commercial games, such as Nintendo or its sibling Game Boy, are isolated activities, and therefore children are losing out on the very valuable social interaction that traditional games have long taught them. According to Jones, children—especially children today—simply do not know how to have fun, because that fun for hundreds of years has been centered around group games. Historically, when a group of people worked hard on a laborious task (picking corn, cutting forest timber, or shucking oysters), they would fill their free time engaging in games of competition involving these same

| Week | Time of Award | Monday | Tuesday | Wednesday | Thursday | Friday |
|---|---|---|---|---|---|---|
| | **FIGURE 9–5   Suggested Schedule for Awarding Reinforcers Over a Six-Week Period** | | | | | |
| 1 | Mid-AM<br>Noon<br>End of Day | edible<br>edible<br>edible | edible<br>edible<br>tangible | edible<br>tangible<br>tangible | edible<br>tangible<br>tangible | tangible<br>tangible<br>PAT |
| 2 | Mid-AM<br>Noon<br>End of Day | edible<br>edible<br>edible | edible<br>tangible<br>tangible | tangible<br>tangible<br>PAT | _____<br>tangible<br>tangible | tangible<br>_____<br>PAT |
| 3 | Mid-AM<br>Noon<br>End of Day | edible<br>tangible<br>tangible | _____<br>tangible<br>tangible | tangible<br>_____<br>PAT | _____<br>_____<br>PAT | tangible<br>_____<br>PAT |
| 4 | Mid-AM<br>Noon<br>End of Day | tangible<br>_____<br>PAT | _____<br>_____<br>_____ | tangible<br>_____<br>PAT | _____<br>_____<br>_____ | _____<br>_____<br>PAT |
| 5 | Mid-AM<br>Noon<br>End of Day | PAT<br>_____<br>PAT | _____<br>_____<br>PAT | _____<br>_____<br>_____ | _____<br>PAT<br>_____ | _____<br>_____<br>PAT |
| 6 | Mid-AM<br>Noon<br>End of Day | _____<br>_____<br>PAT | _____<br>_____<br>_____ | _____<br>_____<br>PAT | _____<br>_____<br>_____ | _____<br>_____<br>PAT |

Mid-AM = award reinforcer in the middle of the morning, Noon = award reinforcer just before lunch, End of Day = give award just before students depart school.

activities (thus we have corn-husking, log-chopping, and oyster-shucking contests). The PAT approach is literally attempting to save children's cultural heritage and get teachers and students to socially enjoy themselves, while at the same time slipping in some academic training and review.

## SCHEDULING REINFORCERS

The awarding of reinforcers—either edible, tangible, or PATs—is time consuming and administratively cumbersome. Most teachers may initially feel it is important to work toward positive behavior, but in practice this has not been easy to accomplish through a hit-or-miss form of giving reinforcers. Figure 9–6 shows a suggested schedule for using and fading the three types of reinforcers. Generally, the teacher follows this schedule over a six-week period (see the explanation of Mars Days in Chapter 13) and one can see in the suggested schedule that type 1 edibles are used heavily the first week, then dropped or faded, moving to type 2 tangibles, and then in the last weeks type 3 PATs are mostly used.

---

**FIGURE 9–7    Score Card**

---

Teacher names the prize on this space (an edible, tangible, or PAT)

Each color represents a team

The numbers can be covered with an "X" when a score is awarded to the team.

| Score Card | | | |
|---|---|---|---|
| Prize _____ | | | |
| Red | Blue | Green | Yellow |
| 1 | 1 | 1 | 1 |
| 2 | 2 | 2 | 2 |
| 3 | 3 | 3 | 3 |
| 4 | 4 | 4 | 4 |
| 5 | 5 | 5 | 5 |
| 6 | 6 | 6 | 6 |
| 7 | 7 | 7 | 7 |
| 8 | 8 | 8 | 8 |
| 9 | 9 | 9 | 9 |
| 10 | 10 | 10 | 10 |

The total number needed to win will be set by the teacher. First, perhaps only 3 points will be required, slowly increasing until 10 is reached. When the objective is less than 10, the teacher will "X" out numbers that will not be used prior to the game beginning.

We see by the suggested scheduling that the reinforcers in the Incentive System of edibles and tangibles will gradually fade. Once the students have developed normal classroom habits, the Rights and Responsibility Game will be stopped—but not the PAT. The PAT should continue throughout the year, with normal classroom teaching and learning becoming more fun and game-like until the learning and the having fun begin to blend into one activity for the students

## SCORING AND THE SCORE CARD

A Rights and Responsibility Score Card would be mounted on the wall (see Figure 9–7 for an example of a suggested card) at the front of the classroom within easy reach of the teacher. A team scores a point in one of three ways: misbehavior by a member of another team, bonus points to all teams, and bonus points for the student who needs encouragement.

*Mr. Hansen is teaching a social studies lesson, when it becomes apparent that Earl and Rod are not paying attention. The boys are off task and are talking so loudly that they are disturbing their neighbors and disrupting Mr. Hansen's lesson. While maintaining his rhythm and continuity of his lesson, Mr. Hansen walks to one side of the chalkboard, where a score chart is mounted representing four teams: red, blue, green, and yellow. The teacher places a check mark under red, blue, and yellow, but does not put a mark under the green team—of which Earl and Rod are members. The boys look up, see what is happening, and realize that they have caused the other classroom teams to "score a point." They quickly return to the lesson, and Mr. Hansen has lost no time or momentum.*

This *scoring of points* on the mounted score card is done in a low-profile manner. Without saying a word, the teacher goes to the Score Card and awards a point to each of the other three teams, and returns quickly to teaching. Notice in the vignette that no reprimand is made to the misbehaving students. If need be, the teacher may make eye contact and square off with the misbehaving students to cue or *body-telegraph* to them that they were the ones causing others to lose points. More likely, however fellow students will signal or cue them about their behavior.

---

### BODY-TELEGRAPHING

Through nonverbal body actions (*kinesics*), the teacher communicates to the observing students that the teacher "means business."

---

## Bonus Points

The teacher awards bonus points to all teams if no misbehavior occurs during a specific time interval, announced as a verbal contract with the class beforehand. The teacher gradually fades this bonus reward by lengthening the time period, so that now the points are rewarded after an entire morning or an entire day.

## Bonus Points for the Student Needing Encouragement

At times, there will be one or two very difficult students whose behavior disrupts the Incentive System, and the team members get so unhappy with them that they do not want or refuse to have such a student on their team. This student has been described as the "best bad kid" in the classroom or in the school (see Section V, The Encouragement System, for further actions in dealing with this discouraged student). In order to prevent the class from making this student the outside aggressor, the teacher begins a bonus-awarding process. Establish a contract with the class and the misbehaving student, agreeing that if he or she can maintain positive behavior for a short period of time (a timer can be set for this interval), all teams will win points.

At first, this time interval is small, such as 5 or 10 minutes, making sure that the difficult student and, in turn, the entire class is able to win. The teacher awards points for all teams so that if the difficult student succeeds, the entire class may applaud the student in a further reward for his actions. Then the Bonus Points Contract is restarted with a slightly longer interval. The time interval for bonus points increases and increases until it no longer is needed and the difficult student can behave in such an appropriate manner that he can be a positive team member. Notice that the misbehaving student doesn't get some independent-individual reward, but he helps all teams get reinforced.

A second variation in working with this "best bad kid" is to give the student his own personal score card with numbers, pinned to his shirt. Each time the student maintains good behavior for a specific time interval, the teacher punches the personal score card with a hole punch. Once the difficult student has reached the same number of holes as the number written on his personal card, all teams cheer him and all teams win a point. This second variation works well for out-of-classroom or open-field activities such as on the playground or in the cafeteria.

The difficult student is then given a new personal score card, with a higher number or an increased time interval, to challenge the student to increase his time on task and his self-control. The social dynamic that you are attempting to create is to prevent the misbehaving student from being rejected by his or her peers or from gaining status by his misbehavior, making him the "best bad kid." You want to have these classmates celebrate and reward him for his ability to grow and become a more cooperative student.

## A WORD ABOUT "WINNING"

Historically, schools have used competition that rewards one individual as "King" or "Queen" of the Christmas Ball, or one team of students winning over large groups of other students. This competition, where few can win, makes the majority of the students "losers." If one is picked as the most attractive, it make the rest feel not as attractive and suggests inadequacy. This contradicts the general philosophy inherent in the Rules and Responsibility Game. Teachers want all students to be winners, and to work as teams and as a class to have everyone be successful.

Games of competition are found in most cultures, but there are cultures that, through their games, teach cooperation rather than "destroying" or beating the other for the benefit or glory of a small group or an individual. It is said that early Eskimo games were played in such a manner that the game continued until all members of the group succeeded or "won." Then, with great cathartic release, all members cheered *their* success. This cooperative gaming is also seen in the movement called New Games, where games selected from other cultures are played for the purpose of cooperation and the success of all participants—no individual or small minority beats others. So, the teacher's approach in refereeing the Rights and Responsibility Game is *not* to get caught up in winning and the destructive form of competition, but to play the game so that all teams can and do win and receive awards. This is especially important in the first few weeks of the Mars Days (the first six weeks of school). The teacher should deliberately work in such a manner by liberally dispensing points or lessening the time period for getting points. This enables all teams to have many early experiences of winning and getting the rewards, before any team has to experience not getting a reward.

## OUT-OF-CLASSROOM SUPERVISION

During these first six weeks of school, the so-called Mars Days, the Rights and Responsibility Game is played by not only the classroom teacher but also the special area teachers in such subjects as art, music, physical education, and media. It also involves all school personnel, including the school crossing guards, bus drivers, and playground and cafeteria supervisors. The art, music, or media teacher who has a defined classroom may color code the tables or desks, arranging them so that when a new class of students enters the classroom, they know exactly where to seat themselves with their team. Remember that the students may arrive in the special-area room wearing a piece of colored felt material, which will show the teacher each student's team. The special-area teacher also has a score card and will play the Rights and Responsibility Game just like the classroom teacher, issuing his or her own rewards.

In this way, there is continuity between the special-area and classroom teachers, and the special-area teachers can send notes back to the classroom teacher telling which teams have "won" points for the classroom teacher to record for "team success at special area."

During open-field supervision such as on the playground or in the cafeteria, the students will be wearing their color tags. If the open-field supervisor gives a student a desist (see Section II, Limit-Setting System) and the student fails to comply, the supervisor sends a pink card to the classroom with the student's name and transgression. At a predetermined time, the classroom teacher will announce the student's name and transgression, and score points for the other teams. The teacher may also choose to do a Plus/Delta meeting with this misbehaving student or his team, with the cafeteria or playground supervisor in attendance.

## The Plus/Delta Meetings

Historically, misbehaving students would find themselves knee to knee or face to face with the teacher, receiving reprimands and criticism regarding their negative behavior and threats of punishment if they failed to desist. In contrast, Relationship-Listening forms of interaction—discussion of problems, finding answers, counseling, mediation, and "talking out" misbehavior, conducted between or among teacher and student(s) or between student and student—are the *ultimate goal of the Rights and Responsibility Game*. The control of students through rewards is only a short-term powerful process, for class control and to teach rights and responsibilities to both the misbehaving and the well-behaving students. The plus/delta meetings are held repeatedly and consistently with the misbehaving student, with a team that needs to deal with one of its misbehaving team members, or with the entire class. They are used throughout the Rights and Responsibility Game. After the first six weeks of school, the rewards are faded and the games disappear, but plus/delta meetings continue throughout the remainder of the school year to help the teacher maintain positive behavior and to gain more mature behavior from the students.

The teacher holds a plus/delta meeting to discuss a topic that involves some incident of social conflict repeatedly occurring within the classroom. "Rod, let's talk about the fight in the cafeteria" (Step 1: Defining the Problem). The teacher then leads the students through the Six Steps to Problem Solving (Step 2: Generating Solutions; Step 3:

Evaluating Solutions, etc.). The Six Steps to Problem Solving provides a structure for helping children think out problems and come up with creative solutions. (See Chapter 8 for a full explanation of the techniques and procedures for carrying out the Six Steps to Problem Solving and a plus/delta meeting.)

## CONTRACTING

The failure to obtain a reward (edible, tangible, or PAT), either by the individual well-behaving team member or by the misbehaving student, is a serious matter because the negative action may destroy the motivation of all the students involved. Keep in mind that it is critical to make sure that all students in the Rights and Responsibility Game get plenty of rewards during the early stages of the six-week schedule.

The awarding of an edible, although a very powerful reinforcer, is quickly consumed and normally quickly forgotten by most students. Thus, the loss of such reward is generally easier for the child to handle emotionally. But the loss of a tangible can be a more serious action, and the loss of a PAT is the most serious. In our earlier example, Rod caused his green team to lose points. Once this occurs, tension will build within Rod's team, and team members will begin to feel "put upon" by Rod's misbehavior. The first plus/delta team meeting, under the guidance of the teacher, is now held to deal with this tension. Participants define the problem, generate solutions, and go through the complete Six Steps to Problem Solving. When they get to Step 4: Deciding on the Solution, the teacher now turns this into a verbal contract and, later, a written contract.

Here is an example:

*Teacher:* "Team, we have now decided on a solution to this problem so that your team will not lose. Do we all agree?"

*Team:* "Yes!"

*Teacher:* "Do we now have a contract?"

*Team:* "Yes!"

*Teacher:* "Now, I need to shake your hands (the teacher does so with each team member) to seal this agreement. (The teacher approaches the misbehaving student.) Rod, do we now have an agreement, a contract, that when [so and so] occurs, you will do [so and so]?"

*Rod:* "Yes."

*Teacher:* (shakes Rod's hand) "Now that we have a contract, and we have all agreed, I will give you today's reward, even though your team lost."

Now if the misbehaving student or the team loses again and again, the tension builds within the group and a second plus/delta meeting in Sphere 2: One to Team is held in a similar manner. But this time, after the contract is agreed upon and hands have been shaken, all well-

| FIGURE 9–8 | One-On-One Meeting Techniques | |
|---|---|---|

**Relationship-Listening Face**

| TBC | Techniques | Examples |
|---|---|---|
| *Looking* | Proxemics | Teacher and misbehaving student are seated on chairs in a knee-to-knee position; teacher makes eye contact. |
| *Naming* | Active listening | "Wow! You have had a disappointing morning, and have lost a reward. You must feel disappointed." |
| | Door openers | "Rod, help me understand what is happening with you." |
| | I-messages | "When students take other's property (behavior), this disrupts the class (effect) and that is disturbing (feeling), and stops me from teaching." |

**Confronting-Contracting Face**

| | | |
|---|---|---|
| *Questioning* | "What-how" questions | "Rod, what did you do? What was the rule? What will happen if you continue to act like this?" |
| | (or, if need be) | "Rod, here is what you did---. The rule is---." |
| | Contracting | "You and I need to work this out! How will you change?" (Shaking hands or a contract signed) |
| | Logical consequences | "If the contract is broken, this consequence will happen,…" |

**Rules and Consequences Face**

| | | |
|---|---|---|
| *Commanding* | Assertive command | "Rod (say name, make eye contact), when this happens, I want you to do so and so" (tell what to do, not what not to do). |
| | Promise a consequence | "If this occurs again, then this will happen." |
| *Acting* | Transporting | *Backup System* begins. |

behaving team members will receive the reward, but the misbehaving student will not. We caution against ever depriving the well-behaving team member of a reward, with this one exception: If the team fails to discuss the problem and is not willing to work together, the entire team might be deprived of an edible or even a tangible, but never a PAT. Well-behaving children will consider it extremely unfair to be deprived of a "big ticket" reward such as a PAT just because they happen to be on the same team as a very difficult peer, and you will soon have very unhappy parents knocking at your classroom door to complain.

Now, if the misbehaving student has failed to receive the reward, the teacher holds a Sphere 1: One-to-One meeting with the misbehaving student following the procedures given in Figure 9–8. The one-on-one personal counseling and advisement session always takes a problem-solving attitude and approach. It escalates through the Teacher Behavior Continuum and the Three Faces of Discipline. Figure 9–8 is an example.

## SUMMARY

The Rights and Responsibility Game, built on the developmental need for the elementary school-age child to compete in a games-with-rules structure, is used as a behavioral Incentive System. It is used first to help the teacher gain classroom control, then to teach the misbehaving student how to move to more productive behaviors, and finally to teach the well-behaving student how to defend his or her rights. The process begins with reinforcers involving external control, which are faded through scheduling in order to finally permit the student go gain self-control. The tension caused by team membership and the loss of points because of a member's misbehavior is used in plus/delta meetings to solve problems and teach the misbehaving student his interdependence with others. Through the entire process of the Incentive System, the teacher's actions are positive and devoid of punishment or reprimands. The tension created by team competition creates the context for the teacher to teach new social skills and positive ways of behavior for the misbehaving student.

The classroom Incentive System can, through the Rights and Responsibility Game, help the students acquire new behaviors, maintain already learned behaviors, and increase the rate of their work activities. The motivation for doing such actions must be built on this developmental interest—that is, group membership and identity, rules, "gaming," and competition for rewards that are real or symbolic.

# References

Goldstein, A. P., Sprafkin, R. P., Gershaw, N. J., & Klein, P. (1980). *Skill-Streaming the Adolescent: A Structured Learning Approach to Teaching Prosocial Skills*. Champaign, Ill.: Research Press.

Jones, F. H. (1987). *Positive Classroom Discipline*. New York: McGraw-Hill.

Kounin, J. (1970). *Discipline and Group Management in Classrooms*. New York: Holt, Rinehart, and Winston.

Piaget, J. (1965). *Moral Judgment of the Child* (Marjorie Gabain, Trans.). New York: Free Press.

U.S. Toy Co. Inc. (1995). *U.S.Toy–1995: Wholesale Carnival, Decoration and Party Catalog*. 1227 E. 119 St., Grandview, MO 64030 (FAX: 1-816-761-9295).

# The Encouragement System

Other systems provide the tools necessary for the classroom teacher to organize her room to reduce the potential for behavioral outbursts, and to provide incentives for the students to perform well and behave properly. But inevitably in the classroom, there will be one particular student (or perhaps more) who has endured so much negative input that he or she has grown frustrated and discouraged. This type of student needs something special to encourage him to participate in the learning environment and to become a fully functioning member of the class.

This system is known as the Encouragement System. It offers an array of techniques for the teacher to use in drawing that one discouraged student out of his shell and into the broader world of classroom life.

# 10

# Finding Acceptance

## THE DESIRE TO BELONG

"Since the child is a social being, his strongest motivation is the desire to belong. His security or lack of it depends upon his feeling of belonging with the group. This is his basic requirement. Everything he does is aimed at finding his place. From infancy on, he is very busy exploring methods of being a part of his family group [later the school group]. From his observations and his successes, he draws conclusions—not found in words, but definite knowingness—'Ah! This is how I can belong. This is how I can have significance.' . . . The desire to belong is his basic goal while the method he devises for attaining his basic goal becomes his immediate goal."—Rudolf Dreikurs

Why is it that some elementary school students in your classroom are so disruptive that they prevent you from teaching and their fellow students from learning? The explanation for their destructive behavior is that they are discouraged.

*It is the first day of school at the beginning of a new year, and Mr. Garcia is casually observing the new group of fifth-graders entering his room for the first time. He finds nothing particularly distinctive about this new group, until Ronald appears. This student is dressed in faded blue jeans that are covered with patches bearing the logo of a popular motorcycle company. Even more noticeable are the two patches running across the seat of his pants bearing the words "Screw You" on one hip pocket and "Mother F--ker" on the other. The rest of Ronald's attire includes a T-shirt and a western-style hat pulled down over his eyes. In order for him to see while walking, he has to lead with his chin and look out over his nose.*

*Mr. Garcia gradually loses sight of Ronald as he visually skims over the remaining faces in the classroom. Suddenly, he hears one girl scream and another student laugh, and then the classroom quiets. Everyone's attention focuses on Ronald, who is slouched down in his seat with his hat pulled over his face. The students glance from the teacher to Ronald and back to the teacher. Seeing that neither Mr. Garcia nor Ronald is going to make any further move, the class members return to their chatting. A few minutes later, Mr. Garcia begins reading through the class roster, calling each student's name and receiving in return a proper acknowledgment such as "I'm here." When he calls out "Ronald Foster," there is no response. He repeats it a second time to no response, but all eyes turn toward Ronald. The teacher asks, "Isn't Ronald Foster here?" Ronald replies, "Yo, chill, man!" The teacher states, "You're Ronald?" Ronald gives the slightest "yes" nod of his head.*

*Mr. Garcia ignores Ronald's lack of a solid response, finishes calling the roll, and finally introduces himself and the content of the course. He turns his back to the class and begins to write the name of the textbook across the chalkboard. Before he can finish, he hears the same girlish scream, but this time with such intensity that it is clear something more serious is occurring. The girl seated in front of Ronald—physically mature for her age—suddenly jumps out of her seat and runs from the classroom. As she passes, it is apparent that Ronald has unfastened her bra.*

*As the year progresses Mr. Garcia will discover that Ronald is a student who will be a continuous and serious discipline problem, costing Mr. Garcia considerable classroom teaching time and stress throughout the school year.*

Ronald Foster's behavior may be viewed as goal directed. There is one central goal for students (as well as adults), and that is the attempt to find social acceptance and recognition. Humans are individual social beings living in a world with others. The things we say, the clothes we choose to wear, how we cut our hair, and how we behave and act are all for purposes of obtaining social recognition from others.

When a student is unsuccessful in obtaining social acceptance and recognition (sometimes as early as his or her infancy and toddler years at home), a pattern of misbehavior begins. Once such a child has entered the school during the elementary years, he or she begins to attempt to find acceptance and recognition among peers through the use of similar negative behaviors. The child now begins to understand, and fairly accurately evaluate, his or her strengths and limitations within the context of the peer culture and school. If poor patterns of getting acknowledgment and recognition were used in the home, the child will attempt to use similar misbehavior patterns in the new school setting.

Ronald's behavior is that of a discouraged student who has not found positive ways of gaining acceptance and who has developed a pattern of behavior designed to get acknowledgment and recognition—even if negative. Subconsciously, children such as Ronald are in essence saying, "If I cannot get recognition for being the best 'good' kid, I will get recognition for being the best 'bad' kid. This will make me someone—others will see and know me as being special." Thus, Ronald's misbehavior is a result of being discouraged, possibly very early in life, in not finding full social acceptance. Out of this feeling of discouragement, he has acquired the motivation and behavior to compensate for this nonacceptance.

If a student like Ronald cannot find acknowledgment and acceptance, he will subconsciously begin to work from four "mis-motivations": attention getting, power, feelings of revenge, and helplessness.

## MIS-MOTIVATIONS

The first mis-motivation of the discouraged student is to attempt to get *attention* by any manner. This will begin with a series of disruptions that stop the class from working and stop the teacher from teaching and that draw all the attention to the student, as in the example of Ronald and the unfastened bra. When you, as the teacher, reprimand and insist that the student stop, he will smile sheepishly and stop the disruption at that moment—but before long the attention-getting student is again doing something disruptive to draw attention to himself. His need for excessive attention through repetitive disruptions seems to "nickel and dime" you into submission, and you feel clearly *annoyed* by his actions and toward him.

The second mis-motivation of the discouraged student is the quest for *power*. The student will engage in a host of classroom disruptions, but when asked to stop, he will challenge your power and authority overtly, by defying you to your face or passively appearing to not see you and continuing with his misbehavior. His response to your request to stop is, "Let's see you make me!" You may use the strongest and most extreme forms of threats and punishments, but the power-seeking student is not fearful of any sanctions and appears to love the center stage that these punishments give him. The teacher's feeling toward this misbehaving student is one of feeling *beaten*. The power-seeking student will challenge your power and take any punishment and appear to delight in it.

The third mis-motivation for the discouraged student is feelings of *revenge*. The revengeful student will do physical or psychological damage to the teacher, fellow classmates, or the school and school building, and appear to take delight in hurting others. It is almost as if the revengeful student is saying, "I have been hurt by the world of others and I am going to get even!" These students are sometimes called the "hit-back-first kid." This means that the revengeful student, when first engaging in social activity with others, immediately concludes that the other person will not only reject him but will do him harm. Therefore, before such outcome can occur, he will hurt the other person first. A teacher will have clear feelings of being *hurt* by this student. At times, such students are psychologically skilled at finding sensitive personal characteristics and knowing how to offend or hurt by their actions and comments.

The fourth and final mis-motivation is that of *helplessness*. The student feels so rejected by others that he retreats into a passive shell, cutting himself off from others and wanting not to be seen or acknowledged. It is as if he is saying, "I know that I am unworthy. Please do not see me or draw attention to me in any way." Such a student will sit as a passive shadow in your classroom, not causing any disruption, and may go unseen because he does not cause any discipline difficulties. However, this is the student who is in the most serious difficulty and needs a clear intervention and encouragement. This is difficult for you, however, because the helpless student is so introverted and nonresponsive that he gives you feelings of *inadequacy* in educating or in dealing with him as a student.

So, the behavior of Ronald Foster is viewed by saying that Ronald is a discouraged student. Somewhere in his past development, he was unable to find basic acceptance, and has developed destructive patterns of behavior based on one of the four mis-motivations. This view, based on concepts of social membership, also gives added justification for the use of The Rights and Responsibility Game and team competition used within the Incentive System. The incentive team competition gives the student practice at being a member of a group.

Mr. Garcia knows that Ronald's motivation is not helplessness, but he may not be sure which of the other mis-motivations Ronald may be working from. In dealing with Ronald, Mr. Garcia would begin collecting data and observing Ronald in school and social settings. One of the central techniques is for the teacher to attempt to analyze how he truly feels toward Ronald. Does he, as the teacher, feel annoyed? (If so, the motivation may be attention getting.) Does he feel beaten? (If so, the motivation may be power.) Does he feel hurt by Ronald's actions? (If so, it is revenge.) Does he feel inadequate? (If so, it is helplessness.)

## Background Information

To begin, the teacher must determine which of the four faulty goals is motivating the student. This determination follows a four-step process, as follows:

1. The teacher observes and collects information about the student in situations involving peers and family.

2. Once the teacher has gathered information about the student, he or she can then hypothesize which of the underlying goals is held by the student.

3. The teacher can verify this hypothesis by reflecting on what feelings arise within the teacher as a result of the student's behavior.

4. Final verification is achieved by confronting the student with a series of four questions and looking for a recognition reflex by the student.

In carrying out this procedure, which will be done as part of the Backup System, the teacher moves through the Teacher Behavior Continuum behaviors of *Looking*, *Questioning*, *Commanding*, and *Acting*.

## Looking

Mr. Garcia, immediately faced with 31 pairs of eyes peering at him, disinvolves himself emotionally from Ronald's behavior. He has noted the first impression of rudeness, braggadocio, and flashiness that Ronald has created. Mr. Garcia makes a mental note to search for more information by checking school records, talking to former teachers, and possibly making a home visit. For now, though, with limited information, he suspects that Ronald's goal may be attention getting, power, or revenge. It certainly is not helplessness!

It is important to remain calm during the beginning encounter with a student operating under any of the faulty goals, and not to give the student what he or she seeks. For example, the worst thing Mr. Garcia could do would be to call out loudly and angrily to Ronald. To do so would give Ronald the attention he seeks (attention getting), or it would accelerate the battle of who will win out (power), or it would drive Ronald into physically lashing out (revenge).

Mr. Garcia can remain calm because he knows rationally that Ronald's behavior is not directed at him personally but is simply Ronald's previously learned mode of responding in groups. Of course, a quite human reaction by a teacher would be to explode, but this urge must be held in check. Examining this emotional urge or feeling toward the student will be most helpful in narrowing down and identifying the student's goal.

## Questioning (Clarifying Teacher Feelings)

Now Mr. Garcia can covertly assess the inner emotions that Ronald's behavior has evoked by asking himself four questions related to the goals:

1. Do I feel annoyed? If so, the teacher may have reason to suspect attention getting as a goal.

2. Do I feel beaten or intimidated? If so, Mr. Garcia may have reason to suspect power as a goal.

3. Do I feel wronged or hurt? If so, Mr. Garcia may have reason to suspect revenge as a goal.

4. Do I feel incapable of reaching the student in any way? If so, the teacher may have reason to suspect helplessness as the goal.

Mr. Garcia analyzes his feelings as *annoyed*, to say the least, and even slightly *intimidated*, which suggests that Ronald's goal was attention getting or power.

Let's see what Ronald's probable responses would have been if the teacher had given free rein to his first impulses. If Mr. Garcia had yelled at him, Ronald might have responded with, "Chill out, chill man, no need to lose it, just chill!" In other words, if Ronald's goal was power, he would have won at that point. He would have "shown up" Mr. Garcia in front of the class, revealing a teacher who becomes easily flustered while he, an 11-year-old student, was more of a man with calm and collected reactions. For the class members, this would be "show time." If, on the other hand, Ronald's goal was to get attention, he would have responded in a different way. Mr. Garcia's yells might have caused Ronald to put his head down sheepishly and grin to himself. The rest of the class would be observing Ronald, and as soon as Mr. Garcia turned away, Ronald's head would be back up, face smiling and looking around to make sure that everyone had seen him. In both cases, Mr. Garcia's primary reaction would have done little to prevent numerous future occurrences.

Mr. Garcia knows he can't play into the student's scheme and is ready now to take specific action. He makes a guess that Ronald's primary goal is to gain attention.

## Commanding

The previous reflective thinking and covert behaviors of *looking* and *questioning* were primarily done to gather information, to narrow down and identify the student's possible goal, and to make a tentative plan for action. A teacher trained in *The Three Faces of Discipline* approach would take only a split second from the time he first witnessed the girl running out of the classroom to the moment he begins action toward Ronald.

Having identified attention getting as Ronald's underlying goal, Mr. Garcia acts in a way that deprives Ronald of the attention related to his misbehavior. Because of the public nature of the results of Ronald's misbehavior, Mr. Garcia is forced to drop the Limit-Setting System and move to the Backup System.

*Mr. Garcia turns to the girl and quietly tells her to come back in the classroom when she is ready and to take another seat away from Ronald. He then turns to the class and states, "Class, I would like to introduce you to some of the special science equipment you will be using this year. In a few minutes I would like you to break up into groups of four people and gather around the tables at the back of the room. When you get settled, open to the first page of your manual, where you will find pictures of the various kinds of equipment. As a group, see if you can first learn the equipment names, then I will join each group briefly to demonstrate how to use some of the more dangerous equipment, such as the Bunsen burner. OK, class, find your groups of four and move to your tables." Turning to Ronald, he adds, "Oh, Ronald Foster, your behavior has told me that you are not ready to work with others. I want you to remain in your seat."*

Having tended to the class and taking away the students who could provide Ronald an audience, Mr. Garcia gives Ronald a command. For now, let's say that Mr. Garcia has employed as a logical consequence the loss of the student's right to engage in an activity as a result of behavior that would be counterproductive to performing that activity. Before Mr. Garcia can conclude definitely that attention getting is Ronald's goal and initiate a long-range plan based on that goal identification, the teacher needs further verification. He can achieve this by returning to overt questioning with Ronald.

## Questioning (Overt)

Ronald is seated alone, slouched down with his hat over his face for nearly half the period. This is a further sign that Mr. Garcia has correctly identified Ronald's goal. If Ronald had wanted power, he would have continued to defy the teacher's rules. If Ronald had wanted revenge, he would have physically retaliated against the girl or teacher.

Mr. Garcia eyes Ronald slowly getting out of his seat and moving toward the work table. There is only one spot open in the groups of four, and he heads toward that spot. When the trio notices that he is ready to join them, one of the girls at the table (the very one that Ronald annoyed) begins to complain and shout, "No, no, you don't! You're not joining our table, turkey." Ronald then turns to another nearby group and is greeted with, "You're not coming into our group. There is dangerous stuff here—you'll get us killed!" With a parting shot, "You're all a bunch of jerks," Ronald returns to his desk. Mr. Garcia moves toward him (*closing space*), takes a seat nearby (*proximity-near*), and, in a voice that cannot be heard by anyone else, begins to question Ronald.

> ***Mr. Garcia:*** *"Do you know why you acted like you did this morning?"* (confronting).
> ***Ronald:*** *(simply shrugs his shoulders)*
> ***Mr. Garcia:*** *"I have some ideas. Would you like to know?"*
> ***Ronald:*** *(nods yes)*
> ***Mr. Garcia:*** *"Could you want special attention?"* (verifying).
> ***Ronald:*** *(For the first time, his eyes look directly at Mr. Garcia, and he gives a slight smile)* (recognition reflex).

During a discussion in a calm setting, it is proposed that the teacher do as Mr. Garcia has done. You should ask the student if he is interested in knowing why he behaves as he does. If the student does not resist, ask one of four questions. Here are the central questions related to each mis-motivation:

| | |
|---|---|
| 1. (Attention) | Could it be that you want special attention? |
| 2. (Power) | Could it be that you want your own way and hope to be the boss? |
| 3. (Revenge) | Could it be that you want to hurt others as much as you feel hurt by them? |
| 4. (Helplessness) | Could it be that you want to be left alone? |

After you ask each of these questions, look (*Looking*) for behavioral verification. If the student smiles, laughs, looks up suddenly, moves his or her shoulders, or shows other signs of response to the implied goal, then you have conclusive evidence that your hypothesis is correct and actions can proceed. You may then formulate a plan and return to appropriate commanding.

Now that Ronald has given the recognition reflex, Mr. Garcia can be confident that attention is Ronald's goal. Mr. Garcia's task now becomes one of finding ways for Ronald to receive attention through constructive social behavior. In other words, he needs to give Ronald the attention that the boy craves. Following are descriptions of treatment for each of the four goals, with a corresponding prescriptive chart for teachers (see Figures 10–1 through 10–3).

**Attention**   A student who seeks attention should not receive it when he or she acts out. To give attention to the student for inappropriate behavior would be playing into the student's plan and would not help the student learn how to behave productively in the group. Instead, the teacher might use some of the techniques shown in Figure 10–1.

**Power**   A student who wishes to possess power should not be able to engage the teacher in a struggle. The teacher who falls for this "bait" and gets pulled into the battle is merely continuing the excitement and challenge for the student. The student becomes increasingly bolder and pleased with trying to test the teacher. The teacher should attempt to remove the issue of power altogether and force the student to look for some other goal for behaving.

**Revenge**   In this case, the teacher is dealing with a more difficult task. A student who feels hurt and wishes to retaliate must be handled in a caring, affectionate manner. It is probable that this student appears unloving and uncaring, and is very hard to "warm up to." But this is exactly what the student needs (to feel cared for). Figure 10–2 discusses some techniques that are helpful with students who seek power and/or revenge.

---

**FIGURE 10–1    Nonsocially Adaptive Students: Attention Getting**

| Student's Motivation | Behavior Characteristics | Teacher's Feelings |
|---|---|---|
| Attention Getting | Repetitively does actions to make him the center of attention. When asked to stop, will comply but will start again later. | Annoyed |

**Techniques with the Attention-Getting Student**

*Minimize the Attention*
Ignore the behavior.
Give "The Eye." (Look straight at the student until he stops.)
Stand and move physically close by. (Move into the personal space.)
Mention the student's name. (Called "low-profile desist" to make the student aware of his behavior but not disrupt the thought process of the other class members.)
Send a secret signal. (Wink or make a similar humorous nonverbal signal the student understands that says, "I see you and I recognize you," but continue your teaching.)
Give written notice. (Have previously made and stored in your lesson plan book small notes with a desist message, humorous if possible, and simply slip it to the student so there is no break in the continuity of your teaching.)
Give an I-message. (A statement containing the teacher's reference to himself or herself as *I*, and then the student's behavior, effect on the teacher, his or her feelings, and a request for the student to desist.)

*Legitimize the Behavior*
Make a lesson out of the behavior. (The math teacher makes spitball throwing permissible by making it a part of the lesson, with the students counting distances, graphing each person's throw, and teaching probability concepts related to hitting a target with the spitballs.)
Extend the behavior to its most extreme form. (A student making spitballs now must make 500. A student who is constantly out of his seat now must stand for the entire period.)
Have the whole class join in the behavior. (When a student does some annoying behavior, such as tapping pencils or burping, the entire class is asked to do so, stealing attention from the attention-getting misbehaving student.)
Use a diminishing quota. (Make a contract that the student can do the attention-getting behavior but 25 percent fewer times in the class period. Put a check on the board for each time he may do it, and while continuing to teach, keep erasing the checks until he runs out of his allotted quota. Continue every day from this point on, dropping the permitted number of times until the behavior becomes zero.)
Do the unexpected. (Steal the attention from the student.)
Turn out the lights.
Play a musical sound.
Lower your voice to a whisper.
Change your voice. (Pretend a silly accent.)
Talk to the wall. (Tell the wall that so-and-so is doing something specifically to get attention and you wish he or she would stop. This steals the attention from the attention-starved student.)

---

*(continued)*

---

**FIGURE 10–1    Nonsocially Adaptive Students: Attention Getting (continued)**

Use one-liners. (These are jokes, maybe about the teacher himself, that do not ridicule or make fun of students.)

Cease teaching temporarily. (Simply stop and say nothing until the attention-getting student stops. Students will stop and look at him but not in a supportive way.)

*Distract the Student*
Ask a direct question.
Ask a favor.
Change the activity.

*Notice Appropriate Behavior*
Thank the student.
Write well-behaved students' names on the chalkboard. (May or may not be a good idea for middle and high school students.)

*Move the Student*
Change the student's seat.
Send the student to the thinking chair. (This chair is located at the back of the room out of the view of other students.)

---

*Source: A Teacher's Guide to Cooperative Discipline: How to Manage Your Classroom and Promote Self-Esteem* (pp. 32–41) by L. Albert, 1989, Circle Pines, MN: American Guidance Service.

---

**FIGURE 10–2    Nonsocially Adaptive Students: Power and Revenge**

| Student's Motivation | Behavior Characteristics | Teacher's Feelings |
|---|---|---|
| Power | Repetitively does behavior to make him the center of attention. When asked to stop, he becomes defiant and escalates his negative behavior and challenges the adult. | Annoyed |
| Revenge | Hurts others physically or psychologically. | Hurt |

**Techniques with the Power and Revengeful Student**

*Make a Graceful Exit*
Acknowledge the student's power. (You may actually say, "You can beat me on this—I have no wish to take you on!")

*Remove the Audience*
Table the matter. (State that you will not deal with this now, but at a later date, decided by you. You can then calm down and assert your power in a different context on your ground.)
Make a date. (Tell the student when you wish to deal with him—time and place).

Use a Fogging[a] Technique
Agree with the student. (Revengeful student: "You're an ugly bitch!" Teacher: "Well, I probably wouldn't win a beauty contest.")
Change the subject.

*Use Time Out*
Time out in the classroom.
Time out in another classroom.
Time out in the office.
Time out in the home.

*Set the Consequence*
Loss or delay of activity.
Loss or delay of using objects or equipment.
Loss or delay of access to school areas.
Denied interactions with other students.
Required interactions with school personnel.
Required interaction with parents.
Required interaction with police.
Restitution:
   Repair of objects.
   Replacement of objects.[b]

*Sources:*
[a] *Your Perfect Right: A Guide to Assertive Behavior* by R. Alberti and M. L. Emmons, 1978, San Luis Obispo, CA: Imact Publishers.
[b] *A Teacher's Guide to Cooperative Discipline: How to Manage Your Classroom and Promote Self-Esteem* (pp. 72–83) by L. Albert, 1989, Circle Pines, MN: American Guidance Service.

**FIGURE 10–3    Nonsocially Adaptive Students: Helplessness (avoidance-of-failure)**

| Student's Motivation | Behavior Characteristics | Teacher's Feelings |
|---|---|---|
| Helplessness | Wishes not to be seen; passive and lethargic, rejects social contact; refuses to comply or try most educational demands. | Inadequate, Incapable |

**Techniques with the Helpless (avoidance-of-failure) Student**

*Modify Instructional Methods*
Use concrete learning materials and computer-assisted instruction.
Teach one step at a time.
Provide tutoring.
Extra help from teachers.
Remediation programs.
Adult volunteers.
Peer tutoring.
Learning centers.

*(continued)*

---

**FIGURE 10–3   Nonsocially Adaptive Students: Helplessness (avoidance-of-failure) (continued)**

---

*Teach Positive Self-Talk*
Post positive classroom signs. (Posted in the classroom are signs such as "I can do it!" or "With a little effort, I'll succeed," etc.)
Require two "put-ups" for every put-down. (Make a rule that for every negative statement that the student says out loud, he or she must say two positive statements.)
Encourage positive self-talk before beginning tasks. (When a task is given, require the discouraged student to make two positive "I can" statements into a tape recorder.)

*Make Mistakes Okay*
Talk about mistakes.
Equate mistakes with effort.
Minimize the effect of making mistakes.

*Build Confidence*
Focus on improvement.
Notice contributions.
Build on strengths.
Show faith in students.
Acknowledge the difficulty of a task.
Set time limits on tasks.

*Focus on Past Success (remind student of past successes)*
Analyze past success.
Repeat past success.

*Make Learning Tangible*
"I-Can" cans.
Accomplishment Albums.
Checklists of skills.
Flowchart of concepts.
Talk about yesterday, today, and tomorrow.
Recognize achievement.
Applause.
Clapping and standing ovations.
Stars and stickers.
Awards and assemblies.
Exhibits.
Positive time-out.
Self-approval.

---

*Source: A Teacher's Guide to Cooperative Discipline: How to Manage Your Classroom and Promote Self-Esteem* (pp. 98–104) by L. Albert, 1989, Circle Pines, MN: American Guidance Service.

**Helplessness**   The student who shows inadequacy or helplessness is the most discouraged. He or she has lost all initiative for ever trying to belong to the group. The teacher must exercise great patience and attempt to show the student that he or she is capable. Some practices that might assist a helpless student are discussed in Figure 10–3.

Returning now to our vignette:

*Ronald is obviously interested in Mr. Garcia's suggestion that he (Ronald) is seeking attention, but he jars Mr. Garcia back to the immediate situation with a sarcastic, "Well, that sounds cool, but there's one big problem. I can't do all these things without equipment, and no one wants me in their group. What do you suggest? Maybe you'll buy me my own table?"*

Mr. Garcia, as a teacher, knows that he must capitalize on using the group as a model to help Ronald adjust. Mr. Garcia informs Ronald that at the end of class today, and on every Friday, there will be a short class meeting—a plus/delta meeting—to discuss problems that are of concern to the members of the class. He adds that Ronald could bring up his problem at that time and see what he and the class might work out.

The Three Faces of Discipline orientation is that schools and classrooms, as part of a democratic society, need to be models or laboratories of that society. In other words, students need to practice democratic principles in school in order to learn how to contribute later to society as a whole. The central process for carrying out this modeling of democracy is the use of the class meeting, which Mr. Garcia refers to as the plus/delta meeting. Regular meetings should be held to discuss everyday occurrences as well as long-range policies.

Voting should be avoided, as it has a tendency to alienate the minority. Instead, decisions should be made through arriving at a consensus of all members. When many people agree with a decision, peer pressure tends to influence the one or two "holdouts" and thus makes the decision unanimous. (We see this at political party conventions. After a hard battle among several candidates, one individual finally emerges a winner and all opposition evaporates. A united party once again emerges.) Let's see how Mr. Garcia capitalizes on the group process.

*Mr. Garcia calls the students back to their seats and tells them that, in his classes, he always has a class meeting on Fridays for the last 20 minutes of the school day. However, since this is the first week of a new school year and they have a lot of problems to work out, they will have a meeting every day this week, beginning today. The class is then encouraged to begin an open general discussion. One or two students bring up different problems pertaining to missing playground equipment, how they are going to be graded, and what to do if they forget their lunch money.*

*Finally, Ronald raises his hand, and everyone turns to look at him. "I have no equipment and I'm in no group." The girl he previously embarrassed shouts, "Serves you right." Mr. Garcia interjects, "What Ronald has done is in the past. What can we do about his not having a group to join?" The class begins in earnest to discuss the issue. Most students express the feeling that if Ronald has no equipment, he cannot pass the activity and that would be unfair. Some students ask members of the trio if they would let Ronald into their group. Again, the girl who had been embarrassed states, "No way! He will bug us and keep us from our work. He is dangerous!" However, the other two members of the group say they would be willing to work with him on a trial basis. Finally, after much discussion, it is decided that the girl will change places with a student in another group and Ronald would now have three people with whom he can work at the science table. Ronald appears greatly relieved to hear this decision.*

Up to this point, everything seems to have been resolved. But what happens if Ronald continues to misbehave? What recourse does the teacher or class have? To answer these questions, we need to look at logical consequences.

## REINFORCEMENT

Although some approaches to discipline rely on the use of punishment, negative reinforcement, praise, or positive reinforcement, some experts substitute natural/logical consequences and the process of encouragement. Each of these will be explained as it applies to Ronald.

### Natural/Logical Consequences

If Ronald should create a commotion after becoming accepted in the group, he could be disciplined as a result of some of the following logical consequences:

1. Have the group of three decide what should be done with Ronald.

2. Have Ronald work alone and have him use the laboratory equipment on his own time (at lunch, during recess, after school).

3. Bring Ronald's misbehavior back to the entire class in a classroom meeting to decide on future consequences.

Specifically, for Ronald, this means:

1. If Ronald has been causing a disturbance by poking students with a pencil, take away all of his pencils and tell Ronald that whenever he needs to write, he'll have to come to the teacher's desk to ask for a pencil.

2. If Ronald has been constantly moving out of his chair and distracting others, tell Ronald that he does not seem to need a chair and take it away from him. Let him stand until he requests to have it back and promises to stay in it.

A *natural consequence* is defined as that which happens as a result of one's behavior. If a student is rushing to get into line and trips and falls, this is called a natural consequence. On the other hand, if a student is rushing and pushing others in order to be first in line and is removed by the teacher to a place at the end of the line, then this would be identified as a logical consequence. In other words, a *natural consequence* is an inevitable occurrence that happens by itself, whereas a *logical consequence* is arranged but directly related to the preceding behavior. The Three Faces of Discipline position is that, in a democratic classroom, students must be responsible for how they behave. There is no room for autocratic punishment that further alienates and discourages a student. Extensive punishment serves as a force to drive a student toward the goal of revenge. Punishment is not seen as being logically related to a student's behavior. It is inflicted as a reaction to personal dissatisfaction felt by the teacher. Punishment says to the student, "You had better behave or I (the teacher) will make life miserable for you." If the student does "knuckle under," it is because of the power of the teacher and not because the student has learned how to be a productive member of the group. If one accepts the Three Faces definition of human behavior as a purposeful attempt to belong, then a teacher who uses punishment blocks a student's purpose. Punishment plays back into the student's misdirected goals. It gives attention, enhances the power struggle, stimulates further revenge, and keeps the helpless student in his or her place.

Additionally, many of today's students are not easily coerced by the use of authoritarian power. Not only does punishment thwart a student's ambition but it simply does not work. Let us further explore the operational distinction between punishment and natural/logical consequences. Sending a student home with a note, keeping him or her after school, paddling, scolding, ridiculing, or standing the student in a corner are all forms of physical or psychological punishment. The teacher's actions are aimed at hurting the student or making him or her feel bad. Punishment is the teacher's vengeance for a committed "crime." On the other hand, students who clean up the mess they created, who are put at the end of the line for shoving, who miss a special rally because of tardiness with their assigned work, or who are barred from using certain materials until they choose to use them properly are all actually involved in the effects of logical consequences. Logical consequences are not always easy to tailor to every disruptive action. However, it is the teacher's task to arrange the situation that follows the disruption in a way that the student can see a relationship between the consequences and his or her behavior.

Finally, it is important to note the differences in a teacher's attitude and manner in the application of logical consequences as opposed to the act of punishment. Two teachers might arrive at the same solution for a problem caused by a student's behavior, but one will be an example of logical consequences and the other will be an example of punishment. Sounds confusing, but it really isn't! For example, during quiet work time, Sue Ann continually pokes Ernie with a pencil. One teacher, Mr. Matter-of-Fact, tells the girl, "Sue Ann, if you do that again, you are showing that you cannot control your pencil, and I will need to take it from you. You will be able to finish your work here in the classroom while others are on the playground." The other teacher, "Mr. How-Dare-You," says, "Sue Ann, I have told you a thousand times not to do that. Can't you understand anything? If I catch you once more, I'll take all your pencils away and you'll stay in at recess. Maybe being alone is the only way that you can work!" Mr. Matter-of-Fact has calmly told the student to use the pencil correctly or give it up. Mr. How-Dare-You acts as though he has been personally affected and that Sue Ann's misbehavior is a direct challenge to his authority. He tries to hammer her down by scolding, questioning her competence, and challenging her. The same outcome has occurred—the student has had the pencil confiscated—but Mr. Matter-of-Fact has used logical consequences and Mr. How-Dare-You has applied punishment.

## Encouragement

At the same time that the class and Mr. Garcia are applying logical consequences to Ronald's behavior, Mr. Garcia is also using the encouragement process. Mr. Garcia asks Ronald to keep inventory of all playground equipment. Mr. Garcia also makes a mental note to greet Ronald warmly each day.

The encouragement process is an attitude taken with a misbehaving student that results in a climate of respect and optimism. One must remember that a student whose goal is attention feels stifled by authority and may retreat to the even more destructive power seeking. When that goal is "beaten down" by an overbearing, punitive teacher, the student may then resort to the goal of revenge to retaliate. When revenge is crushed by ever more coercive means, we may finally have the most pathetic result—a student who has simply given up and has internalized the goal of helplessness. This lowering of goals is the result of a student becoming further discouraged. Not only does the student retreat further back into gloom and despair, but so does the teacher. The vicious cycle compounds the problem.

The role of the teacher is to stop this dissipation of hope by using encouragement. This is accomplished by teacher actions such as:

- Emphasize improvement rather than a perfect product.

- Criticize the student's actions, but not the student (i.e., "I like you but I don't like to hear you shouting").

- Keep the student in a group with other students who are willing to help. Determine those peers who are most accepting and tolerant of the student in question. Seat the student with them and arrange for him or her to work with them in groups. Find a companion or friend for the student.

- Refrain from having the student compete against others. Do not compare the student to others ("Why can't you behave like Walter?") or constantly single out or praise others who outperform the youngster. Deemphasize grades; try to grade the student on effort and growth, not rank in relation to others. Avoid contests for the best-behaved student or citizen of the week, where the student has little chance of winning.

Praise as a way of promoting positive reinforcement is generally not a desirable method. Encouragement is much broader than behavior modification's use of verbal praise or material/situation rewards as conditioning to achieve appropriate behavior. More than three decades ago, Dinkmeyer and Dreikurs wrote, "Unfortunately, even the well meaning and sincere educator may often fail to convey much needed encouragement if he tries to express his approval through praise. . . . Praise may have a discouraging effect in the long run, since the student may depend on it constantly and never be quite sure whether he will merit another expression of special approval and get it."

Dinkmeyer and Dreikurs, on whose work this Encouragement System is based, are not saying that praise should be totally avoided, but rather that too much praise makes a student dependent on the teacher. The student who is "won over" by the teacher to work quietly due to the teacher's praise ("Oh, look at Hillary! What a fine student to be working so quietly! I am so proud that you are being so quiet.") has not learned social behavior. Instead of learning how to act out of consideration for others, the student instead is learning how to act for purposes of receiving the teacher's special compliments and dispensations. In other words, the student behaves well, but for all the wrong reasons. If the teacher is removed from the scene, the student's behavior will deteriorate. The student needs to internalize the correct motivation for being well behaved (acting as a productive member of the group) in order for it to be lasting.

In addition, the student who sees himself or herself as a failure and is motivated by revenge or helplessness will tend to disbelieve the authenticity of the teacher's words. A student who refuses to work and gives up on carrying out any order may have reason to speculate on why the teacher makes such an effort to praise him or her ("Oh, Sam, look what a good job you did! You make me so pleased when you hang your coat up!" Or, "Margie, it's great the way that you answered that question!"). The student will, in effect, believe that the teacher is overcompensating and that he or she is being singled out because he or she is indeed inferior. The student may think, "Why make such a big deal about hanging my coat up or answering a simple question? The teacher must think I'm a real loser." Thus, the result will be the opposite of what the teacher intended (a further sign that reaffirms the student's sense of inferiority). In this vein of thought, Dreikurs and Grey wrote of the fundamental difference between the act of reward and the act of encouragement. Few realize that, at times, success can be very discouraging. The student may conclude that, although success was achieved once, it could not happen again. The student's recent "success" may become a threat to his or her future ability to succeed. Worse, such an event often conveys to the student the assumption (actually shared by most of his or her teachers and fellow students) that he or she is worthwhile only when he or she is successful.

What we have, then, is the premise that praise or other forms of reward seem to heighten a student's anxiety always to have to "measure up." It puts constraints on a student who feels such pressure. He or she feels comfortable only when being successful. The discomfort with being unsuccessful further discourages a student from feelings of being accepted and of being an acceptable person. He or she feels accepted only when successful, but not when something less than success occurs as a result of efforts expended. The student who needs to learn to be a member must learn to accept his or her individual self as being a person capable of both success and failure but who, despite outcomes, is still worthy of being loved and accepted by others.

A student who is always dependent on being rewarded for what he or she does is in a bind when it comes to taking a risk. The individual who is learning how to belong must be encouraged to try new ways of behaving. The student who learns that it is safe and rewarding to be meek and passive will not easily venture into the unknown by being assertive and active. He or she won't venture into untried areas. This is the danger of having "fail-proof" programs or "praise-laden" teachers.

The teacher must not stress the concept of success, but instead promote a climate of always accepting the student as worthwhile. This happens when a teacher uses encouragement rather than reinforcement as praise. Following are two contrasting lists that give examples of praise versus encouragement. Praise focuses on the teacher being pleased by the student and on the student achieving a completed product. Conversely, encouragement focuses on the student and on the process of the student trying.

| **Praise** | **Encouragement** |
|---|---|
| "I (teacher) like what you have done." | "You're trying harder." |
| "Great job! What a smart person you are." | "You must be happy with (playing that game, being with others, etc.)." |
| "You get a star (token, free time) for doing that." | "It must be a good feeling to know you're doing well." |
| | "You have every reason to be proud." |

## ACTING AND ISOLATION

Forms of teacher intervention such as paddling or shaking a student must be rejected. Such treatment is seen as a form of punishment that would drive a student further away from social cooperation. Discomfort experienced as a natural consequence (without the possibility of serious harm) may be allowed. Some examples of this might be the student who rushes to be first in line and in his or her haste falls and is bruised, or the student who repeatedly provokes the class gerbil and is bitten. On the other hand, there are some natural consequences that can follow when a student precariously tilts back in the chair, or when a "90-pound weakling" begins to taunt and enrage a 250-pound high school football tackle. These could be dangerous consequences, and the teacher would be wise to prevent them from occurring. It is important to note that a teacher should carefully judge the natural consequence before deciding to act or not act in a given situation.

Isolation, through various forms of time out, must also be used judiciously by the teacher. The Three Faces of Discipline advocates the use of isolation only as a logical consequence. We saw that Ronald was isolated temporarily by Mr. Garcia when his behavior was immediately disruptive of others. However, Ronald was given the opportunity to rejoin the group once he decided that he wished to belong.

It is evident that if being part of a group is the ultimate goal for all individuals, then each person needs to learn to relate successfully to others. A student only learns such relationships by practicing appropriate behaviors with others; he or she does not learn cooperation by being lectured to or having to sit alone. For these reasons, instead of relying on isolation, the teacher is required to look constantly for ways to encourage attachments between the offending student and other members of the class.

## ENCOURAGEMENT AND THE OUTSIDE AGGRESSOR

*In art class, the students are allowed to select their own seats among the many tables in the room. Five girls have been sitting together at a round table for four weeks so far. Amy, a pleasant new student at the school, has been sitting by herself but has started to become friendly with some of the girls at the "in" table. After class, Marcia, one of the girls at the table, tells Amy to make sure to get to art class early tomorrow and to grab a seat at the round table. She confides that she and three others will also be early so they can all sit together. The next day, Amy and the four girls are already seated by the time Julie, a past member, walks in. She seems startled and walks up to Amy and says, "Pardon me, but you're in my seat!" Amy isn't too sure what to say and looks around at the other girls who are smiling at her. Marcia looks up at Julie and says, "We've invited Amy to join us. I'm sure you can find somewhere else to sit where you'll fit in." Stunned, Julie walks away.*

*During art class that same day, the teacher is placing paints before Julie when one pot accidentally tips and spills, making a small yellow paint mark on Julie's blouse. Julie shouts at her teacher, "Look what you did, you damn stupid old cow!" The entire class quiets while "the gang" giggles and laughs at Julie.*

The incident with Julie and "the gang" shows clearly that Julie has lost her past friends and companions and is now being socially isolated. The Three Faces of Discipline position would be that Julie's acting out (the verbal aggression, "you old cow") was a result of built-up revengeful feelings being directed at an innocent party: the teacher. All misbehavior by children in your classroom—whether attention-getting power acts, revengeful acts, or passive behavior—is seen by the Three Faces as a failure to find social acceptance. However, rarely does one get such a clear observation as in the Julie incident to actually verify this position. Instead, one typically sees a repetitive host of misbehaviors and aggressive actions that on the surface do not appear to be related to immediate behavior by other children. For example, a student hits other students without any provocation. Children's first feelings of acceptance come out of the home setting with parents and siblings. If they felt they were rejected in early family interaction, they assume that they will be rejected in a classroom situation and will set out with negative actions *to prove* that others do not like them.

The less skilled teacher might bring "the gang" aside and verbally reprimand and lecture them for their actions, applying large doses of guilt for their behavior. Such actions might unknowingly make members of "the gang" even more hostile to Julie, and now they will be revengeful toward her in more subtle ways that the teacher will not see or detect. Instead, Julie needs to acquire social skills that will enable her to find acceptance.

This is another example of the phenomenon of the outside aggressor, first introduced in Chapter 5. The teacher may employ a number of techniques to be proactive in helping children acquire social skills to overcome this potentially significant problem. Reaction to the outside aggressor is an expectable, normal behavior among students. The teacher's role, of course, is to develop ways through which students can learn to be social in a more healthy manner and to help children like Julie find belonging and acquire social skills. This can be done through beneficial use of social engineering.

## SOCIAL ENGINEERING

*After the "we don't want you in our group" incident, but before any outburst such as the "you old cow" verbal aggression could occur, Mrs. Anderson calls Julie to the art table. She has seen Julie being made the outside aggressor and summons her in a voice loud enough for "the gang" to hear. She states, "Julie, we are going to make the centerpiece for the holiday pageant, and I am going to let you be the chairperson of this project. You may choose helpers to work with you!" Every member of the class is eager to be on this committee, and everyone begins waving hands to be chosen. Julie chooses six nearby students. Members of "the gang" see what is happening. Their facial expressions show that their excitement has been deflated, and they begin to wander over to the art table and look on as this new project is being organized. They loiter about, and then gradually plead in a whining voice, "Mrs. Anderson, can we be on the committee, too?" The teacher responds, "I don't know. I am not the chairperson of this project—Julie is! You will have to ask her."*

*The gang approaches Julie and asks, "Can we join your committee?" Julie hesitates for a few seconds, then smiles and says yes. The teacher hovers nearby, watching all the committee members working on the art arrangement, her presence helping Julie to maintain her power. Later, when the pageant programs are printed, Julie's name is listed as the chair of this committee, and she has her photograph taken while working on the project for the local newspaper and classroom scrapbook. During a subsequent class discussion, Mrs. Anderson will encourage other students to express their joy at being a part of the project and working under Julie's leadership* (encouragement).

In the use of *social engineering*, the teacher considers a student who is acting out or misbehaving and views that student as being powerless, lacking the skill to find social belonging. The teacher deliberately "engineers" or sets up activities whereby children such as Julie are empowered and helps them enjoy the experience of successfully working within a group. The teacher deliberately points out to classmates, genuinely, how the student has given and contributed to making the classroom a happy and accepting place.

Thus, you deliberately engineer positive experiences for misbehaving children. After the centerpiece experience, you may question Julie with Confronting-Contracting "what" questions, such as, "Julie, what did you do as committee chair? What worked for you as you worked with friends? What did not? What will you do next time when you want friends?" Notice that you do *not* tell Julie how well she did, or make any value judgments, or offer a prescription for her in further interactions. Through your questions and counseling of children who are having social difficulty, you want them to become reflective after social experiences, to become consciously aware of their own behavior, to evaluate their success, and to come up with ideas of how they may be even more effective the next time.

---

## FRIENDSHIP CHARTS (SOCIOGRAMS)[2]

Since the Three Faces theory places membership and belonging as the primary motivator, teachers may wish to study the social makeup of the class with the use of a Friendship Chart (sociogram, see Figure 10–4). This may be done by asking the students to state preferences for other members of the class in response to such questions as: Who would you like to sit beside? Who would you like to work with on an art project or math problems? Which student would you most like to visit at home? Which boys or girls do you like least? Based on the results, the teacher constructs a diagram similar to Figure 10–4.

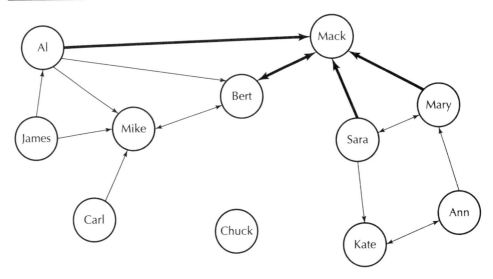

**FIGURE 10–4   Friendship Chart**

*Symbols*

A ←————— B:   B chooses A, but A does not mention B

A ←————→ B:   A and B choose each other

A ■————▶ B:   A dislikes B

A ◀■————▶ B:   A and B dislike each other

*Explanation*

There is a clique centering around Mike, as leader.

Al is a *fringer* in this group; only James has chosen him.

Carl, James, and Chuck are both *isolates*; neither has been chosen by other students.

Mack is a *reject*; two boys and two girls dislike him, and he has no friends.

There are three pairs of mutually chosen friends (Sara and Mary, Kate and Ann, and Mike and Bert).

There are two boys who mutually dislike each other (Bert and Mack).

*Definition of Terms*: *fringers* may consider themselves a member of a group but are chosen only by one member of the group; *isolates* have no close friends; *rejects* are disliked by others

Even the best designed social engineering plan cannot be expected to eliminate all problems associated with children who are at risk of becoming outside aggressors. If you look closely at the problem child's classmates and school personnel, you can begin to see that after a period of time you may have unintentionally made this child the outside aggressor in your classroom. He or she gets blamed by *all* students and staff for *all* accidents and negative occurrences. Others, including teachers, do not want him at their table or sitting near them at social events. Most everyone, including adults, has unknowingly begun a process of "shunning" the problem student.

This shunning and unwanted status as the object of the outside aggressor phenomenon now severely complicates the intervention and dynamics of ever helping this student to change. The difficult student has dug a deep social hole that he will never be able to climb out of by himself. You must now address a new question: How can you reduce or even eliminate this collective anger and shunning toward the student?

## THE MOST WANTED

A staff meeting, as described in Chapter 8, must be called to involve all adults who come into daily contact with the difficult student. (If you are one teacher by yourself, you may need to sit down during a quiet period and in essence have this meeting with yourself.) At the start of this meeting, it might be helpful if members of the group of adults are permitted some time to express their honest feelings toward the student. Staff members who are frightened by their own negative feelings toward the difficult student might receive some reassurance if they hear a skilled and respected teacher state, "I am wondering how you are feeling about Ronald Foster these days. I must confess that at times I find myself getting angry and even frightened by him. At times I don't want him in my class, and at times I am having a hard time liking him." The first step in changing the staff's negative behavior toward a difficult student is to get honest feelings "out on the table."

As already noted, the problem student has dug a deep social hole that he cannot climb out of by himself. Because he feels rejected, he sits about day in and day out, his negative actions evoking further rejection from classmates and adults. The problem student is still in the formative years of development, and these years—along with the stormy adolescent years rapidly approaching—are the most robust years for making an impact on his development that will serve him—or misserve him—for the remainder of his life. As the expression goes, "Love begins with love!" The very nature of your job, and *your central role* as teacher, is to make a lasting contribution to these difficult children. Almost all adults can recall one significant experience where a teacher befriended and helped them at a difficult point in their life. You, as a teacher, must understand what a lasting impression this can have and how it can produce long-term positive results for the student's well-being.

That is the challenge—and the opportunity—before you as you deal with this one particularly difficult problem student. If you do not do it, who will? Literally anyone can teach a student who has been well mothered and fathered, but it is the difficult student who enables you to "earn your stripes" as a teacher. This is a big responsibility but you may be this student's only and last hope—for once he gets into the real adult world, rarely will he find another person willing to take the time to help him.

Now, exactly how do you do this? You do it in a staff meeting by using the Confronting-Contracting procedures. You ask, "What am I and his classmates really doing to Ronald Foster?" The answer is that you are, unknowingly, shunning him and making him the outside aggressor. You want most staff members to verbally express past incidents in which they have moved away from this problem student. Mrs. Anderson confesses, "I am embarrassed to admit it, but one time when I was seated at the table with a group of students, we had one chair remaining at our table. I saw Ronald approaching, and—again, I'm embarrassed to admit it—but I grabbed another student and had him take this free seat so that Ronald would not be at my table." This outward admission is most important! (The teacher working alone might want to write this out.) Mrs. Anderson's candor may then encourage other staff members to share similar experiences or feelings.

The next question is, "What can be done to change?" The answer is that for the next two weeks, Mrs. Anderson will put Ronald, as her difficult problem student, on the Most Wanted list. Unlike a police Most Wanted list, however, this list will single Ronald out for special *positive* behavior. Perhaps you have witnessed the behavior of staff and students when you had a visiting student, maybe from another country. Visitors enjoy special status while spending the day in the classroom. Everyone rolls out the "red carpet" for them: They are greeted warmly at the door, shown where to be seated, and told how and where things work. Placing your difficult student on a Most Wanted list means treating him as an honored guest throughout a two-week period. When every staff member—even those who do not have him in their group or classes—sees the difficult student passing by, they are to say hello, make eye contact, say the student's name, and make some pleasant verbal overture. The teacher helps him and invites him to be a part of any group activities. During *every* time period throughout the day for the two weeks, some adult should be helping the student as if he were new to school procedures and practices—a stranger visiting without friends. At any discussion groups involving the entire class, the teacher will point out to classmates any and all positive behavior by the difficult student as statements of encouragement.

Almost as if a whistle has been blown, all adults deliberately change their behavior toward the difficult student. If you, as the teacher, don't change, then classmates and the student himself cannot change. You thus help the problem student "climb out" of the deep social hole in which he was imprisoned by changing the entire social environment in the school. At first, you are likely to feel phony acting in such a manner, but you must push through such feelings and commit yourself to perform these "motor actions." A campaign of welcoming the student day in and day out can have a real impact to change a problem student's behavior and help him gain a feeling of acceptance. In contrast, if you do social engineering techniques (described previously) but the school climate— the actions of the other adults and classmates—still shuns the difficult student as an object of outside aggression, it will be unlikely that progress can be made. At the end of the two-week period of the Most Wanted program, another staff meeting must be held. This will be a follow-up meeting to evaluate the success or lack of success of the welcoming process. The remainder of the staff meeting should follow the Six Steps to Staffing (described in Chapter 8) in which teachers and staff focus on the student's problem behaviors and address what actions can be taken by each of them individually to deal with misbehavior. Also, it is given that the welcoming and accepting attitude toward the difficult student should and must continue, even if not in such a ritualistic manner.

## THE ENCOURAGEMENT PLAN

An Encouragement Planning Form (Figure 10–5) is provided to guide the teacher through the planning process for establishing a clear plan to encourage one particular student. Each step requires the teacher to take some action, then write the results on the form, thus using the concepts of mis-motivation, questions that the teacher would ask herself, thinking through actions for social acceptance, and other concepts previously described.

| FIGURE 10–5   Encouragement Planning Form | |
|---|---|
| Name of Student | Date |
| Step (a) Observe and describe the student's behavior. | Step (b) Ask oneself, "Do I feel…" |
| 1. | |
| | (check one)___annoyed?  ___beaten? ___incapable? |
| 2. | |
| | (check one)___annoyed?  ___beaten? ___incapable? |
| 3. | |
| | (check one)___annoyed?  ___beaten? ___incapable? |
| Steps (1) and (2) Confront the student (write your verbal statements): | |
| | |
| Step (3) Verify the goal ("Could it be that you want: special attention, to be the boss, to hurt others, to be left alone?") | What is the student's goal?: |
| Step (4) Make a plan | |
| | |
| | |
| | |
| Step (5) Use the classroom group ("How could a class meeting/discussion enlist peers to help?") | |
| | |
| | |
| | |
| | |

*(continued)*

| FIGURE 10–5    Encouragement Planning Form *(continued)* | |
|---|---|
| Step (6) State natural/logical consequences to be used. | Step (7) State encouragement strategy. |
| 1. | 1. |
| | |
| | |
| | |
| 2. | 2. |
| | |
| | |
| | |
| 3. | 3. |
| | |
| | |
| | |
| Step (8) Describe social engineering strategies: | Describe a Most Wanted strategy |
| | |
| | |
| | |
| | |
| | |
| | |
| | |
| | |

## SUMMARY

The central position of the Three Faces of Discipline model is that students need to find acceptance or membership with others. The Rights and Responsibility Game serves as a start-of-the-year school process to deliberately structure this gaming activity to teach all students ways to gain group membership. The Encouragement System is a process of focusing on the one or two very difficult students who the Incentive System fails to help. The teacher now views the student as needing encouragement. The Teacher Behavior Continuum (Figure 10–6) summarizes the steps that teachers may use to help such students. These steps begin with observing and gathering data on the student, then determining the goal that motivates the misbehaving student. Finally, the teacher sets out a plan to help meet this goal in a socially acceptable manner.

# FIGURE 10–6  Teacher Behavior Continuum and Encouragement System

| Looking | Naming | Questioning | Commanding | Modeling | Reinforcement | Acting and Isolation |
|---|---|---|---|---|---|---|
| (a) observe and collect information about the student<br>• with peers<br>• with family<br>• with other teachers | | (b) Ask oneself "Do I feel..."<br>(1) "annoyed?" (Attention getting)<br>(2) "beaten?" (Power)<br>(3) "hurt?" (Revenge)<br>(4) "incapable?" (Helplessness) | (1) According to the hypothesized goal, give logical consequence. ("Class, continue. Ronald, you have shown by your behavior that you are not ready to join the group.") | (5) Use the classroom as an example of democratic living. Allow classmates to discuss and propose ways to help the student. | (6) Natural/logical consequences<br>• do not punish<br>• arrange outcome as immediately related to student misbehavior | Use as a natural/logical consequence and/or in times of danger |
| (c) Recognition reflex after verifying questions (smiles, laughs, looks up, shrugs shoulders, etc.) | | (2) Confronting "Do you want to know why you are behaving like this?" | | | (7) Encouragement<br>• Recognize student's attempts to improve, not the end product ("You are trying...")<br>• Avoid teacher praise ("I like what you have done...") | |
| | | (3) Verifying "could it be that you want...<br>• special attention"<br>• to be the boss"<br>• to hurt others"<br>• to be left alone" | (4) Make a plan according to the verified goal. | | | |

# References

Albert, L. (1989). *A Teacher's Guide to Cooperative Discipline: How to Manage Your Classroom and Promote Self-Esteem*. Circle Pines, MN: American Guidance Service.

Dinkmeyer, D., & Dreikurs, R. (1963). *Encouraging Children to Learn: The Encouragement Process*. Englewood Cliffs, NJ: Prentice-Hall.

Dreikurs, R. (1964). *Children: The Challenge*. New York: Hawthorn Books.

Dreikurs, R. (1968). *Psychology in the Classroom: A Manual for Teachers*, 2nd. ed. New York: Harper & Row.

Dreikurs, R. (1972). *Discipline Without Tears: What to Do with Children Who Misbehave*. New York: Hawthorn Books.

Dreikurs, R., & Loren, G. (1968). *Logical Consequences*. New York: Meredith Press.

**Books written for parents on the STEP Program (Adlerian-Dreikurs based theory):**

Dinkmeyer, D., and McKay, G. D. (1976). *Systematic Training for Effective Parenting (STEP)*. Circle Pines, MN: American Guidance Service.

Dinkmeyer, D., & McKay, G. D. (1981). *Padres Eficaces Con Entrenamiento Sistematico (PECES)*. Circle Pines, MN: American Guidance Service.

Dinkmeyer, D., & McKay, G. D. (1983). *Systematic Training for Effective Parenting of Teens (STEP/Teen)*. Circle Pines, MN: American Guidance Service.

Dreikurs, R. (1964). *Children: The Challenge*. New York: E. P. Dutton.

# Endnotes

1. Isaacs, S. (1972). *Social Development in Young Children*. New York: Schocken Books.

2. Redl, F., & Wattenberg, W. W. (1951). *Mental Hygiene in Teaching*. New York: Harcourt, Brace, pp. 209–211.

# The Management System

Discipline is not affected only by what goes on within the classroom; it is also affected by the classroom itself. How the room is set up and how the teacher makes classroom resources available to students will have a profound impact on the kind of discipline that will be necessary—and effective—with the students who will spend their school year within that room.

The key method of eliminating many discipline problems is understanding and skillfully using the technology of management of (1) the design of classroom objects, furniture, and materials; (2) the establishment and teaching of rules; and (3) the method and techniques for beginning the school year and orienting the students to integrate all of the systems previously learned.

In short, a very direct correlation exists between the effective use of skilled management techniques and the prevention of many of the typical discipline incidents that disrupt the school day and year. The Management System provides these techniques.

# 11

## Design of the Classroom

The scene is a round table at which a group of five second-grade boys is seated for art class. The art teacher places eight large markers and a collection of art paper and materials in the middle of the table for the boys to use. A marker rolls across the table and falls to the floor, and four of the boys pursue it. They are now out of their chairs and underneath the table, scrambling on hands and knees to find the runaway marker. Two boys find it at the same time, and now fight over who it belongs to. A third student hits his head on the underside of the table as he forgets where he is and tries to stand. The fourth student is still crawling on hands and knees, until he gets his fingers stepped on by a passing classmate. Unknowingly, the crawler is "mooning" anyone who looks, which inspires the fifth boy to sprinkle art glitter down the crack of his backside. The teacher is immediately drawn to this group, and as a result, one-third of the students have their hands raised, wanting the teacher's attention and complaining that they do not have the needed materials. Chaos, conflict, and total class disruption are seen here, and major discipline problems are on their way! Whose fault is this? The fault lies with a lack of understanding of the *concept of classroom*.

In a direct instruction classroom, students typically are bolted to a desk and chair for long periods of time and must ask permission before they may get up and move about or do any other task. Such a regimented classroom can be organized with little care for classroom concepts. But when 20 or more students are freely moving about in a fairly limited space with a host of learning centers and a wide variety of equipment, this space and materials must be planned with scientific precision.

Consider any space where large numbers of people gather for a specific purpose, and you will find that the space uses a concept of design that either facilitates this activity in a smooth and safe manner (a grocery store, hospital, cafeteria) or hinders the activity to the point that it can cause injuries (construction work on city streets or even the second-grade art room). At the high school level, teachers have to deal with industrial arts classrooms, home economics classrooms, an art room, a band room, a chemistry lab, and even a gymnasium—each of which is a

**211**

complicated and demanding space with a wide variety of materials, furniture, and equipment. There are concepts for arranging space in all these rooms, as well as various elementary classrooms, that most teachers have not learned formally—the concept of classroom.

It is imperative that the teacher who wishes to create a supportive classroom, with a minimal amount of the kind of conflict seen in the marker example above, actually creates a paper floor plan/map of the classroom area, as demonstrated in Figures 11–1 and 11–2. It is suggested that at the end of each day for the first 10 days a new classroom design is used (at the beginning of the school year or after the classroom has been rearranged), the teacher should mark the floor map with small check marks, indicating where some difficulty has occurred (such as the marker incident).

---

### FLOOR MAPPING

Drawing a schematic map of the classroom in order to provide the best design for the classroom space.

---

Many city traffic departments maintain a bulletin board map of the city streets, and place straight pins on the map to show where accidents occur. After a short period of time, it can clearly be seen on the street map that a handful of intersections accounts for an overwhelming percentage of accidents. The solution: Physically alter the troublesome intersections by using an understanding of traffic flow to prevent accidents from happening, thereby saving the considerable costs of accident damage and perhaps saving lives.

The teacher will be surprised to discover that the same process will occur on her classroom map. The students may literally be falling over the equipment or one another. The check marks, indicating points of conflict and difficulty, will begin to cluster at key spots on the classroom map, perhaps near a certain science station, supply cupboard, or water source. The solution: Alter the space by moving equipment and materials around with the concepts described here, thereby eliminating large numbers of incidents that call for disciplinary action or require the teacher to "put out a fire" (as with the rolling marker).

**Scientifically Designed Classroom (Double E Classroom)**
**(see Figure 11–1)**

1. Desks/chairs are clustered into four obvious groupings—double E arrangement (teams: red, blue, green, yellow).

2. The teacher's desk is placed to the side of the room and is not a barrier between the teacher and students. The desk is close to the door, permitting the teacher to take messages delivered at the door. Also, when seated at the desk, the teacher can easily see off-task behavior. (A back-of-the-room desk, located where F table is positioned, is even better for this supervision.)

**FIGURE 11–1    Double E Classroom**

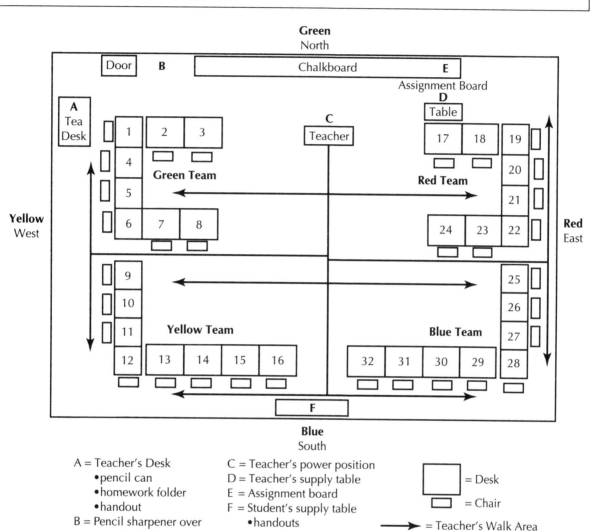

A = Teacher's Desk
•pencil can
•homework folder
•handout
B = Pencil sharpener over waste baskets

C = Teacher's power position
D = Teacher's supply table
E = Assignment board
F = Student's supply table
•handouts
•pencil can

☐ = Desk
▭ = Chair
⟶ = Teacher's Walk Area

3. The pencil sharpener and waste paper basket are placed near the door.

4. The chalkboard is located at the front of the room, and the assignment board is located to the right.

5. The teacher's power position (C) is established as a position to obtain student attention.

6. Open space in front of the teacher permits the teacher to quickly move in front of every student with a minimum of steps (proximity: far, near, intimate).

7. Color directionality: Walls are designated North–green, East–red, South–blue, and West–yellow, which can be used to create a student's sense of directionality in the classroom and assist in storage of materials.

*Concepts and Principles vs. Techniques*

Not every teacher will want to copy the technique exactly; for example, not every teacher has to have the classroom in a Double E. However, the concepts and principles should be used to guide the teacher to create a classroom arrangement and techniques that are in keeping with the Three Faces of Discipline framework.

1. Establish an X, Y, Z pattern on the desks of the students. Generally, X should be a high-achieving student, Y a middle-achieving student, and Z a low-achieving student. (*Note*: Some teachers also choose to have an alsternating boy-girl arrangment.)

2. Misbehaving students should be placed at desks 8, 24, 16, and 32.

3. Well-behaving and dependable students are placed at desks 6, 10, 11, 12, and 13, and at 22, 26, 27, 28, and 29.

4. During the first six weeks of the school year or a new semester, the teacher should feel free to repeatedly change students' desks so a skilled and effective cluster of students is obtained.

5. Pseudomature students or similar students who need excessive attention may be most effectively seated at desks 14, 15, 30, and 31. They are in direct facial position to the teacher, thus receiving *Looking* from the teacher, but the back-row position permits the teacher to determine the distance (proxemics) she will give or withhold with these students. Never place such students in desks 1, 4, 19, or 20 because they will repeatedly act out to get the teacher's *Looking* and the teacher will be drawn off to the extreme right or left.

The arrangement of furniture and equipment within the classroom space establishes a structure that will control proximity or physical closeness of teacher to student and student to student, and, if improperly designed, can actually prevent the teacher from seeing the students who need her visual and personal investment (TBC's *Looking*). What follows is a description of a scientifically designed classroom arrangement that in seconds allows desks to be moved to create all three spheres of relationships.

Classroom space in most elementary, middle, and high schools generally supports a limited number of basic classroom teaching and learning activities: (1) lecture or direct group instruction (one-to-all relationship); (2) small group direct instruction (one-to-group relationship); (3) independent student group work (may involve one-to-one); and (4) independent work (may involve one-to-one helping).

The typical middle or high school classroom is set up for lecturing and direct instruction, with six rows containing six desk and chairs all facing the chalkboard, with the teacher's desk in front, a waste paper basket and a pencil sharpener near the door, and one prominently located bulletin board. Which educational architects designed this classroom? Jones,[2] a leading discipline expert, would say it was the janitor. This room arrangement of furniture permits the janitor to move without stopping to run a dry mop from the door, up and down the rows and out the door again, leaving the floor "clean." The pencil sharpener and waste basket can be reached from the doorway and emptied quickly. But the furniture arrangement in rows forces a one-to-all (teacher to students) relationship and communicates coldness and distance that can make the students feel as if they are nothing more than numbers who will be herded into their stall-like seats, force-fed a diet of academic content, and herded to the next feeding carrel when the bell rings.

So, how can you, as the classroom teacher, arrange the desks and chairs so that direct instruction (such as a lecture) may occur with as much intimacy as possible? The answer lies with the construct of spatial proximity (*proximity far*, *proximity near*, and *proximity intimate*) as well as eye contact. Intimacy is expressed at an eye-to-eye nonverbal level from the first moments of life; an infant meets her parent eye to eye and face to face and later through "peek-a-boo" play in which the parent's eyes are "lost" and then joyfully "found" again. The traditional arrangement of desks in a row inhibits the teacher's freedom to physically move close to students. This prevents the TBC's *Looking* while the teacher is lecturing, blocking the teacher's visual investment in her students. The construct of the Double E configuration is recommended whenever possible.

Using Figure 11–1 as a guide, you may arrange the desks and chairs in the E and reverse E pattern. Once the desks are properly arranged, you can then follow these directions:

1. *Floor (Visual) Prompts*: Using a permanent marker (or tape), draw circles on the floor around the feet of desks 1, 12, 28, and 19. These marks will serve as visual prompts for the students as to where the desks should be located, thus providing anchor desks for other students to use in arranging their rows. Small symbols may be placed on the wall in eight key locations to serve as visual prompts for desk alignment, permitting most students to look front and back or left and right to find two or three alignment points to know if their desks are in line. If possible, the teacher may have lines painted in a Double E arrangement on the floor so that the front legs of each desk can be placed on the line prompt.

2. *Teacher's Desk*: The teacher's desk (letter A) is never placed in the front of the room because you want the students and their desks to be as close as possible to the front chalkboard and to the teacher (at letter C). Placing the desk in front of the room would create a barrier between the teacher and the students. The desk located near the door and off to the side provides easy access for the teacher. Placed on top of the desk would be a pencil can (extra old pencils to be borrowed by students) and a homework folder (students will always know where to place their written work as they arrive and depart past this desk). Students will also be taught to pass by this table to look for and pick up any handouts.

3. *Waste Can / Sharpener:* At the B location will be a pencil sharpener and a waste basket underneath it. Students moving in and out of

the room will repetitively pass these two items and can use them quickly—and the janitor will love it.

4. *Assignment Board:* One end of the chalkboard is always dedicated to an Assignment Board (E). The students will be able to depend on finding their current assignments in writing here, listed in descending order of priority by the teacher.

5. *Storage:* A small table (D) placed before desk 17 will serve as a storage place for items the teacher needs to have nearby while lecturing. This is *not* a space to be shared by students.

6. *Table F:* A table or flat surface holds any materials that the teacher displays and wishes the students to inspect.

7. *Seat Assignment:* After sufficient time, the teacher will be able to identify those students who are going to be discipline problems and those who will be very well behaved with a strong, dependable academic ability. The problem students will be placed in desks 3, 8, 16, 32, 24, and 17. This will keep these difficult students in the proximity-near position, only a few steps from the teacher, who will place herself in the teacher's power position (C). Students who are very well behaved and have strong academic ability will be seated at desks 11, 12, 13, 29, 28, and 27. These desks will be in proximity-far, so the teacher will want to have very independent and trustworthy students in these seats.

8. *Adding Desks:* The map (Figure 11–1) shows seating for 32 students, but more than this number can be added by placing them in this order:
   - Desks 33 and 34 are placed between seats 6 and 7, pushing seats 7 and 8 deep into the middle of the room.
   - Desks 35 and 36 are placed between seats 22 and 23, pushing seats 23 and 24 deeper into the middle of the room.
   - If still more desks must be placed into this arrangement, remove table F and create a row of desks centered in the back of the room and directly facing the teacher.

9. *Pathways:* Notice that the arrow lines show the teacher's walking area, permitting her to "*work the crowd*" and see all students without being embedded in furniture. Notice the openings between seats 9 and 6, 22 and 25, and 16 and 32; these permit the teacher to move behind the students and *camp out from behind.*

**Classroom Mapping Activity (see Figure 11–2)**

1. Cut out silhouettes of furniture.

2. Draw classroom walls on grid paper (1 square = 1 foot).

3. Draw in or color with markers to show rugs or permanent items such as doors, windows, water fountains, shelving, etc.

FIGURE 11–2 **Classroom Mapping**

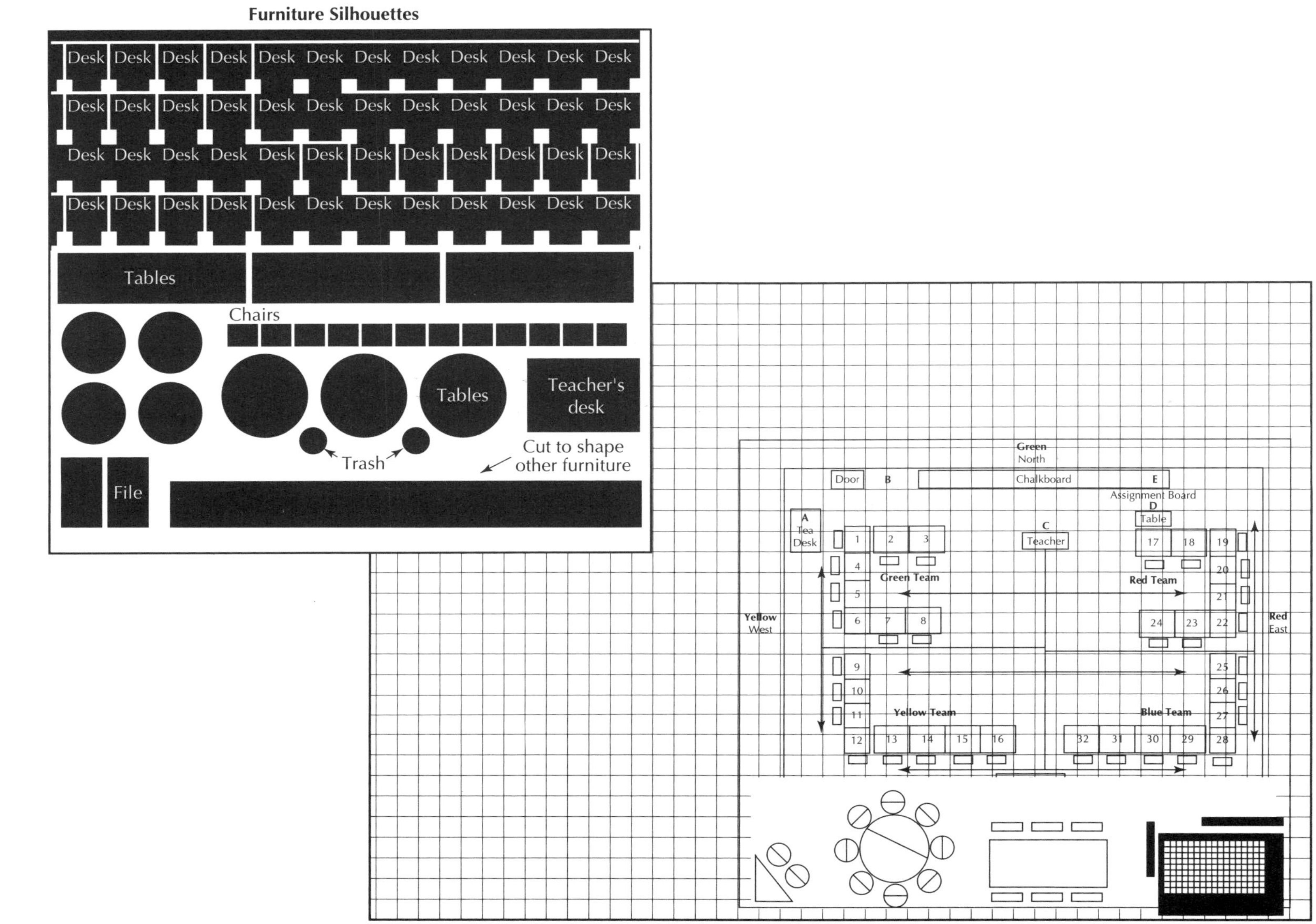

Furniture Silhouettes

4. Arrange silhouetted furniture in a classroom design:
   a. Permit quick proximity to all students.
   b. Allow for effective transitions between groups of students.
   c. Determine, based on the map, the degree of openness-closeness.

5. During the first weeks of school or the semester, place a small check mark on the map where a discipline difficulty has occurred. These checks will cluster, indicating that you may need to move the seating of certain students or change the space with regard to "control of error."

## THREE SPHERES OF RELATIONSHIP

A classroom that brings together students and a teacher involves degrees of relationships, and it is the quality of those relationships that will enable students to feel welcomed and accepted. Adults who are put in charge in institutional settings (nurses in hospitals, guards in prisons, and teachers in schools) or businesses (airline counter attendants, store check-out personnel), when under day-in and day-out stress, may begin to show *institutional behavior*. They begin to deal with the public in a mechanical manner, showing curt speech, flat expressionless behavior, and an unthinking administration of the rules. They exhibit little consideration of the needs of the individual with whom they are dealing and communicate no warmth. If we are not very careful, this same attitude begins to be seen in the behavior of teachers in the elementary, middle, and high school classrooms, especially if the classroom is imbalanced with too many students, not enough help for the teacher, and a lack of equipment and classroom materials.

The airline counter attendant is burned out because she has to manage too many passengers (in a classroom it would be students). A snowstorm has grounded five flights and she must deal with literally hundreds of angry passengers—the situation is obviously out of balance. Teachers working in an imbalanced classroom (too many kids, not enough equipment or materials) can begin to become burned out and take on institutional behavior. Students may spend eight hours a day traveling to and from school and assigned to classrooms, and they feel the need for significant emotional investment by administration and teachers. To go days, weeks, or months being cared for or taught by adults and teachers who are depressive and burned out can have a real and lasting destructive effect on groups of students. We cannot permit this to occur in schools and classrooms, and thus we use the *three spheres of relationship* construct to determine how to best use time with students.

There are three basic spheres in a teacher's relationships with her students: Sphere 1: One to One, Sphere 2: One to Group, and Sphere 3: One to All (see Figure 11–3). Viewed in reverse order, we see that the *one-to-all* sphere is a lecture format where the students must sit passively, refrain from communicating, and listen to the teacher speak. They feel no affection coming from the teacher and feel depersonalized—thus one teacher to all students. This is the traditional mode of teaching such subjects as math, English, history, and so on.

| FIGURE 11–3 | Spheres of Relationship | |
|---|---|---|
| One to One | A teacher interacts with one student (knee to knee); a private meeting. | The student receives near total emotional attention from the teacher and may dominate conversation. |
| One to Group | A teacher interacts with a small group of 4 to 8 students. | The student feels more emotional connectedness with the teacher and peers, but needs to share conversation with peers. |
| One to All | A teacher speaks or teaches to the total group of students. | The student feels little emotional contact (a spatial distance) with the teacher, and must generally inhibit the desire to talk and instead must simply listen. |

The *one-to-group* sphere occurs where the teacher is seated together with a group of four to eight students and there is conversation among all members of the group. An example of this would be when the teacher is working with a cooperative group of students at a science table. There is much more warmth felt among this smaller group, but the students do have to share the teacher's warmth and attention with their table mates—one teacher to a group of up to eight students.

The *one-to-one* sphere is the time where the teacher and student are totally invested in one another, screening out others. The student can receive total warmth and attention from the teacher and is free to dominate the conversation. Such Relationship-Listening techniques as active listening, door openers, and acknowledgments can be very helpful in communicating with students during this *one-to-one* sphere of relationship, and to a lesser extent with a group of students in the *one-to-group* sphere.

The anger and excessive need for attention that many students feel today is a result of the institutional behavior they see as emotionless and lacking in caring. They may have first felt this in group daycare as a very young child, and seen a continuation from a host of elementary school teachers—and perhaps even from busy parents who have not given them attention and time at home. Children today, sometimes referred to as *latchkey children* because they wear a house key around the neck to let themselves into the empty home after school, are spending large amounts of time alone. The dramatic increase in discipline problems reflects the large number of students wanting a relationship and social interaction with adults. If it does not come to them through positive behavior, they become discipline problems and get it in the negative form. These students are saying by their behavior, "Please see me!"

We cannot leave it to chance and hope that every child will get sufficient personal time with a teacher, because the quiet and less assertive student will inevitably fall through the cracks. In staff meetings and during teacher planning time, we must use the three spheres construct in planning the student's day to assure that every child will have a relationship with the teacher in each of the three spheres. The Double E classroom arrangement demonstrates how the teacher may physically have students move into and out of groups with little confusion or discipline activities. Most discipline incidents occur during transitions, and a clear understanding of how to make these movements will eliminate much of this difficulty.

## Making a Group of Two

The students transition into groups of two by simply turning toward their partner, following basic combinations. The partners are:

**Pair Grouping**

| Group | | | | |
|---|---|---|---|---|
| North-East (Red Team) | 1 and 4 | 5 and 6 | 7 and 8 | 2 and 3 |
| Group South-East (Blue Team) | 9 and 10 | 11 and 12 | 13 and 14 | 15 and 16 |
| Group North-West (Green Team) | 17 and 18 | 19 and 20 | 21 and 22 | 23 and 24 |
| Group South-West (Yellow Team) | 25 and 26 | 27 and 28 | 29 and 30 | 31 and 32 |

Notice that the students located in desks 12 and 28 present a problem. Should they be seated facing north toward the chalkboard, or east and west so they will be seated beside their partner for group work without needing to continually move? The answer depends on which location enables these two students to see the chalkboard best (alternatively, the teacher may simply elect to give them a choice).

## Making Groups of Four or Eight

The Double E desk arrangement also permits quick movement into group work that might involve four or eight students in a group (see Figure 11–4). For example, this can be done by having desk 2 pull back and put the front of that desk against the back of desk 4; repeat the process with desk 3 joining desk 1, desk 8 joining desk 5, and desk 7 joining desk 6. This creates an easy group of eight. To have groups of four, simply force a space between desks 4 and 5, and create two groups of four with desks 4, 1, 2, and 3 sliding north in the classroom. This can be done in like manner with the remaining three large groups. Numbers 9, 10, 11, and 12 should swing to join the stationary 13, 14, 15, and 16, and in like fashion, desks 25, 26, 27, and 28 swing to their counterparts 32, 31, 30, and 29. It will be quite important to teach the students which desks move and which stay in place during changes.

## Making Groups of Three

A group of three (see Figure 11–5) can also be formed from the basic E arrangement, but usually is done by keeping all desks in place and having one student carry his or her chair and place it behind the chairs of two other students, centered between the two receiving chairs and desk. The teacher will need to clearly identify which students are to move and which pair is to receive a third member. This may be done as follows:

### Green and Yellow Team

| Student moving chair behind pair | 3 | 2 | 11 | 10 | 9 |
|---|---|---|---|---|---|
| Pair receiving student above | 5 and 6 | 1 and 4 | 14 and 15 | 12 and 13 | 7 and 8 |

### Red and Blue Team

| Student moving chair behind pair | 17 | 18 | 27 | 26 | 25 |
|---|---|---|---|---|---|
| Pair receiving student above | 21 and 22 | 19 and 20 | 31 and 32 | 30 and 29 | 24 and 23 |

Numbers 32 and 16 are still without partners, so 32 moves his seat to number 16, thus forming a pair; if three people are required for the activity, the teacher joins this pair.

If the desk and chair is a single piece of furniture that cannot be moved as simply (or quietly), the following combinations can be used quickly:

### Green and Yellow Team

| Student moving desk-chair combination | 1 | 8 | 7 | 13 | 12 |
|---|---|---|---|---|---|
| Pair stationary and receiving student above | 2 and 3 | 4 and 5 | 6 and 9 both moving | 10 and 11 | 14 and 15 |

### Red and Blue Team

| Student moving desk-chair combination | 19 | 24 | 23 | 29 | 28 |
|---|---|---|---|---|---|
| Pair stationary and receiving student above | 17 and 18 | 20 and 21 | 22 and 25 both moving | 26 and 27 | 31 and 30 |

FIGURE 11–4 A Group of Four and Eight Arrangment

FIGURE 11–5 A Group of Three Arangement

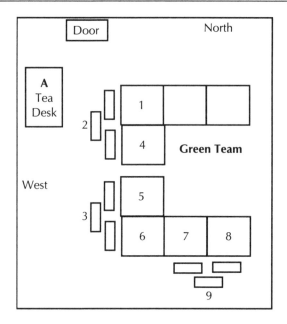

Numbers 32 and 16 are still without partners, so 32 moves his seat to number 16, thus forming a pair; if three people are required for the activity, the teacher joins the pair.

In the description of the movements from the basic Double E arrangement, we have used an arbitrary class size of 32 students for purposes of example. Each teacher's class size will vary dramatically, so it is important to understand the smooth organized movements between the pairs and groups of 3, 4, and 8, and make minor adjustment to the preceding movements to accommodate the particular number of students involved.

This Double E basic lecture classroom is a well-engineered design and has these advantages:

1. The teacher is not behind any barriers and can move quickly from her power position in order to use *proximity-near or intimate* and eye contact. During instruction, students will be able to feel the presence and greater intimacy from the teacher because the teacher will actually come to them and make eye contact.

2. With the simplest command, the teacher can have each member of a pair turn and face each other or move to groups of 3, 4, and 8 to immediately begin working as a team and just as quickly return to a lecture arrangement.

3. Misbehaving students are in the closest proximity to the teacher at all times, permitting the teacher to use eye contact and be close to the student's *comfort bubble*. Misbehaving students generally need this attention and feeling of closeness.

4. Students can use the visual prompts (marks) on the floor and walls of the room and can centrally place their desks without repeated directions or nagging from the teacher.

5. Students can obtain handouts and turn in assignments in a predictable manner and as a matter of routine.

6. The assignment board always communicates to the students what work they should be doing as seatwork and in what order. As soon as they walk through the door, they will begin the first item as a matter of routine at every class period. If the students work quickly, there is always a catch-all general assignment at the bottom of the assignment list (such as reading a library book) (see Figure 11–6).

7. The seating arrangement creates four spatially clustered teams (Northeast, which we will label the Red Team, Southeast as the Blue Team, Northwest as the Green, and Southwest as Yellow) that can be used as competitive teams as a part of the Incentive System (explained previously).

8. When students are taking a test and need to be seated so they are not tempted to look at another student's paper, every odd-numbered desk can be pulled backward one desk length and every even-numbered desk pushed forward one desk length. In a matter of seconds

the students can be in, and out, of a test seating arrangement, moved by the teacher's simple verbal prompt: "Testing positions."

9. The Double E seating arrangement permits total group discussion because, with the exception of just eight students (2, 3, 7, 8, 17, 18, 24, and 23), every student can see anyone who is talking, and with a slight turn of the head most of the eight can see a high percentage of their classmates.

10. Unknowingly, we have suggested that students perform a very dangerous action—pick up and move a chair. I can now see a high school weightlifter who enjoys the challenge of lifting bar bells, and who also has some difficulty with cognitive complexities, picking up a desk and/or chair over his head, carrying it over his fellow students' heads, and tripping on the way, with the chair crashing down with full force on an unsuspecting classmate's head. "Oh, they would know better than to carry chairs in such a manner," say some teachers.

---

**FIGURE 11–6   North-Green Wall**

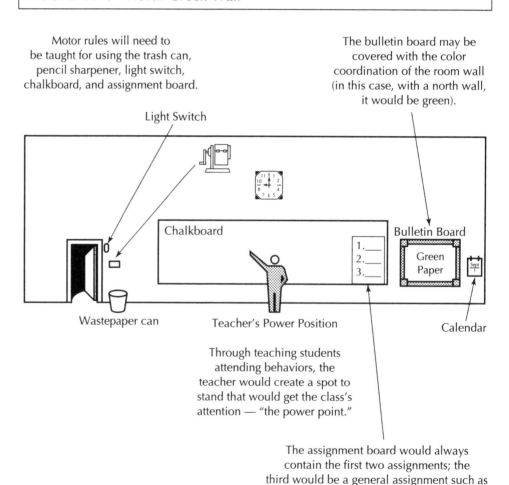

Motor rules will need to be taught for using the trash can, pencil sharpener, light switch, chalkboard, and assignment board.

The bulletin board may be covered with the color coordination of the room wall (in this case, with a north wall, it would be green).

Light Switch

Chalkboard

Bulletin Board

1. ___
2. ___
3. ___

Green Paper

Sept

Wastepaper can

Teacher's Power Position

Calendar

Through teaching students attending behaviors, the teacher would create a spot to stand that would get the class's attention — "the power point."

The assignment board would always contain the first two assignments; the third would be a general assignment such as "When done with the first two assignments, read a book!"

Jones, the discipline expert who has given us many of the management ideas, would say, "In your dreams." This needs to be taught to all students before any chair moves an inch—this is nuts-and-bolts classroom management. (Chapter 12 describes the three-step lesson used to teach such motor rules.)

---

### MOTOR (OR SPATIAL) RULES

Automatic motor actions suggested by the room or zone in which the student is located (such as throwing paper in the trash when done with it, closing the door behind you, or putting things away when done).

---

To summarize, the Double E basic desk arrangement does almost everything the teacher needs. It supports a lecture format or direct group instruction (a one-to-all relationship), small group direct instruction (one-to-group—with two, four, or eight members), and independent student group work (may involve one-to-one). It also provides the open walkways that permit the teacher to get immediately to a student (may involve one-to-one helping).

A concept of classroom means engineering the basic furniture and equipment in the classroom to serve a predetermined function. When the teacher has developed a clear understanding of the desk arrangement, the students can be taught key classroom verbal prompts during the first days of school. Within seconds, a classroom full of students can be positioned for a new form of teaching and learning.

## THE CONCEPT OF CLASSROOM TRANSITIONS

Except for fire drills (which are practiced in advance), teachers are advised never to issue a command for the entire group to perform in one mass action—an entire gym class, an auditorium of 1,000 students, or a classroom of 32. The aggressive student will bolt for the door, knocking over others and possibly even causing injury. In addition, you can never be sure that your prompt command is understood by everyone, when forgetting is symptomatic with students. Therefore, it is best to view any classroom group, for purposes of making any transition, through the *concept of transitional threes*. One-fourth of the group is requested to move first; the teacher and other students watch this group to see if these students are performing the correct actions. Then a second group—involving approximately one-half of the class—is asked to move, before the final one-fourth is asked to clean and organize the area before making the transition.

The fifth-grade teacher has all 32 students seated at their desks in a Double E configuration. Having completed a directive lesson, he now needs all the students to move to the science tables at the back of the room. With the help of students, he has previously prepared each of these tables with beakers, delicate instruments, and a host of similar sensitive materials. If he commands, "Class, move to the lab tables," there will be a mass exit from the desks, with students pushing to be seated with friends. This, of course, carries a likelihood that something will get broken or someone will get injured.

Instead, the teacher follows the concept of transitional threes, dismissing one-fourth of the class first. "Class, in just a few minutes I will dismiss you in groups to move to the back tables to carry out your science experiments. You will remember that what you are to do and in what order is written here on the Assignment Board. Follow these directions, please. Now, don't move until I tell you, but Blue Team will move first. Remember, I have already assigned you a spot at the science tables. Remember that on these tables are delicate items, so I want you to move slowly and safely to your seat and *wait until everyone is seated at their places before you begin.* Blue Team, you may move carefully to your science tables, now. Class, let's watch them. Mark, I see you turning on the Bunsen burners. The rule is to wait until everyone is seated. Would you please return to your classroom seat." Having sent one-quarter of the students as the first group, the teacher observes to see if they are modeling the proper behavior. If they are not, the teacher reteaches the rule or may take other corrective actions (such as sending Mark back to his classroom seat).

At this time, the teacher is assured that everyone has seen the rules properly carried out by the first group and now feels comfortable with dismissing the second, larger group consisting of about half the class. "Would the Red and Yellow teams move carefully to the lab tables, now. Finally, I would like the Green team to erase the board, pick up any waste papers laying on the floor, arrange the desks, and then move to your science positions." Finally, the teacher says, "Mark, you may now take your spot at the science table."

When the class moves out of a special zone, the last group to be dismissed is responsible for ordering and cleaning up that space before moving on. For example, in physical education class, the final group may be asked to pick up the bases, bats, balls, and any other equipment and carry the items to the storage area.

The teacher checks his watch and sees that there is only five minutes left before the students must leave for the school assembly in the auditorium. Because everyone is working and visually and sensorily invested in the table activity, he does not broadcast across the entire class by shouting, "OK, now every one listen up—here is what I want you do." Such broadcasting-shouting will produce a number of negative effects. For one, the teacher would be modeling shouting in the classroom, encouraging the students to follow this example. Second, since the students are engrossed in their work, only a few will really hear the instruction and will take forever to give proper attention. Instead, the teacher moves into each group and gives the announcement as *preparatory to a transition.* "Students in this group, you have three minutes to finish up and get ready to return to your seats. See the steps for cleaning up that I have written on the chalkboard—all of these steps need to be accomplished. When I see your group done cleaning, I will dismiss you to your classroom seats."

Getting out the door when the bell rings is a powerful incentive for students. The directions as given use that incentive to create a contingency contract. "Do this (clean up) and you will get this reward (able to depart)." On the chalkboard are the verbal prompts for guiding the students through the steps of cleaning up, thus taking the burden off the teacher or requiring the teacher to nag. The teacher now *works the crowd,* watching for how the students are cleaning up, tutoring if necessary, and waiting until three-fourths of the students are ready. Seeing that three-quarters are now ready, the teacher dismisses one table first (group one), then dismisses all but the last table (group two), and then asks this last table to order and clean whatever items need to be taken care of. Students are now in their classroom seats when the bell rings.

Again, the teacher will use the *concept of transitional threes*. This routine of dismissal will be rotated with each of the four teams having a chance to go first, but always moving out as three separate groups—the *concept of transitional threes* in action.

A number of summary points need to be made about handling transitions. The students need to know where they are going and what action they will perform once they get there. It is necessary to teach this to them before the transition begins and to have a verbal prompt, such as the list of steps on the chalkboard. There could also have been activity cards placed on each table for that group to follow, particularly if each group will be doing different work. The teacher dismisses in three groups, monitoring behavior. Finally, the teacher is now free to *work the crowd*.

At first glance, this may seem a bit too structured. But remember: Many of today's children are growing up with a lack of home structure to teach behavior concerning how to work with regard to time, rules of behavior, and care of property. We are presenting principles of classroom management, a management technology; once these structures are learned by students during initial Mars Days (see Chapter 13), the teacher can partially relax some of the structure because the steps have been learned as habits and the students can show self-control. By the third day of class and thereafter, when the dismissal bell rings, no student stands to go running out the classroom door; instead, all students wait and know the structure of how dismissal will unfold. The world for them is predictable, understandable, and secure. Jones says, "Either the teacher sets the classroom agenda or the students will set the agenda!"

## VERBAL PROMPTS

When people live together in a closed space, over time they develop an "in"-group language to the point where one member might give a verbal statement (a prompt) and all members, having shared past experiences, understand that a host of future actions will occur. A group of friends is traveling in the fall in the Northeast, and at every rest stop they see a huge display of fresh red apples for sale. Later, when one member feels a need for a rest stop, he simply gives the verbal prompt, "Apple time." Everyone laughs and knows exactly what that passenger wants to do. However, a stranger having recently joined that "in" group may not understand. These short abbreviated verbal prompts save the group time and effort. Rather than saying three paragraphs to explain what is wanted and what will happen next, one member simply utters one word or phase ("Apple time") and everyone understands. This type of group familiarity must quickly be developed in the first minutes of each semester with a new group of students. Thus, we have the concept of Mars Days (described in chapter 13), where we pretend that these students have just come from another planet, and we teach the abbreviated verbal prompts to facilitate good transitions.

### Group Transition Prompts

- *Order and Clean:* This prompt is given by the teacher at the beginning of each class and is the last prompt before students depart, getting all students to slightly move their desks by using the floor and wall prompts.

- *Testing Positions:* Moving odd-numbered desks back one length and even-numbered desks forward so the students will not be tempted to look on classmates' papers.

- *Pair Groups*: Odd- and even-numbered partners will turn to face each other and work together.

- *Groups of Threes:* One-third of the students will move their chairs behind a preassigned pair.

- *Groups of Eight:* Certain students will move their desks against a counterpart's desk to form eight-desk clusters.

- *Groups of Four:* Groups of four should only be reached after the students first move to groups of eight, with a second prompt moving them to have the group separate to fours.

## CONCEPT OF DIRECTIONALITY (MATERIALS)

Orienting oneself in space, even classroom space, involves *directionality*. In arranging space for purposes of having a *concept of classroom*, the teacher can use the directions of north, south, east, and west. The side of the classroom with a chalkboard, where the teacher is situated to make announcements or lecture, usually becomes the north wall, with the other compass points lining up accordingly. We have now organized desks and chairs, formed students into groups of twos, threes, fours, and eights, and have shown how to make transitions between spaces. Now it is time to gain control of materials. Materials are a specific problem in classroom management because they have to be kept in some order to access them when needed. They have to be stored for their care and safety while at the same time 30 or more students are taking them from storage, using them, and hopefully returning them for future use. This materials management problem is solved by the concept of directionality and the concept of storage (left to right, top to bottom).

Simply put, any student using any material that is not fixed to the wall or floor knows what to do if the teachers says, "Please put this item away." The student should (1) turn and walk to the wall where the item is stored and (2) be able to place the item on shelving or in the drawer where it is stored. *Every* student should be able to do this with *every* item *every* time—a quality system.

---

## COLOR CUEING

A systematic method of marking toys and other play materials with colored marks so that the students can readily identify the object and its proper shelf or storage location.

---

## VISUAL PROMPTS

We are at Happy Harry's Crab House. After imbibing large quantities of the local grog, we find that we must go to the "necessary" room. As we approach the two doors, we must choose between two doors, Gulls and Buoys—no small task under the circumstances. How do we know which door to choose, other than deciphering the "cute" verbal signs? The answer is symbolic visual prompt, through the symbol of a man or woman placed at eye level on the outside of the bathroom door. Today there are hundreds of *visual prompts* that positively control our behavior. A symbol of a cigarette inside a red circle with a crossing red slash tells us that smoking is not permitted in that area; a blue sign with a white wheelchair emblem tells us that the parking space is reserved for drivers who are disabled.

You may use a similar visual prompt system, in the form of color coding, to positively control students' behavior when they use materials in your classroom (see Figure 11–7). Some classrooms have scores of reference books, dozens of hand tools with a host of related pieces, a huge collection of equipment, and a wide variety of supplies. Large numbers of today's students come to school without an orderliness or structure in the objects they use and live with at home, and you are now asking 30 of them to do this at school. Needless to say, this can be a major challenge. The solution is to teach students to use color prompts and symbolic visual prompts to help make sure each article finds its proper storage location.

First, through the spatial concept of directionality, arbitrarily declare the north wall to use all green prompts, the south wall to use blue prompts, the east wall for red, and the west wall for yellow. Use construction paper, tape, wallpaper boarders, or any other solidly col-

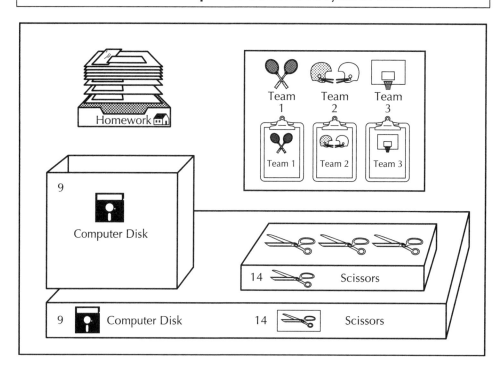

**FIGURE 11–7    Visual Prompts: Color/Number/Symbol/Word**

ored item with these four colors, placing them on the appropriate walls in a decorative manner so it becomes obvious that each wall has its own specific color. Once this has been established, every material or the container used to bring items out from storage will be marked with a colored prompt, corresponding to the color of the wall on which it is stored. Once these items have been used by the student and are ready to be put away, the student needs only to look at it and think, "Oh, yellow!" and can stand and turn to the west (yellow) wall and know that these items belong somewhere on that wall (see Figure 11–8).

The next step in the materials return and storage is to place the item in the pre-designated location for that item. Materials can be stored on or near a wall in a number of ways:

- Hung from hooks, nails, or velcro

- Self-standing on the floor or flat on a shelf

- Stored on shelves within containers

- Stored in drawers, blocked by a visual barrier

- Stored on shelves behind doors, blocked by a visual barrier

## Hung Items

Most everyone has seen the industrial arts teacher's display of hand tools. A hole is drilled through the tool's handle for the purpose of hanging it on a nail or hook; the item is placed against the wall and a silhou-

**FIGURE 11–8 Visual Prompts: East-Red Wall**

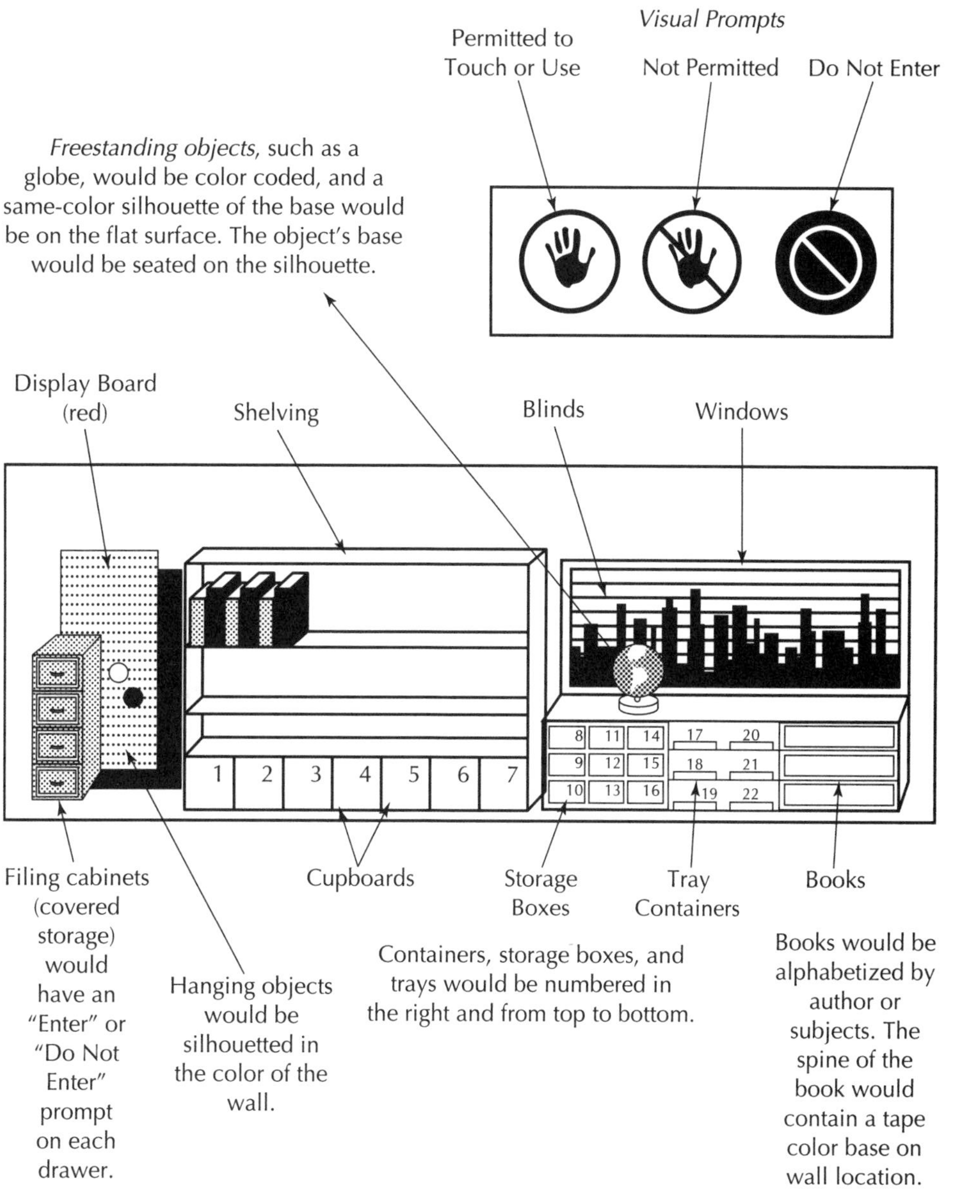
Visual Prompts
Permitted to Touch or Use
Not Permitted
Do Not Enter
Freestanding objects, such as a globe, would be color coded, and a same-color silhouette of the base would be on the flat surface. The object's base would be seated on the silhouette.
Display Board (red)
Shelving
Blinds
Windows
1 2 3 4 5 6 7
8 9 10 11 12 13 14 15 16
17 18 19 20 21 22
Filing cabinets (covered storage) would have an "Enter" or "Do Not Enter" prompt on each drawer.
Hanging objects would be silhouetted in the color of the wall.
Cupboards
Storage Boxes
Tray Containers
Books
Containers, storage boxes, and trays would be numbered in the right and from top to bottom.
Books would be alphabetized by author or subjects. The spine of the book would contain a tape color base on wall location.

ette drawn around it so that when the tool is taken away, a symbolic prompt for a hammer, saw, or similar tool can be seen. This silhouette of the hammer is then painted to match the color of the wall on which the hammer will be stored. Each of the hanging items must be marked with the same color by using such marking devices as paint, plastic tape, or even small dabs of fingernail polish. Now, when Jeff the carpenter needs a hammer, large yardstick, and similar items, he will know where to find them and—more important for a host of reasons, safety being the biggest one—he will now be able to turn to the correct wall, find the symbol prompt, and hang the item back on the wall. This silhouetted symbol prompt can be used in a similar manner for all other classrooms with similar wall displays of equipment.

## Free-Standing Items

A globe used for geography lessons may be stored at the south-blue wall, either standing freely on the floor or on the flat surface of a shelf. The teacher locates the globe at a logical predetermined location and uses the base of the globe to paint a silhouette in that wall's color. Unfortunately, the base produces a common round silhouette that would not immediately identify the globe as the source of the shape. Therefore, the teacher cuts out a picture of a globe from a school supply catalogue and glues this to the center of the circle (symbolic prompts) and might actually write in block letters the word *globe*. To keep the paper letters or picture from being accidentally torn off through wear, the teacher covers it with clear epoxy paint. A similar process is used for all free-standing items that will be stored on flat surfaces or shelves. Each of these free-standing items is also marked with the color of the storage wall on which it is housed.

## Containers on Shelves

Many types of items come in large quantities that would be impossible to color-code individually, while others are expendable (i.e., color construction paper) and must be kept together and housed in storage containers. In such a case, the container itself is marked with the wall color and the color prompt is placed where the container is to be stored.

## Drawer Storage

Drawer storage presents two problems. First, when the drawer is closed, the student is unable to see what is inside. This can be solved by cutting a picture from a supply catalogue and gluing it to the outside of the drawer (*visual prompt*), including the object's written name (*verbal prompt*). Don't depend on name only. Second, if small items (paperclips, pencils, rubber bands, etc.) get scattered about, it can be quite frustrating just "scratching" through the mess trying to locate them. Inside the drawer, all small items should therefore be stored in small cardboard boxes, each with the name of the item written in block letters. Covers should be torn off these boxes so the items can be seen and not be covered by a second barrier. This way, if you are looking for a rubber band and find the drawer with its symbol, only to open it and find an empty box with the words *rubber band* written inside, you can stop your search, knowing that there are none available. That may be frustrating, but it would be even more frustrating to search for another 10 minutes, never to locate one, and still not know if you have searched in the right location. As a further visual prompt for students, you may also place the visual prompt of touch or don't touch (Figure 11–9) on the outside of the drawer.

FIGURE 11–9    Visual Prompts (Touch and Don't Touch)

## Storage Behind Doors

Often, items are stored behind closed doors, thus creating a barrier as to what is to be found inside. This is especially a problem when it comes time to put away items that belong behind these doors. To solve this problem, use visual prompts (picture of the items) and verbal prompts (item names). Once the doors are open, treat the shelf storage just like any other shelf organization with the use of prompts.

## THE CONCEPT OF STORAGE AND DISPLAY

Manipulative objects stored in containers or on shelves need to be arranged in such a manner that students can predictably retrieve them and return them. The materials are placed on the shelves in a left-to-right and top-to-bottom organization. The first materials located in the container on the top left shelf would be the ones with the least academic or physical challenge. Moving to the right on the same shelf, the containers would contain increasingly difficult materials, dropping to the shelf below and repeating the same left-to-right arrangement based on difficulty or complexity. For example, if the teacher is arranging puzzles on the shelf in a first-grade classroom, the puzzle placed in the first left position would be a 4-piece puzzle, moving to the right on the same shelf would be a 6-piece puzzle, then 8- and 12-piece puzzles. Moving to the second shelf, a 16-piece puzzle might be first, continuing to the right in a similar fashion. The most difficult manipulatives would always be found in the right corner of the bottom shelf.

## CONTROL OF ERROR

Let's return to the earlier example of the disruption caused by the rolling marker and the second-grade boys in art class. To view a different approach to this situation, let's change scenes to a different classroom, where the teacher has taken the markers and cemented the marker caps upside-down in an empty, cleaned tuna can. The markers can then be placed back into the cemented caps and placed on the table for the students to use, providing a number of benefits. The students may take out, use, and replace the markers, always knowing where they belong. In addition, storing the markers in fixed caps prevents them from rolling off the table. And, since the markers are now always stored facing down, gravity will keep the tips moist for quick use by the students. There is now less likelihood that the markers will be laying about on a table or in a box, accidentally marking the table or drying out in the open air. The teacher in this classroom has deliberately engineered into the activity and materials the invaluable concept of *control of error* (see Figure 11–10). The students are less likely to make a mistake or have a problem using the material, and the teacher has prevented potential discipline situations such as those created by having students scrambling on hands and knees under the table and across the floor chasing a runaway marker.

Every space and all materials must be evaluated to determine if they can be creatively engineered, using the concept of *control of error,* so that students may be free to actively use materials with little concern for breakage or for the kinds of accidents that may disrupt daily classroom activities. Educational games with many pieces that tend to get lost can be stored and used on small cafeteria trays. Legos, with their greater expense and number of pieces to control, may be used on a larger cafeteria tray (2 feet by 3 feet), or a Lego table can be purchased to help confine the pieces and make them easier to control. Smocks for painting,

**FIGURE 11–10   Control of Error**

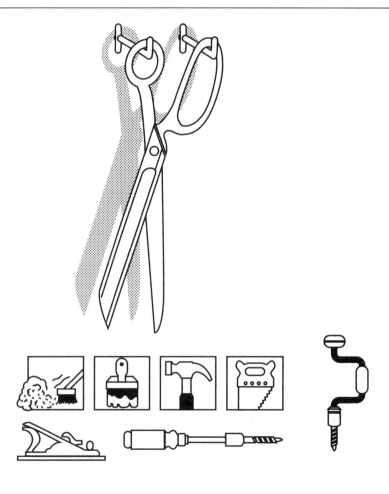

plastic eye shields for hammering at the carpentry table, mouth guards for the water fountain to prevent students from sucking on the outlet— all these provide control of error.

---

### CONTROL OF ERROR

Arranging and putting together materials in a manner that minimizes the chances that students will break, spill, or have accidents while using them.

---

## Bulletin Boards

The best bulletin boards are those that teach. Try to have the students in your class do the bulletin boards. See if student projects based on the subject matter can be designed so that the final products make good displays on bulletin boards. Never use bulletin boards or wall space to display students' work, which would allow a comparison revealing best to worst students. This is humiliating to the student who has done poorly and uncomfortable to the insecure adolescent who has done well and might be "put down" for this by peers. Local and national teacher conferences regularly feature educational materials such as teacher "hint" books. Try to find ones that demonstrate a wide array of bulletin board designs. If all else fails, buy the art teacher lunch and see if you can convince him or her to use your classroom space to display seasonal art projects normally done in the art class.

## Posting Class Rules

Posting four to six class rules—positive statements saying what to do rather than what not to do—is a very common practice. An example would be:

Rule 1: Bring all needed materials to class.

Rule 2: Be in your seat and ready to begin work when the bell rings.

Rule 3: Respect and be polite to all people.

Rule 4: Do not talk or leave your desk when someone else is talking.

Rule 5: Respect other people's property.

Rule 6: Obey all school rules.[3]

Tradition and such discipline models as Assertive Discipline say that these four to six rules should be permanently posted on the bulletin board. I question the wisdom of this for a number of reasons:

1. After 10 days, the students visually saturate on the list and really stop paying attention to it, rendering it ineffective as a verbal

prompt. So use it during the first three weeks of school, or during Mars Days, and then take it down. Put it up again when new Mars Days are employed—normally after long holidays, when good spring weather "springs," or any time you feel that these rules are not being obeyed and need to be retaught using this list as a verbal prompt.

2. Rules have to be taught through the process of Say, Show, and Check-Do (see Chapter 12), and once they are learned as habit, the posted list is of very little value.

3. The list of the four to six rules appears as the teacher's holy written commandments, and, if posted permanently, can seem repressive. In addition, the list will begin to weather and yellow and become esthetically offensive to look at day in and day out.

## Pets and Plants

Both pets and plants can add interest to a classroom, but they are meaningful to students only if they care for the creatures themselves. If pets and plants are your hobby and you do not permit the children to look after them, they will see these fascinating items as *your* possessions, and the pets or plants will be ignored. Mount a record-keeping chart near the plant or pet and require the caregiver to record the amount of water and food given so you can assure yourself that the living items are properly being cared for.

## Audiovisual and Similar Equipment

During the first six weeks of a new school year (Mars Days), when you are using a new piece of audiovisual equipment for instructional purposes for the first time, teach one of the four teams how to use the equipment. Conduct this "training" as you are working with the equipment so you do not lose time doing so, and continue the processes until all groups are trained. From that point on, give two members of the groups responsibility for running the equipment, and rotate this responsibility among all groups and all students.

## Care of the Windows and Blinds

You may notice that at 10 A.M. during the fall and spring months, the sun streams into your classroom, making a blinding glare on the chalkboard and overheating the classroom. Place the care of windows and blinds on a Student Job List, and teach and assign the yellow and blue teams (nearest to the windows) to care for the windows and blinds. Teach them to watch for certain daily patterns and take appropriate actions to eliminate the problem.

## Turning Lights On and Off

When using the *concept of transitional threes*, teach the last group when departing the room to turn off the classroom lights and teach the first group when arriving to turn them back on.

## Teacher's Desk, Filing Cabinets, and Bookcases

The second-best location for the teacher's desk, if it cannot be placed as shown in Figure 11–1, is at the back of the room and near the west wall. When seated, you will be able to visually scan the students, but they will not need to see you. In fact, if you repeatedly catch the eyes of a student while the class is doing seatwork and you are completing paperwork at your desk, it is a sign that some students are off task and "something is going on." Decide whether the top and inside of your desk belongs only to you or whether the top is to be shared with students (picking up hand-outs and depositing homework); the inside space should only be accessed by you. This is your choice, but during the first days of the semester, students need to know the rules regarding the use of the top and inside of your desk, as well as filing cabinets, bookcases, and similar storage areas.

## Storage of Hand-Carried Items

Some students are packrats, carrying excessive items that take up too much desk space and surrounding floor space. They may have to carry these items in a backpack or gym bag. You want desktops to be free for students to work on, and you want the aisles to be clear so you can *work the crowd*. Caution the students against bringing excessive items that are not needed for your instruction. When they are brought despite your warnings, you may solve it one of two ways: You may send the offending student back to her locker (if the school has these) to deposit these items and then, as a *logical consequence*, keep her after the bell rings, to work for two minutes before she is permitted to leave. (Remember, getting out of the door as soon as possible is a real incentive for most students).

Second, you can place a large open storage box at the back of the classroom, put a small box of sticky labels nearby, and permit the student to stick a label with her name on the item and place the item in the box. Don't lecture about it; simply point to the item and point to the box (*visual prompt*)—the student will understand. Put a disclaimer on this box, stating that you are not responsible for these items if they are stolen. Teach this during the first days of the semester.

## Pencil Sharpening

The rule regarding pencil sharpening is the teacher's preference. If you are annoyed by the grinding sound of the sharpener or suspect the students are playing games with "going to the sharpener" in order to pass a friend a note, you will need to teach your pencil-sharpening rules the very first day of school. As a back-up position, some teachers find a supply of grungy old broken pencils and put them in a pencil can for students to borrow. Jones suggests that if you do not have grungy pencils, actually break up some good ones so they are not appealing.

Have two cans, one marked "in" and one marked "out." When a student's pencil breaks, he puts his "pointless" good pencil in the "in" can and takes a grungy one from the "out" can. At the end of the period, the student can return the teacher's pencil and retrieve his own. For a student who does not have a pencil, some teachers require that the student actually take off one shoe and place it on the table by the "in" can. When the student has returned the teacher's pencil, he can retrieve his shoe. No pencils "walk" off this way and the "shoe leaving" becomes a disincentive as the student feels rather awkward hopping around the classroom.

## Paper Headings

There should be a uniform heading, common to all teachers in the school, that students are taught to automatically put at the top of all work papers and tests. A good example would be:

| | |
|---|---|
| Last Name, First: | Date: |
| Subject: | Teacher's Title (Mr. Mrs. Ms. Dr.) and Last Name: |

A large model of this heading is written on display paper and posted above or on the chalkboard, and taught to all students during the first days of a new semester. During the first two weeks, the students are repeatedly reminded about the heading; at the end of the second week, the model is taken down and the verbal prompting stops. On the third week, with red pencil, the teacher circles all papers missing any parts of the heading (fading to a visual prompt) as a practice reminder. The teacher then announces that beginning on the fourth week and from then on, the students will lose one point for lacking a completed heading (a disincentive). If this one point makes a difference between a higher or lower grade, or a B or B+, the student always receives the better grade so that he or she is not downgraded and punished through the use of grades because of behavior rather than through a demonstration of knowledge in academics. This heading will permit the teacher to easily alphabetize the papers so scores can be recorded in the grade book.

## SUMMARY

Many constructs and concepts exist to help the teacher design a classroom balanced with appropriate materials and methods for their proper arrangement. But the steam that makes this classroom engine run remains the teacher. Making use of the balanced classroom, she now has the freedom to create a ballet of teacher movement, supervising this space by her presence and ability to look on. The teacher, finally, plans for ways that every young student may get a share of her emotional investment and skilled help. The blend of space, objects, and teacher presence and emotional investment "speaks" clearly to students, telling them that they are safe, secure, and wanted in this classroom environment.

# Related Readings

Frost, J. L., & Klein, B. L. (1979). *Students Play and Playgrounds*. Boston: Allyn and Bacon.

Gerhardt. L. A. (1973). *Moving and Knowing: The Young Student Orients Himself in Space*. Englewood Cliffs, NJ: Prentice-Hall.

Kritchevsky, S., and others. (1969). *Planning Environments for Young Children: Physical Space*. Washington, DC: NAEYC.

Wolfgang, C. H., & Wolfgang, M. E. (1992). *School for Young Children: Developmentally Appropriate Practices*. Boston: Allyn and Bacon

# Endnotes

1. It is highly recommended that before you begin to arrange or reevaluate current play materials and classroom space, you should obtain and read Kritchevsky's *Planning Environments for Young Children: Physical Space*. In addition, you should obtain a free planning guide from either Childcraft Education Corp., Kaplan School Supplies, or Creative Playthings, which will also provide free slides or videotapes on organizing and selecting materials for your classroom. Kritchevsky's pamphlet-like book, the Wolfgang and Wolfgang book, and the supply company planning guides recommend a checklist of materials and suggest methods of "mapping" your room before you actually move heavy equipment and furniture. The guides provide a measured grid system with silhouetted cut-out pieces simulating furniture and equipment; these can be laid proportionally on the grid to make a classroom map to assist your organizing.

2. Jones, F. (1987). *Positive Classroom Discipline*. New York: McGraw-Hill.

3. Emmer, E. T., Evertson, C. M., Sanford, J. P., Clements, B. S., & Worsham, M. W. (1984). *Classroom Management for Secondary Teachers*. Englewood Cliffs, NJ: Prentice-Hall.

# Rules and Authority

## 12

"Oh, my!" You look out at the sea of faces in your classroom filled with students. *It is the first minute of the first hour of the first day of the school year.* You may be an experienced teacher starting your final year before retirement or a first-year teacher facing your very first classroom alone, without the help of a supervisor. The feeling is not unlike standing on the side of a swimming pool ready to dive in, and realizing that there will be a shock to your body system—it may be pleasant or it may be unpleasant. You do not yet know the course of the journey that is about to begin.

Whether you realize it or not, the dynamic interaction between you and your students that is about to occur this first day will lay the foundation for interactions for the remainder of the year.[1] So, somewhere deep in the back of your mind you hear a voice repeating the old saying, "Don't smile until Christmas!" However, a clear understanding of the Three Faces of Discipline techniques will give you new insights into the first day's dynamics and will provide procedures, practices, and guidelines for preventing this first "dive" into the new school year from being an unpleasant "belly-flop." Instead, it can help make the new school year a pleasant and productive experience.

## RULES ARE SITUATIONAL AND SPATIALLY BOUND

Daily activities are filled with disciplined behavior. People enter a restaurant, are seated, place their order, eat, pay, and depart. People enter church or synagogue, are seated, listen, sing, pray, and depart. People arrive at a weekend football game, are seated, perhaps eat and drink, cheer, and depart. In each of these situations, the sequence and range of behavior was highly productive and socially accepted. In each case, the person was playing a role (customer, worshipper, fan) and there were well-defined rules for the behavior involved in playing these roles.[2] But what if we mix these behaviors? What if after the minister's sermon a worshipper screams out, "Go big Saints!" demands a beer and popcorn with his communion wafer, and gives the minister a tip as he leaves? This clearly would be seen as inappropriate, undisciplined behavior, and nearby worshippers would probably wish to see the offender given the name of a very good psychiatrist.

Each of these behaviors can be completely socially acceptable. What has made them unacceptable is their spatial context—that is, their occurrence in a church with its well-defined parameters of behavior. Acceptable behavior, then, is spatially bound. People obey or follow rules because they have learned a repertoire of motor rules and use them appropriately, based on the spatial context cues, or *prompts*, that have been modeled for or taught to them by authority figures. This is especially true for classrooms, where both teachers and students play roles governed by rules that give structure for "how to behave."

The difficulty for all students in the first minutes and hours of the first day of class is that they do not know the rules.[3] Young first-graders may be completely unfamiliar with a school environment, while even in the later elementary years (and beyond) the students have not yet learned their new teacher's rules. As a result, they may attempt to use "home" or "street" behaviors and play roles that you, as the teacher, might find unacceptable for "school behavior." Older students have been in many classrooms with many teachers, and the rules have varied dramatically. They are asking the core question: "What will the rules be for this classroom and this particular teacher?" They want to know the structure of how this school, this classroom, this teacher will work. The student on the first day of class is like a visitor to a foreign country, wanting to know how to act in this new classroom culture.

## RULES ARE TAUGHT FORMALLY OR INFORMALLY

It is 20 minutes into the first day of classroom activity, and the class has been asked to fill out information cards. John's pencil point has broken and needs to be sharpened. He cannot complete the required task and wonders what to do. He bravely gets out of his seat and takes five steps toward the pencil sharpener. The teacher intercepts him with a stern, "Where are you going, young man? Sit down! You do not get out of your seat without my permission!" All eyes bounce back and forth between John and the new teacher. The tension in the room mounts. John has informally learned his first rule.

The teacher has not explained the classroom rules regarding use of the pencil sharpener, and experienced students subconsciously now recognize that this teacher is going to play the game of "Gotcha"[4] or "Minefield." Only the teacher will know the rules of what is permitted, and the students will have to guess and test their behavior to see what will be permitted and what will be punished. For these students, then, the classroom is like a minefield; they will never know where to place their feet safely. This unpleasant game will be played for many weeks until finally the students have tested and learned all the rules. However, many "mines" will have to be stepped on to expose all the rules, and the students understandably are left "shell shocked," tense, and angry.

## MOTOR RULES

Carol has just finished eating her lunch in the school cafeteria. She stands, picks up her tray, and begins to walk to the disposal window. Suddenly, she stops, whirls around, and returns to her seat. She positions herself at the back side of her chair and, with a controlled use of her lower body, pushes the chair under the table and out of the aisle. Carol is well disciplined and will be highly prized and praised by her teachers. Carol has also demonstrated the use of a *motor rule*.[5] To be well disciplined at church, at a football game, in a restaurant, or in a classroom means simply knowing and using—almost unconsciously or automatically—a host of motor rules that are socially acceptable for the spatial context.

When students come into the classroom on the first day of school, they simply are entering a new world or culture shaped by the teacher's concepts of what is right or wrong. In some classrooms, students are permitted to sharpen their pencils at any time; in other classrooms (John's, for example), it is a major offense. What is called for in the first hours and days of the new year is *not* the teacher keeping the values and rules a secret from the students, forcing them to play the game of "Gotcha" or "Minefield" in order to learn the rules informally. Instead, the teacher must make these motor rules clear to each student and teach them in an overt, formal manner. To state it clearly, the host of motor rules for each classroom must be taught directly to the students by the teacher. Once the students learn the motor rules, they understand where all the "mines" are placed that might cause them to get into trouble, and they are confident they can avoid them. In other words, they feel safe knowing the rules.

### Teaching Motor Rules

Perhaps as a result of the wide acceptance of Lee Canter's *Assertive Discipline*[6] practices, a common practice in many classrooms is for four to six rules to be written on the chalkboard. As well intended as they may be, such rules as "Raise your hand before speaking out" and "Be courteous to others" are not enough and may not even be understood by children if they are simply taught through a process of "talk." It is highly unlikely that teachers will get the motor actions or motor rules that they desire merely from "talking" their rules. This is like trying to tell yourself where your car is parked in a multilevel parking garage. Consider the visitor to Walt Disney World who is advised over a public address system that his car is parked in a lot named after one the Seven Dwarfs. Later, he cannot remember whether it was Sneezy, Dopey, Grumpy, or whoever, because he had been talked to but had not truly learned the name because he had been "taught" at a shallow verbal level. The teaching of motor rules requires a three-step teaching process (Say, Show, and Check or Do)[7] that requires motor enactment or motor modeling of the rule so that it becomes second nature, such as pushing in the chair after eating in the cafeteria (Figure 12–1).

As you teach motor rules, your instruction progresses through three steps as follows:

## Step 1: Say

"Students, if you need to use the pencil sharpener, please do it when you first come into the room. The sharpener is placed on the inside of the door. Because of the noise it makes, I do not want the pencil sharpener to be used while I am lecturing or while you are working. If an emergency occurs and you cannot do your work because your pencil is broken, I have placed a can of sharpened pencils on my desk. You may get up, put your broken pencil in the can, and take one of mine. At the end of the period, return my pencil and retrieve yours—and try to do it without distracting others."

## Step 2: Show

Once the students are told what the rules are, you move to Step 2: *Show*, demonstrating the motor rules.

"Now, let me show you what I mean. Pretend that you are all taking a quiz, and I am writing tomorrow's assignments on the chalkboard. John, let's say your pencil breaks; would you now get up and show us what actions you would take?" (John, through the *behavioral rehearsal*,[8] demonstrates the motor action correctly.)

## Step 3: Check or Do

You now show the students the negation, or the opposite behavior that you disapprove of, and then end by again modeling the correct way to perform the proposed actions. You ask the low-level question to get a unison response from the entire class to have them evaluate the motor response.

| FIGURE 12–1 | The Three-Step Lesson | |
|---|---|---|
| Step 1 | *Say* | The teacher verbally labels or encodes the object or process being taught. |
| Step 2 | *Show* | The teacher models by displaying the object, or having a student act out the process. |
| Step 3 | *Check* or *Do* | The teacher requires a student or students to physically demonstrate the ability to choose the correct procedure from among a series of options. The teacher always ends the lesson by demonstrating the correct example. |

*"Now, did John take the proper actions, class?" The students respond, "Yes."*

*"Now, just for fun, let's do it again, John, and this time you show us what is* not *the rule. Go to the pencil sharpener and really make some noise as you sharpen your pencil during class." (John models the negation, breaking the rule. The class laughs at his behavior, and you join in with your laughter.) "Class, was that the correct behavior?" (The class responds, "No!" and they all laugh again.) "Now, Robert, you show us again what you are to do if you break your pencil point and need a pencil to do your work." (Robert performs the correct actions desired.) "Was Robert correct, class?" The class responds, "Yes."*

For older students, you might have to use a sense of humor to carry out this teaching of motor rules through the three-step process, but you still clearly communicate the desired behavior. You will also monitor the rule closely[9] the first two or three weeks, to stop any rule breaking that has been learned as a habit. If need be, the rule is retaught through another process of Say, Show, and Check or Do. You need to clearly teach the many motor rules of the classroom environment and practices, and you need to do it in the first minutes, days, and weeks at the beginning of each school year or semester.

## WHAT SHOULD THE CLASSROOM MOTOR RULES BE?

The establishment of motor rules in the classroom and the demand for students to desist[10] their rule breaking is a projection of your own values.[11] Within each of us, as teachers, are varying degrees of need for control, perhaps derived from our earliest training by such adults as parents and teachers. When an adult is eating at a table with a 2½-year-old child who throws mashed potatoes across the table, the adult immediately intervenes—hopefully in a kind and gentle manner—to get the child to desist, clearly setting a limit by saying "No." All requests to desist are a form of saying "No" to a student's behavior. All our "No's" are a projection of our values. Therefore, your values will determine whether students will be required to raise their hands before they speak out, or get permission to leave their seats to sharpen a pencil. For students, particularly at the beginning of the school year, it generally is not of high importance what you say "No" to, but it is important that they know what these "No's" are. Once the students are aware of your "No's," your behavior becomes orderly and predictable and they are not frightened of unpredictable actions. Why is it that some teachers are "hard-nosed" with very strict rules, while others allow considerable autonomy by students—yet both types are respected and loved by students and maintain effective discipline? It is because students know these teachers by their orderly and predictable use of limits or desists ("No's").

What about the teachers who maintain poor discipline and in turn receive little or no respect from students? These are the "loosie-goosie" teachers who one day communicate an acceptance of great freedom and use minimal motor rules, and the very next day "slam-dunk" the students by surprising them with a desist and a demand to obey a rule that they never heard of before.[12] The students will say, "We can never tell where he's coming from!" They mean that this "wishy-washy" teacher's desist requests for behavior through motor rules are disorderly and unpredictable. This puts the students living in the classroom version of a minefield, where the teacher periodically and unpredictably drops "bombs" on them. What is even more deadly is that once the students in this "wishy-washy" teacher's classroom feel they know where the mines are, the next day the mine is moved. (The rule suddenly is not enforced, or is enforced differently, and the students never know why.)

At the practical level, motor rules will cluster under the large headings[13] of walls and objects, rituals, transitions, and student groupings (these techniques are detailed in books on cooperative learning[14]):

1. *Teaching the Walls and Objects*: The teacher begins at the doorway and teaches the motor rules for all objects on the walls, or furniture and equipment positioned against the wall. (For example, *light switches:* Are students permitted to turn lights off and on? *filing cabinets:* Are students permitted to open, use, and explore their contents? *windows:* Are students permitted to raise or lower windows and window blinds? *materials:* What may students do with classroom books and other random materials? Are they permitted to take objects from the teacher's desk, or to go into the teacher's desk drawers?)

2. *Teaching the Rules for Student Rituals*: The teacher tells the students how to perform routine actions, such as raising their hands, signaling that they wish to leave their seat or leave the room, putting a standardized heading on papers, and the like.

3. *Teaching the Rules for Movement or Transitions*: The teacher explains procedures for periods between activities, such as arriving on time, departing, moving from desks to special-area tables, fire drills, handing in and passing out materials, and so on.

4. *Teaching the Rules for the Grouping of Children*: The teacher explains how students are to work when assigned to groups, including each student's responsibility to the group.

These procedures, which are designed to become motor rules, may seem on the surface to be overly controlling. It becomes imperative for the students' well-being, as well as for that of the teacher, to think out how much autonomy students will be granted in each particular classroom and under what circumstances. You can then communicate what you need and expect of students by teaching the motor rules through the three-step process. The worksheet found in Figure 12–2 (at the end of this chapter), titled Materials/ Prompts/ Motor Rules, may be used by the teacher before school begins to clearly determine in writing just what the rules will be regarding various classroom materials and objects. The worksheet also requires the teacher to apply the previously learned principles related to directionality (color coding of walls) and visual prompts. The worksheet, with its list of rules, would then be used to teach motor rules on the first day of the school year.

## Establishing Teacher Authority and Leadership

Even when motor rules are taught, they do not become truly valid to a classroom full of students until they are tested.[16] The students wonder, "Ha! He told us these rules, but does he really mean it? Will he back up his word?" In the erratic classroom of the wishy-washy teacher, there is a void of established authority and leadership. All productive groups require leadership and authority. Closely watch the children's sandlot games and you will see peer leaders emerge from the group to toss the coin to see who goes first; teams are formed with all children yielding authority and leadership to one individual for the temporary life of the game.[17] Normally in games, the other team becomes the "person or people to exclude,"[18] and being a member of a team brings acceptance and belonging because each player has an opposing team of "enemies" to "hate."

Similar actions happen in classrooms. When a teacher fails to establish himself or herself as a leader, a powerful personality (usually one student) will become assertive to fill the void, much to the teacher's detriment. The teacher completely loses control. In fact, when groups of students become uncontrollable, they normally make the classroom teacher the "outside aggressor" (see Chapter 10). Once the teacher loses control in the first few days of school, it probably will be next to impossible to regain control by reestablishing his or her authority or leadership. This is why Jones would say, "Pay in pennies now or pay in dollars later in remediation."[19] This means, of course, that you should take time immediately to establish a classroom management system, and you will need less time in the long run to stop in order to deal with discipline incidents.

If you watch these sandlot games closely, you will find that when a new set of peers comes together to play, the children heatedly argue the rules for many minutes before the games begin. Once the rules are agreed on, they become spatially context bound: "These are the stickball rules for our street, our neighborhood, or our playground!" These rules reflect the children's definition of reality for that space. When they are joined by a new child from "outside the neighborhood" who might have played with a different set of rules, play stops and the rules again are debated until everyone—especially the new player—is in agreement that "these are the rules." This need to preestablish rules and create a sense of fairness reflects the school-age child's budding sense of moral development[20] and social understanding. These developmental needs will be brought into the "game of school" or the "game of classroom."

The common denominator or social dynamic that is central for establishing teacher authority and leadership is a clash.[21] This occurs when a student violates a rule, accidentally or deliberately, to test the rule's validity and the teacher as the leader. Daily positive and productive educational experiences with students are the building blocks for a good teacher-student relationship, but the clashes between the student and the teacher, and their positive resolution, provide the cement that binds these building blocks of relationships together.

The clashes between husband and wife, between friends, between parent and child, and between teacher and student are all pivotal points in social relationships. Critical to maintaining a relationship is one person's use of power to raise an issue, and the use of minimum power to get a change in the other's behavior while still maintaining the second person's dignity. In contrast, the excessive use of power and "slam-dunking" the other person destroys the other's self worth and destroys the relationship. The careful use of power in setting limits and expressing a desist will be a critical element in successful discipline.

It is the third week of class. The students have been taught the motor rules, and your classroom procedures and activities are running smoothly. Just as things seem to be going so well, here comes John, and it is clear to you and all the class that he has broken an established rule. John is testing the validity of your rules and your skill as a teacher. This is the clash! You must initiate a desist request, and the manner and skill with which you do it will provide the cement—the information about you—that will bind the class behind your authority and produce a quality relationship between you and your students. If this challenge is poorly handled, everyone in the class—not just misbehaving John—will fear being slam-dunked or punished unfairly in the future, and therefore will protect themselves by withholding their affection and cooperation.

Poorly handling the desist request is likely to turn the teacher into the class *outside aggressor*. In Transactional Analysis[22] terms, the comment, "Where are you going, young man? Sit down! You do not get out of your seat without my permission!" is clearly a PARENT statement full of demeaning guilt that communicates the student's unworthiness. This use of *Guilt Induction ("GI'ing")* is a psychologically destructive process that strikes the student directly in the conscience, flooding the child with guilt that will soon turn to anger. An ADULT statement, in Transactional Analysis terms, would permit the teacher to be assertive and initiate a desist request in such a manner that it addresses the reality problem at hand and is free of guilt. An example would be, "I need you to stay in your seat during tests so other students will not be distracted."

ADULT-based techniques can initiate a skilled desist request in a way that cements the relationship. The central motivation for most students is the desire for belonging,[23] the wish to be valued and accepted by teacher and peers. For the older students, acceptance by peers is more valued than the teacher's acceptance. The risk in asserting a desist request is that it may be loaded with guilt that communicates nonvaluing or nonrespect for the student as an individual. When it is done in front of peers, it threatens the student's prestige among those peers.

## POWER AND DEGREES OF DESIST CONTROL

We have seen how teacher techniques can be placed along a continuum of degrees of power and control, and through the Three Faces of Discipline construct can be placed under the broad headings of Relationship-Listening, Confronting-Contracting, and Rules and Consequences. With this power continuum in mind, it is suggested that you first apply a desist request with minimum intrusion, as with the Relationship-Listening attitude and techniques. If this fails to be effective, you can then move to increased power or intrusion using Confronting-Contracting procedures, and then finally to maximum control with Rules and Consequences desist techniques.

## ATTENDING BEHAVIORS

The teacher complains, "These students just will not listen!" This may be true for large numbers of students who are raised on large diets of television and in environments that do not require close attention. If this complaint is accepted as valid, the job then becomes one of teaching these students attending behaviors. This is done through the use of teaching techniques called *prompts* and *fading*. For example, the teacher wants the class to become quiet so that directions may be given, so she proceeds as follows.

## PROMPTS

1. "Clang, Clang, Clang." (The teacher uses a bell or whistle, blinks the lights, hits a note on the piano, etc., as an aversive stimulus [auditory prompt] that will get the students' attention.)

2. "Class!" (The teacher gives a verbal prompt by labeling who she is addressing.)

3. "Stop!" (The teacher gives a verbal prompt as a command.)

4. "Look at me!" (Second command; the teacher points to her eyes as a visual prompt.)

5. The teacher scores a point (reinforcer) on the Incentive System's Score Board for all teams that comply. (See Chapter 9 on the Incentive System.)

6. The teacher now "squares off." (See Chapter 3, Looking.)

7. The teacher repeats steps 1, 2, 3, 4, 5, and 6, as directed above, three times (do three cycles).

### Fading

The teacher continues to "square off" and wait. These nonverbal prompts signal the students that their attention is wanted, but the teacher will gradually fade this out:

| Request | Teacher Actions |
|---------|-----------------|
| First | Does three cycles of items 1–6 above. |
| Second | Does only two cycles of numbers 1–6. |
| Third | Does one cycle of numbers 1–6. |
| Fourth | Does two "Clangs" and numbers 2–6. |
| Fifth | Does one "Clang" and numbers 2–6. |
| Sixth | Fades (stops doing) "Clang" but does 2–6. |
| Seventh | Fades (stops doing) 2, and begins with 3–6. |
| Eighth | Fades 3, and begins with 4–6. |
| Ninth | Fades 4, and begins with 5 and does 6. |
| Tenth | Fades 5, and then squares off and waits. |

From this point on, the teacher needs only to square off at the power position in the classroom, which is shown on the Classroom Map (Figure 11–1 in Chapter 11). This is the repeated location at which the teacher regularly stands to begin nearly all activities or to get the attention of the entire class before directions are given. The teaching of attending behaviors begins with aversive stimuli and involves "training" the students, but with the fading techniques, the teacher gradually leads the students to respond to her language and physical presence. Attending to others' language progresses from simply training, as might be done with animals, to the human process of communication through language that teaches the listening skills necessary for the teacher to instruct and for the students to comprehend and attend.

## SUMMARY

Let's return to the sea of faces of your new group of students on the *first minute of the first hour of the first day of the school year.* You are now ready to dive into the school year with an understanding that the students are eager to quickly learn who you are, what "No's" you use, and the motor rules you want in the spatial context of your classroom. You understand that rules are broken soon after they are made, and you know that soon you will need to make desist or limit-setting requests. You now understand that there is a range of power in limit setting, from minimal to quite assertive demands for appropriate behavior and action, and you may wear one of the three faces. The more genuine and relaxed you can be in using desists and the power inherent in them, the more skilled you will become as a teacher.

# Endnotes

1. Brophy, J., & Good, T. L. (1974). *Teacher-Student Relationships: Causes and Consequences.* New York: Holt, Rinehart and Winston.
2. Smilansky, S., & Shefatya, L. (1990). *Facilitating Play: A Medium for Promoting Cognitive, Socio-Emotional and Academic Development in Young Children.* Gaithersburg, MD: Psychosocial & Educational Publications.
3. Kounin, J. S. (1970). *Discipline and Group Management in Classrooms.* New York: Holt, Rinehart, and Winston.
4. Berne, E. (1964). *Games People Play: The Psychology of Human Relations.* New York: Grove Press.
5. Piaget, J. (1965). *The Moral Judgment of the Child.* Marjorie Gabain, trans. New York: Free Press.
6. Canter, L. (1992). *Assertive Discipline: Positive Behavior Management for Today's Classroom.* Santa Monica, CA: Lee Canter & Associates.
7. Engelmann, S. (1980). *Direct Instruction.* Englewood Cliffs, NJ: Educational Technology Publications.
8. Willoughby-Herb, S., & Neisworth, J. T. (1983). *HICOMP Curriculum.* Columbus, OH: Charles E. Merrill.
9. Kounin, *Discipline and Group Management.*
10. Ibid.
11. Spitz, R. (1957). *No and Yes.* New York: International Universities Press.
12. Canter, *Assertive Discipline.*
13. Evertson, C. M., Emmer, E. E., Clements, B. S., Sanford, J. P., & Worsham, M. E. (1984). *Classroom Management for Elementary Teachers.* Englewood Cliffs, NJ: Prentice-Hall.
14. Johnson, D. W., Johnson, R. T., & Holubec, E. J. (1986). *Circles of Learning: Cooperation in the Classroom.* Edina, MN: Interaction Book Company.
15. Wolfgang, C. H., & Wolfgang, M. E., (1992). *School for Young Children: Developmentally Appropriate Practices.* Boston: Allyn and Bacon.
16. Johnson, Johnson, & Holubec, *Circles of Learning.*
17. Herron, R. E., & Sutton-Smith, B. (1971). *Child's Play.* New York: John Wiley and Sons.
18. Isaacs, S. (1968). *Social Development.* New York: Schocken Press.
19. Jones, F. (1987). *Positive Discipline.* New York: McGraw-Hill.
20. Piaget, *The Moral Judgment.*
21. Spitz, *No and Yes.*
22. Berne, *Games People Play.*
23. Driekurs, R., & Cassel, P. (1972). *Discipline Without Tears.* New York: Hawthorn Books.

**FIGURE 12–2  Materials/Prompts/Motor Rules**

| | Materials | Visual Prompt (number silhouette) | Check Column Indicating the Wall on Which the Materials Are Located | | | | Interior Items | Motor Rules |
| --- | --- | --- | --- | --- | --- | --- | --- | --- |
| | | | North (green) | East (red) | South (blue) | West (yellow) | | |
| 1. | Door | | | | | | | |
| | a. Hallway passes | | | | | | | |
| 2. | Light Switch | | | | | | | |
| 3. | Pencil Sharpener | | | | | | | |
| 4. | Trash Can | | | | | | | |
| 5. | Chalkboard (chalk, erasers) | | | | | | | |
| 6. | Filing Cabinets | | | | | | | |
| | a. Cabinet #1 (name): | | | | | | | |
| | b. Cabinet #2 (name): | | | | | | | |

(continued)

**FIGURE 12–2  Materials/Prompts/Motor Rules (continued)**

| Materials | Visual Prompt (number silhouette) | Check Column Indicating the Wall on Which the Materials Are Located | | | | Interior Items | Motor Rules |
|---|---|---|---|---|---|---|---|
| | | North (green) | East (red) | South (blue) | West (yellow) | | |
| c. Cabinet #3 (name) | | | | | | | |
| 7. **Teacher's Desk/Chair** | | | | | | | |
| a. Teacher's grade/lesson plan books | | | | | | | |
| b. teacher's purse/briefcase or similar property | | | | | | | |
| c. drawers | | | | | | | |
| d. top items (assignment boxes, pencils, etc.) | | | | | | | |
| e. Item #1 (name): | | | | | | | |
| f. Item #2 (name): | | | | | | | |
| g. Item #3 (name): | | | | | | | |
| h. Item #4 (name): | | | | | | | |

| | | | | | | | |
|---|---|---|---|---|---|---|---|
| 8. | **Shelved Materials** | | | | | | |
| | a. Open shelves | | | | | | |
| | (1) Free-standing items (microscope, globe, etc.) | | | | | | |
| | (2) In containers | | | | | | |
| | (3) On trays | | | | | | |
| | (4) Stacked (such as puzzles) | | | | | | |
| | b. Closed (doored) shelves | | | | | | |
| | (1) Free-standing items (microscope, globe, etc.) | | | | | | |
| | (2) In containers | | | | | | |
| | (3) On trays | | | | | | |
| | (4) Stacked (such as puzzles) | | | | | | |
| 9. | **Windows** | | | | | | |

(continued)

**FIGURE 12–2  Materials/Prompts/Motor Rules (continued)**

| Materials | Visual Prompt (number silhouette) | Check Column Indicating the Wall on Which the Materials Are Located | | | | Interior Items | Motor Rules |
| --- | --- | --- | --- | --- | --- | --- | --- |
| | | North (green) | East (red) | South (blue) | West (yellow) | | |
| a. Blinds/curtains | | | | | | | |
| 10. **Water Fountain** | | | | | | | |
| 11. **Sink** | | | | | | | |
| a. Towels | | | | | | | |
| b. Soap | | | | | | | |
| c. Trash can | | | | | | | |
| 12. **Restroom** | | | | | | | |
| a. Toilet | | | | | | | |

| | | | | | |
|---|---|---|---|---|---|
| b. Tissue | | | | | |
| c. Sink | | | | | |
| d. Towels | | | | | |
| e. Soap | | | | | |
| f. Trash can | | | | | |
| g. Other (name): | | | | | |
| 13. **Exhibits** | | | | | |
| a. Flora | | | | | |
| (1) Name: | | | | | |
| (2) Name: | | | | | |
| (3) Name: | | | | | |
| b. Livestock (rabbits, fish, hamster, etc.) | | | | | |
| (1) Name: | | | | | |

(continued)

FIGURE 12–2   Materials/Prompts/Motor Rules (*continued*)

| Materials | Visual Prompt (number silhouette) | Check Column Indicating the Wall on Which the Materials Are Located | | | | Interior Items | Motor Rules |
|---|---|---|---|---|---|---|---|
| | | North (green) | East (red) | South (blue) | West (yellow) | | |
| (2) Name: | | | | | | | |
| (3) Name: | | | | | | | |
| c. Other | | | | | | | |
| (1) Name | | | | | | | |
| (2) Name | | | | | | | |
| (3) Name | | | | | | | |
| 14.  **Display Tables** | | | | | | | |
| a. Name: | | | | | | | |
| b. Name: | | | | | | | |
| c. Name: | | | | | | | |

|  |  | | | | | | | |
|---|------|---|---|---|---|---|---|---|
| 15. | **Student Coat Racks** | | | | | | | |
| 16. | **Student Storage Bins (Wall)** | | | | | | | |
| 17. | **Student Desk** | | | | | | | |
| | a. Desk surface use | ■ | | | | | | |
| | b. Desk storage | | | | | | | |
| | (1) Book arrangement | | | | | | | |
| | (2) Loose paper | | | | | | | |
| | (3) Pencil/erasers | | | | | | | |
| | (4) Loose items | | | | | | | |
| | (5) Personal items | | | | | | | |
| | c. Notebook organizer | ■ | | | | | | |
| | d. Chairs (carrying of) | | | | | | | |
| 18. | **Audio-visual Equipment (Permanent)** | | | | | | | |

(continued)

**FIGURE 12–2  Materials/Prompts/Motor Rules (continued)**

| Materials | Visual Prompt (number silhouette) | Check Column Indicating the Wall on Which the Materials Are Located | | | | Interior Items | Motor Rules |
|---|---|---|---|---|---|---|---|
| | | North (green) | East (red) | South (blue) | West (yellow) | | |
| a. Name: | | | | | | | |
| b. Name: | | | | | | | |
| c. Name: | | | | | | | |
| 19. **Apparatus/ Equipment** | | | | | | | |
| a. Computer | | | | | | | |
| (1) Keyboard use/care | | | | | | | |
| (2) Diskette storage/care | | | | | | | |
| (3) CD-ROM use/care | | | | | | | |
| (4) Desk storage/care | | | | | | | |
| (5) Mouse storage/care | | | | | | | |

| (6) Printer storage/care | b. Name | (1) | (2) | (3) | (4) | c. Name: | (1) | (2) | (3) | (4) | (5) |
|---|---|---|---|---|---|---|---|---|---|---|---|
|  |  |  |  |  |  |  |  |  |  |  |  |

**259**

# The First Days of School

## Teaching the Basics of Good Classroom Discipline

# 13

In our adult world, spatial location communicates a specific set of motor rules and behavior. Because we are well socialized, we respond appropriately. In a movie theater, we act with certain defined motor rules; at a football game, we act in an entirely different way.

A great number of today's students are growing up without being taught a sensitivity to spatial rules in their home setting. Teachers may remark about many of today's students, "Where do these kids come from—they don't know how to act! Are they from Mars?" Well, compared to the way the teachers were raised and taught value systems, these students may just as well come from Mars, considering the dramatic gap between the teachers' values and those of the students. The new mission of the quality school is now clear: We must teach students to be socially sensitive to expected and "proper" social behavior based on where they are and the social context of the moment. Developing this awareness is a skill, and once students learn it, they will be ready for the life experiences of a working world filled with rule-based environments. We start this all-important educational process by declaring *Mars Days*.

If a student had come to a classroom from a foreign land, or another planet, you would not expect him to know your habits, routines, and cultural dos and don'ts. Similarly, you cannot expect many of today's students to know how to behave in your classroom. Therefore, it may be best to consider them as having just stepped off a spaceship from Mars. In dealing with these "Martians," you cannot expect them to know anything about how your classroom works, so you directly teach it to them. Declare Mars Days (1) during the first six week of a new school year or semester, (2) when a large number of new students enter the school or classroom and will not know the routine, (3) after a long holiday break that has kept the students away from the school and school routines, and/or (4) when classroom behavior generally begins to deteriorate and you find yourself dealing with too many discipline incidents (too many "fires" to put out). Too many accidents, especially in the hallways or cafeteria, would also signal a need to declare a schoolwide Mars Day.

## ORIENTATION DAYS AND WEEKS

During the first six weeks of the school year (what we have labeled Mars Days), the classroom should follow a schedule similar to the one seen in Figure 13–1 (found at the end of the chapter). On the first day of the first week (presumably Monday), you assign seats based on the numbering system described in Chapter 11. Next, teach the Rules and Responsibility Game (see Chapter 9) as a part of your Incentive System. Finally, on that very first morning, teach the motor rules from the planning form (Figure 12–2) through the Three-Step Lesson (Figure 12–1). While conducting any transition within the classroom—such as moving to groups or departing the classroom—you would teach transitional prompts using the three-step concept for making transitions (see Chapter 12). At the end of the morning, just before lunch this first day, award a small Type 1 Reinforcer (edible) as a part of the Rights and Responsibility Game. Once this has been accomplished, a new "game" begins.

After lunch, hold a plus/delta classroom meeting, encouraging the students to openly discuss what went well during the first half of the day. Place a summary statement under a "Plus" column on the chalkboard. Students should also be encouraged to tell what they did not like or any problems they faced, with these listed under a "Delta" column. (*Delta* is the mathematical or scientific notation for a problem that needs a solution or a change that needs to occur—hence the name plus/delta discussion.) This is an honest discussion and the teacher must be prepared to hear criticism about her own actions, be willing to list this on the board, and then invite the students to come up with solutions as to how to make classroom change, thus moving the problems in the Delta column into positives on the Plus side.

Finally, at the end of the day, another reinforcer (Type 2-Tangible) is awarded and a second plus/delta meeting is held. Do not erase listed items from the board, but leave them there for review the next morning.

During the second day (Tuesday), conduct another lesson on motor rules (see Figure 13–1), but this time choose only half the previous day's list of rules, focusing on the rules you know are more difficult for the students to use and remember. The previous day's plus/delta results are also reviewed. Next, introduce the Assignment Board (see Chapter 11) and how it is to be used, giving the class one or two easy assignments. Again, all transitions are taught as a three-step process. At the end of the morning, another Type 1 Reinforcer is awarded.

Most of the items on the Orientation Week (Mars Days) chart (Figures 13–2 through 13–6) will now be self-explanatory. What is important to see as you progress through the six weeks is that items are faded with time. Reinforcers gradually change from time-consuming Type 1 and 2 reinforcers to the use of Type 3 PATs, with preferred activity time finally being relegated only to Friday afternoons. Rules are taught less and less frequently until they eventually fade out as well.

## SUMMARY

A program of orienting students into the new classroom setting, the concept of Mars Days, is typically conducted over a period of 6 weeks. For most elementary school classrooms, this six-week period will be sufficient. However, depending on the age of the students or the number of very difficulty children in the class, the teacher's professional judgment may indicate that Mars Days may need to be extended to 8 or 10 weeks, or even longer. (On the rare occasion, the teacher may need to use the Mars Days structure for the entire school year.)

The goal of a Mars Days program is to gradually fade the need for the Rules and Responsibility Game with its reinforcers, replacing it with a process through which the students solve difficulties and conflicts—especially discipline problems—through the use of plus/delta meetings. Obtaining the ability to discuss problems though the use of language, within the context of group membership, is the ultimate goal of the Three Faces of Discipline philosophy.

**FIGURE 13–1  Orientation Week 1 (Mars Days)**

Teacher assigns seating in a boy-girl, boy-girl arrangement, and in teams. Once the teacher knows the students better, seating may be rearranged to balance teams by sex, race, ability, and difficulty of behavior.

Teach the motor rules through a Show, Say, and Check/Do three-step teacher process. Also teach the Rights and Responsibility Incentive Game.

Teach transitions as a three-step process to in- and out-of-room movements.

| | Monday | Tuesday | Wednesday | Thursday | Friday |
|---|---|---|---|---|---|
| Begin Day | ☐ Assign Seats & Teams (number system)<br>☐ Teach Rules & Responsibility Game<br>☐ Teach Motor Rules (100% of rules) | ☐ Teach Motor Rules (50% of rules)<br>☐ Review Monday's (+/–) Meeting Results<br>☐ Teach Assignment Board | ☐ Teach Motor Rules (4 rules only)<br>☐ Teach and Use Assignment Board | ☐ Use and Monitor Assignment Board<br>☐ Teach Motor Rules (2 rules only) | ☐ Use and Monitor Assignment Board<br>☐ Teach Motor Rules (rules as needed)<br>☐ Award Reinforcer (Type 1) |
| During A.M. | ☐ Teach Transitional Prompts 1. Depart/return from classroom | ☐ Teach Transitional Prompts | ☐ Teach Transitional Prompts | ☐ Teach Transitional Prompts<br>Hold (+/–) Meeting with Losing Team | ☐ Teach Transitional Prompts<br>Hold (+/–) Meeting with Losing Team |
| Just Before Lunch | ☐ Award Reinforcer (Type 1) | ☐ Award Reinforcer (Type 1) | ☐ Award Reinforcer (Type 2) | ☐ Award Reinforcer (Type 2) | ☐ Award Reinforcer (Type 2) |
| Just After Lunch | ☐ Hold (+/–) Meeting | ☐ Hold (+/–) Meeting | | ☐ Hold (+/–) Meeting | |
| During P.M. | | | Hold (+/–) Meeting with Losing Team | Hold (+/–) Meeting with Losing Team | Hold (+/–) Meeting with Losing Team |
| End of Day | ☐ Award Reinforcer (Type 2)<br>☐ Hold (+/–) Meeting | ☐ Award Reinforcer (Type 2)<br>☐ Hold (+/–) Meeting<br>☐ Review and Use Assignment Board | ☐ Award Reinforcer (Type 1)<br>☐ Hold (+/–) Meeting<br>☐ Use and Monitor Assignment Board | ☐ Award Reinforcer (Type 3)<br>☐ Hold (+/–) Meeting<br>☐ Monitor Assignment Board | ☐ Award Reinforcer (Type 3)<br>☐ Hold (+/–) Meeting |

Hold a +/– Class Meeting

Teach and begin using the Assignment Board

Award Reinforcer Type 3: PAT

Award Reinforcer Type 2: Tangible

Award Reinforcer Type 1: Edibles

**FIGURE 13–2 Orientation Week 2 (Mars Days)**

| | Monday | Tuesday | Wednesday | Thursday | Friday |
|---|---|---|---|---|---|
| Begin Day | ☐ Reassign Seats & Teams (number system)<br>☐ Teach Motor Rules (50% of rules) | *(Fade to Reinforcers, Types 2 & 3)*<br>☐ Teach Motor Rules (4 rules only)<br>☐ Review Monday's +/– Meeting Results | ☐ Teach Motor Rules (2 rules only) | ☐ Teach Motor Rules (rules as needed) | ☐ Teach Motor Rules (rules as needed) |
| During A.M. | ☐ Teach Transitional Prompts | ☐ Teach Transitional Prompts<br>Hold +/– Meeting with Losing Team | | Hold +/– Meeting with Losing Team | ☐ Teach Transitional Prompts<br>Hold +/– Meeting with Losing Team |
| Just Before Lunch | ☐ Award Reinforcer (Type 1) | ☐ Award Reinforcer (Type 2) | | ☐ Award Reinforcer (Type 3) | |
| Just After Lunch | ☐ Hold +/– Meeting | ☐ Hold +/– Meeting | | ☐ Hold +/– Meeting | |
| During P.M. | ☐ Teach Transitional Prompts | ☐ Teach Transitional Prompts | Hold +/– Meeting with Losing Team–contracting | ☐ Teach Transitional Prompts<br>Hold +/– Meeting with Losing Team–contracting | ☐ Teach Transitional Prompts<br>Hold +/– Meeting with Losing Team–contracting |
| End of Day | ☐ Award Reinforcer (Type 2)<br>☐ Hold +/– Meeting<br>☐ Monitor Assignment Board | ☐ Award Reinforcer (Type 2)<br>☐ Hold +/– Meeting<br>☐ Monitor Assignment Board | ☐ Award Reinforcer (Type 2)<br>☐ Hold +/– Meeting<br>☐ Monitor Assignment Board | ☐ Award Reinforcer (Type 2)<br>☐ Hold +/– Meeting<br>☐ Monitor Assignment Board | ☐ Hold +/– Meeting<br>☐ Award Reinforcer Type 3 |

**FIGURE 13–3  Orientation Week 3 (Mars Days)**

| | Monday | Tuesday | Wednesday | Thursday | Friday |
|---|---|---|---|---|---|
| Begin Day | ☐ Reassign (elective) Seats & Teams (number system)<br>☐ Teach Motor Rules 2 rules only | *(Fade to Reinforcers, Type 3)*<br>☐ Teach Motor Rules (rules as needed)<br>☐ Review Monday's +/– Meeting Results | | | ☐ Teach Motor Rules (rules as needed) |
| During A.M. | | ☐ Teach Transitional Prompts<br>Hold +/– Meeting with Losing Team | | Hold +/– Meeting with Losing Team | Hold +/– Meeting with Losing Team |
| Just Before Lunch | ☐ Award Reinforcer (Type 2) | ☐ Award Reinforcer (Type 3) | | | |
| Just After Lunch | ☐ Hold +/– Meeting | ☐ Hold +/– Meeting | | ☐ Hold +/– Meeting | |
| During P.M. | ☐ Teach Transitional Prompts | | ☐ Teach Transitional Prompts<br>Hold +/– Meeting with Losing Team–contracting | Hold +/– Meeting with Losing Team–contracting | ☐ Teach Transitional Prompts<br>Hold +/– Meeting with Losing Team–contracting |
| End of Day | ☐ Award Reinforcer (Type 3)<br>☐ Hold +/– Meeting<br>☐ Monitor Assignment Board | ☐ Award Reinforcer (Type 3)<br>☐ Hold +/– Meeting<br>☐ Monitor Assignment Board | ☐ Hold +/– Meeting<br>☐ Award Reinforcer (Type 3)<br>☐ Monitor Assignment Board | ☐ Award Reinforcer (award PAT points)<br>☐ Hold +/– Meeting<br>☐ Monitor Assignment Board | ☐ Hold +/– Meeting<br>☐ Award Reinforcer (Type 3) |

## FIGURE 13–4 Orientation Week 4 (Mars Days)

| | Monday | Tuesday | Wednesday | Thursday | Friday |
|---|---|---|---|---|---|
| Begin Day | ☐ Teach Motor Rules (2 rules only) | ☐ Teach Motor Rules (rules as needed) ☐ Review Monday's +/– Meeting Results | ☐ Hold +/– Meeting | | ☐ Teach Motor Rules (rules as needed) |
| During A.M. | | Hold +/– Meeting with Losing Team | | Hold +/– Meeting with Losing Team | Hold +/– Meeting with Losing Team |
| Just Before Lunch | | ☐ Award Reinforcer (Type 3) | | ☐ Award Reinforcer (PAT points) | |
| Just After Lunch | | | | | |
| During P.M. | ☐ Teach Transitional Prompts | | Hold +/– Meeting with Losing Team–contracting | Hold +/– Meeting with Losing Team–contracting | Hold +/– Meeting with Losing Team–contracting |
| End of Day | ☐ Hold +/– Meeting ☐ Award Reinforcer (Type 3) ☐ Monitor Assignment Board | ☐ Award Reinforcer (Type 3) | ☐ Hold +/– Meeting ☐ Award Reinforcer (Type 3) ☐ Monitor Assignment Board | ☐ Award Reinforcer (Type 3) | ☐ Hold +/– Meeting ☐ Award Reinforcer (Type 3) |

**FIGURE 13-5 Orientation Week 5 (Mars Days)**

| | Monday | Tuesday | Wednesday | Thursday | Friday |
|---|---|---|---|---|---|
| Begin Day | ❑ Teach Motor Rules (rules as needed) | | | | ❑ Teach Motor Rules (rules as needed) |
| During A.M. | | Hold +/− Meeting with Losing Team | | Hold +/− Meeting with Losing Team | Hold +/− Meeting with Losing Team |
| Just Before Lunch | | | ❑ Award Reinforcer (PAT points) | | |
| Just After Lunch | | | | | |
| During P.M. | | | Hold +/− Meeting with Losing Team–contracting | Hold +/− Meeting with Losing Team–contracting | Hold +/− Meeting with Losing Team–contracting |
| End of Day | ❑ Hold +/− Meeting<br>❑ Award Reinforcer (Type 3)<br>❑ Monitor Assignment Board | ❑ Award Reinforcer (Type 3) | ❑ Hold +/− Meeting<br>❑ Monitor Assignment Board (for individual students only) | | ❑ Hold +/− Meeting<br>❑ Award Reinforcer (Type 3) |

## FIGURE 13–6 Orientation Week 6 (Mars Days)

| | Monday | Tuesday | Wednesday | Thursday | Friday |
|---|---|---|---|---|---|
| Begin Day | ☐ Teach Motor Rules (rules as needed) | | | | |
| During A.M. | | Hold +/− Meeting with Losing Team | | Hold +/− Meeting with Losing Team | Hold +/− Meeting with Losing Team |
| Just Before Lunch | | | | | |
| Just After Lunch | | | | | |
| During P.M. | | | Hold +/− Meeting with Losing Team–contracting | Hold +/− Meeting with Losing Team–contracting | Hold +/− Meeting with Losing Team–contracting |
| End of Day | ☐ Hold +/− Meeting ☐ Award Reinforcer (Type 3) ☐ Monitor Assignment Board (for individual students only) | | ☐ Award Reinforcer (Type 3) | | ☐ Hold +/− Meeting ☐ Award Reinforcer (Type 3) |

# Index